W9-APZ-261

MAYAKOVSKY AND HIS CIRCLE

PG
3476
M3
S543

WITHDRAWN

MAYAKOVSKY
AND HIS CIRCLE

by Viktor Shklovsky

Edited and Translated by Lily Feiler

Illustrated

DODD, MEAD & COMPANY

NEW YORK

RITTER LIBRARY
BALDWIN-WALLACE COLLEGE

Copyright © 1972 by Lily Feiler
All rights reserved
No part of this book may be reproduced in any form
without permission in writing from the publisher

ISBN: 0-396-06701-8
Library of Congress Catalog Card Number: 72-5649
Printed in the United States of America
by The Cornwall Press, Inc., Cornwall, N.Y.

To my husband, Alfred W. Feiler

Acknowledgments

I want to thank Miss Rose Raskin of Columbia University whose erudition, literary taste, and advice throughout my work on this translation were of immeasurable value and who has taught me much more than mere translation techniques. I am deeply grateful to Professor Robert Sheldon of Dartmouth College for his encouragement, his stylistic corrections and suggestions based on his thorough understanding of all of Shklovsky's work. I wish to express my gratitude to Professor Victor Erlich of Yale University, without whose initial support this book would never have been published and whose comprehensive knowledge of the Formalist school helped direct my research. I also want to thank Cathy Temmerson for her assistance in my research.

Contents

Illustrations

Preface

We all have our habits. I usually start a book with a landscape.
Yalta.
End of April.

*   *   *   *

The crows are gray, their wings black.

Very modestly, cyprus trees are blooming; sparrows alighting on steep branches raise a cloud of yellow dust.

Sad as it is, the bloom of the almond tree is almost over and it had bloomed for quite a while. The white wings of the blossoms lie on the ground, and the wind sometimes whirls them into a light snowstorm.

The heavy, diligent smell of the small-leafed plum-tree hangs in the air. One more page of spring—the 76th.

Youth is gone, gone are the friends. There is almost no one to write letters to or to show the manuscript to. The leaves have fallen and they are not last autumn's leaves.

Here leaves fall steathily, almost imperceptibly, like words being replaced in a language: the tree, too, covers itself with new, upright, seemingly leathery, prickly leaves.

Everyone exits in his own way. Tynyanov, Polivanov, Yakubinsky, Eichenbaum are gone.

The pages are turning. I'll try to turn them back, to re-read them.

Old age likes to re-read.

Old age is ending.[1]

This is the "landscape" against which Viktor Shklovsky sets himself in 1970, at 76, in the introduction to his most recent collection of essays, *Bow-String: About the Dissimilarity of the Similar,* published in Moscow. It is one of his favorite literary devices. Instead of stating facts, relating events and describing a mood or person, he transmits his message indirectly through a metaphor, a seemingly unrelated story or an unusual detail. If a mood of nostalgia and melancholy pervades this introduction, the essays of the book deal with his old love, the ever-present concern to which he dedicated his life: the meaning of literary form, structure in art and literature as a dynamic force in life connecting the past with the future.

Viktor Shklovsky appeared on the Russian literary scene as a very young man in the winter of 1913–1914, when he addressed the Futurist poets with his own attack against all literary traditions. This speech, "The Place of Futurism in the History of Language," mentioned in *O Mayakovskom* [Mayakovsky and His Circle], was published in 1914 under the title *Resurrection of the Word.* It represents the first analysis of its kind, Shklovsky being the first to formulate the innovative tenets of a new creed, Russian Formalism, whose subsequent development was the result of intensive intellectual teamwork. Two centers of the Formalist group came into existence: in Petersburg, Shklovsky, with E. Polivanov, L. Yakubinsky and O. Brik, created the OPOYAZ [Society for the Study of Poetic Language]; the Moscow Linguistic Circle was founded by R. Jakobson and P. Bogatyryov. These were groups of young, brilliant and dedicated students of linguistics and literature who rebelled against the academic school of biographical and historical criticism, and out of whose midst came some of the most prominent Russian linguistic scholars and literary critics of this century. The young Shklovsky—witty, sometimes whimsical; sharp, sometimes aggressive —coined many of the new definitions and became one of the most influential Soviet literary personalities.

The basic Formalist doctrine was defined in the early collections, *Studies in the Theory of Poetic Language* (1916 and 1917) and *Poetics: Studies in the Theory of Poetic Language* (1919).[2] The attack was directed against both the traditional critical school, with its emphasis on content and social meaning in literature, and the new Symbolist school, with its emphasis on philosophy, mysticism and musicality. The Formalists sought a reinterpretation of literature that would stress the importance of purely linguistic elements and artistic devices: sounds and words, structure and style. At that time, Malevich and Kandinsky in art, and Khlebnikov and Mayakovsky in poetry, were overthrowing the old and experimenting with the new. Now, the Formalists were creating a new terminology and methodology of literary criticism and assigning art a new role in life. Art was to be judged on its own terms, completely apart from all political and social issues. As Shklovsky put it in his often-quoted passage: "Art was always free of life, and its color never reflected the color of the flag which waved over the fortress of the city."[3] And while it was to be independent of any outside forces, art was to change life by permeating it with a new awareness. Shklovsky believed that "in art, man fights for the poetry of his heart, for his happiness."[4]

From the very beginning of his involvement with literature, Shklovsky was close to the Futurist poets—Mayakovsky, Khlebnikov, Kruchyonykh—who had revolutionized poetry with their linguistic experimentation and their use of transrational language. Now the poets, in turn, became interested in the Formalist studies that dealt with words and sound patterns in poetry. Not that the Formalist critics limited their studies to poetry; they also analyzed the structural features and specific narrative devices of prose fiction. They saw the chronological order of events, the story line and even the main characters as subordinate to the method of presentation of literary materials. Formalist literary criteria and Shklovsky's modernist, experimental theory of prose opened utterly new vistas for the creative writer.

As the Communist rule took shape a basic difference developed between these two groups: the Futurists wanted their revolutionary art to serve the Communist state and help create a new society; Shklovsky and the Formalists needed the Revolution to break down the traditional understanding of art, but they wanted a free art standing on its own.

During the first years of the Soviet regime and the civil war, Shklovsky fought with and against the Red Army, but he never abandoned his literary cause. Around him gathered a group of young prose writers and, in 1920, in the House of Arts in Petrograd, regular discussions were held under his guidance on the survival of free art in the new society. This group, which included some of the most talented young Soviet writers (M. Zoshchenko, V. Kaverin, K. Fedin, L. Lunts and others) called themselves the Serapion Brothers. In 1922, with the rising tide of political pressures and the trials of dissidents, Shklovsky, fearing that he would be accused of counter-Revolutionary activities (previous charges against him had been dismissed only thanks to Gorky's intervention), fled to Germany. In Berlin, he wrote his haunting, compelling account of those years, *Sentimental Journey*,[5] as well as *Zoo, or Letters Not about Love*.[6] The latter is a fascinating, personal book about post-war Berlin, about being an émigré, about literature and, above all, about his unrequited love for Elsa Triolet.

Upon his return to the Soviet Union in 1923, made possible through the intervention of Mayakovsky and Gorky, he joined Mayakovsky and his friends in LEF [7] and became one of the main contributors to their magazine by the same name. Formalism was at the height of its influence and popularity. In these years, when the lines of literary controls were still fluid and dissent did not mean treason, Shklovsky influenced many young Soviet writers and worked with other Formalists on a reinterpretation of literature. Some of his major works were published in those years: *On the Theory of Prose* (1925), *The Third Factory* (1926) and *The Hamburg Account* (1928). Also published was *Materials and Style in Leo Tolstoy's WAR AND PEACE* (1928), which introduced a new element into Shklovsky's literary analysis: sociological material.

Ominous signs, however, had been appearing since 1924–25. Formalism was attacked for its asocial, escapist attitude. Mayakovsky himself, while appreciating the linguistic contributions of the OPOYAZ writers, urged more social consciousness in art. After 1928, with the acceptance of the First Five-Year Plan and Stalin's ascendence to absolute power, literature and art had to be regimented. The instrument used to bring dissident writers into line was, first, the Russian Association of Proletarian Writers (RAPP), and later, the Writers' Union. Formalists were severely criticized and recantation became the only way to survive. Shklovsky's article "A Monument to a Scientific Error," in the *Literary Gazette* (January 27, 1930) represents his capitulation to outside pressure. Formalism became a major crime for Soviet writers and artists and the charge is still used today to indict writers and artists in disfavor.

Shklovsky survived the dark period of the thirties. He published little; he wrote movie scenarios, scripts for documentaries and some reportage. However, he contributed something more important than any book. Nadezhda Mandelstam, the widow of Osip Mandelstam, testifies to this in her recent memoirs: "In Moscow there was only one house to which an outcast could always go. . . . The Shklovskys' house was the only place where we felt like human beings again. This was a family that knew how to help lost souls like us." [8] It is no secret that to give shelter to people like the Mandelstams was a risk: it meant possible disgrace, deportation or worse.

From the mid-thirties on, Shklovsky witnessed an unexpected development. His friend Vladimir Mayakovsky, whose original, personal poetry he had admired but who, in his lifetime, had been attacked by Marxist critics as a "petty bourgeois individualist and anarchist, who had never understood the Revolution," Vladimir Mayakovsky, who, in his last years, had been hindered from producing his plays, had been ostracized and hounded by RAPP critics, had committed suicide, and whose name had been rarely mentioned since 1930—this same Vladimir Mayakovsky was suddenly resurrected by an editorial in *Pravda* on December 5, 1935. In this editorial, Stalin was quoted as having said: "Mayakovsky is the best, the most talented poet of the Soviet epoch. Indifference to his memory and to his work is a crime." This was the signal that was to transform the dead poet into a model for young poets to follow. Mayakovsky's early lyrical, rebellious poems were neglected; his Futurism was explained as a mistake of his youth; his commitment to the ideas of LEF was disregarded; his passionate, complex personality was streamlined. Mayakovsky emerged as The Poet of the Communist Revolution, inspired by Lenin and Stalin, guided by Gorky, and was used to enforce conformity in art. His suicide was attributed to an illness, to an error, and became almost an accident. Pasternak, recalling this period, wrote: "Mayakovsky was beginning to be propagated compulsorily, like potatoes in the reign of Catherine the Great. That was his second death. For that he is not to blame." [9]

In 1940, on the occasion of the tenth anniversary of Mayakovsky's suicide, many books were published in honor of the poet. But Shklovsky's book, *O Mayakovskom,* published that same year in Moscow, differs from all the others. Apparently, Shklovsky had been working on his reminiscences of this period for quite a while—probably since the poet's suicide. A section of his book *Diary* [10] has the same title and deals with the same material.

O Mayakovskom is obviously a tribute to the man he knew so well and the poet he admired. Mayakovsky is surrounded by his old friends: the Futurist poets and the Formalist writers, the avant-garde artists and the experimental filmmakers. He is alive again with all his contradictions and complexities. However, perhaps the greatest attraction of the book is that, aside from some inserted apologies for his "errors," Shklovsky writes like Shklovsky again.

Shklovsky's books do not fit into established categories; they do not use conventional forms of narration. If *Sentimental Journey* has been called an "anti-fiction novel," and *Zoo* a quasi-novel, *Mayakovsky and His Circle* [*O Mayakovskom*] could be called an "anti-memoir memoir." The best description of it has been given by the author himself when he wrote about Sterne's *Tristram Shandy:*

But when you begin to examine the structure of the book, you see first of all that the disorder is intentional and, in thise case, poetic. It is strictly regulated, like a picture by Picasso. Everything in the book is displaced; everything is transposed.[11]

"Defamiliarization," Shklovsky's most original contribution to Formalist theory, is discussed in the chapter "OPOYAZ" and he uses it successfully throughout the book as his own artistic device. Shklovsky's concept of "plot," as the sum-total of related events shaped by different and often "displaced" artistic devices, is brilliantly demonstrated by his own writing: his sudden shifts of mood, his digressions, quotations from other writers and recurring poetic metaphors.

Shklovsky's original, staccato style is not always easy to follow, but his technique gives meaning and depth far beyond the facts he relates. One of his favorite devices, the recurring leitmotif, is used to establish Mayakovsky as the poet who addressed the future, whose poetry will survive into the future, but who could not find fulfillment, recognition or happiness in the reality of his day. His typical one-sentence paragraphs, that shift from irony to nostalgia, from minute descriptions to broad generalizations, evoke the atmosphere of a period when people were driven toward the new because the old set of values, both in life and art, had collapsed.

More than any straightforward, traditional narration, Shklovsky's *O Mayakovskom* will give any reader the feeling of participating in the excitement of a very special period, while a reader familiar with Russian literature and the inside events of that time will also perceive different layers in the narrative. Many passages, phrases and images are lifted from Mayakovsky's poems; others echo poems by Pushkin, or paraphrase lines from a poem by Pasternak. Some of Shklovsky's allusions are hard to follow. For instance, in describing Mayakovsky's relationship to Lili Brik, the great love of Mayakovsky's life, he inserts the following lines:

A tired buffalo retreats into the water.

An elephant, perhaps, really warms himself in the sand. But he had no place, there was no sun for him, and his love was a heavy load.

A reader who knows Mayakovsky's passionate poem of 1916 addressed to Lili Brik, from which these images are taken,[12] will have additional insight.

Another element that adds poignancy to some of the more personal passages dealing with the poet's life is Shklovsky's genuine affection for him, their long and close friendship. The poetic prose and metaphors of the chapter "Norderney" transmit a shared intimacy, a mood of youthful, carefree optimism. It adds to our understanding to know that, at that time, Mayakovsky and Shklovsky were in love with two sisters, Lili Brik and Elsa Triolet. They both felt manipulated and unhappy in their love—but, still, there was "the sea and the wind." When, after the poet's suicide, Shklovsky invokes "the sea of Norderney," it takes us back to a vision of the poet at a time when everything still seemed possible, when, regardless of personal disappointments, he was inspired by his art and the cause it served.

Shklovsky's Mayakovsky emerges not only with all his personal traits, but also comes to stand for the mood that inspired his generation in Russia: the despair, the commitment, the hope and the doom. After the poet's suicide, Shklovsky makes the following comment: ". . . he died, having explained how the love boat crashes, how man perishes—not of un-requited love, but because he had ceased loving." It seems obvious that Mayakovsky, who had served Lili Brik and Communism with equal devotion, had not only ceased loving but had lost faith in his cause.

Mayakovsky's "Landscape" had been the swift, moving Rion river in spring; Shklovsky's today is the gray autumn and the prickly leaves—this seems to imply more than just the contrast of personal physical aging.

A few points have to be made about this translation of *O Mayakovskom*, the only one in English. Though it makes its appearance more than thirty years after the original, its relevance for the American reader is perhaps clearer today than ever before. Not only because it introduces us to Maya-kovsky and the LEF, a group which initiated some of the most challenging and original ideas in modern art, but also because the book as a whole evokes a period of artistic and social turmoil.

The mood it describes is one we know very well. Khlebni-kov's predictions on the rebellion of things could be used as slogans by ecologists today; Rodchenko's experimentation with photography and Constructivist reliefs are part of our own art scene; the disconnected, absurdist movie sequences are familiar to us all. Even the problem of "free love," dis-cussed in Lenin's letter to Inessa Armand, has not yet been resolved in our society. Moreover, if, today, Formalism is largely submerged in the Soviet Union, its substantive legacy is very much alive outside its borders. It has developed and changed with the years; divergent schools have merged within its general framework. In America, we have had New Criticism. Recently, in France, the "Structuralists" have in-corporated the seminal insights of Russian Formalism and openly acknowledge their indebtedness to that school. Viktor Shklovsky's contribution to the initial formulation of this body of thought remains important and his *bons mots* and definitions are quoted by literary critics all over the world.

Shklovsky's book came out in 1940, at a time when Soviet literary controls seemed a little more relaxed. Since 1934, the doctrine of "Socialist Realism," requiring a tendentious literature in the service of the Communist Party, has been official policy, enforced by the compulsory Writers' Union. During the years of the political purge trials (1936–38), writers suspected of disloyalty were denounced, accused and arrested. Babel, Mandelstam and many others disappeared or went into hiding. The Stalinist terror was on. In the period of the Second World War, however, Soviet writers felt that they could hope for more freedom. But the return to Stalinist controls of literature in 1946 dashed these hopes. Again and again there have been periods of "thaw" followed by reprisals and a tightening of literary controls. There is no simplistic explanation for the pattern of Soviet controls of the mind. This is why we are all the more appreciative when, during one of these "thaws," a book like *O Mayakovskom* is allowed to reach us. Shklovsky has not written in the same personal style since.

When the book appeared, Shklovsky was severely criticized by the critics for overemphasizing Mayakovsky's ties with the Futurists and LEF, and for failing to portray him as The Poet of the Revolution. Fadeyev, a major Soviet novelist and high-ranking member of the Writers' Union, accused Shklovsky of still clinging to his Formalist concepts and of having "separated Mayakovsky from the Revolution and even from poetry, while enclosing him within a narrow sphere of cliques and family relationships." [13] The reviewer of the influential periodical *October* found it absurd that Shklovsky should imply "that the worldview of the best poet of the Soviet epoch was formed not by the Bolshevik Party with which Mayakovsky had been connected since his youth, not by Lenin's books, which he had read, not by the entire atmosphere of imminent Revolution, but by people like Shklovsky, Brik, Khlebnikov. . . ." [14] Again Shklovsky was accused of trying to rehabilitate Formalism.

In spite of this, a second edition of *O Mayakovskom* appeared in 1964 (reissued again in 1966) as part of Shklovsky's autobiographical collection entitled *Zhili-byli* [Once Upon a Time].[15] The revised edition contains no new material, while large and important passages are omitted. Two rather typical deletions deserve to be quoted.

In the revised edition, the chapter "On Blok" ends with the following paragraph:

He belonged to the new mankind which had inspired *The Twelve* and *The Scythians*. He was not abolished. Because art does not pass.

The rest of the original chapter, which conveys Blok's utter isolation and lack of "air" in the new society, has been left out.

The chapter, "I Continue," which discusses Gorky's relationship with Mayakovsky, their quarrel and their subsequent estrangement, is carefully cut in order to create the impression that only a personal, regrettable incident broke up their friendship. But the text of the present edition clearly indicates that, though Gorky admired some of Mayakovsky's poems, he remained critical of others all his life and that their conflict was very deep. Also, ambiguous phrases, like "later on, the two of them were destroyed one by one, separately," or clear statements, like "had they been united not in museums, but in life . . . the course of Soviet literature would have been different," are left out.

Many more examples could be given, but these suffice to demonstrate that only the first edition deserves to be translated. So that the reader can appreciate the nature of Soviet censorship, we have provided brackets for the deleted passages.

The poems quoted by Shklovsky have been rendered in a literal translation that follows the typographical arrangement of the original.

In Shklovsky's text no sources are given for the poetry, but I have felt that references should be added wherever possible.

LILY FEILER

New York, N. Y.

PART ONE

Composed of ten chapters, which tell about the village of Bagdadi, about the School of Painting, Sculpture and Architecture in Moscow, about the Futurist [1] artist David Burlyuk, about poets and their aspirations. This first part also tells about the future friends and comrades of the great poet Vladimir Mayakovsky.

Chapter 1

Introduction

There are different ways of beginning a book about a poet if it is not a biography.

Nor is it necessary to begin a biography at the beginning. Biographies can begin in various ways.

There are biographies which tell about boy geniuses—about seven-year-old musicians giving concerts, about Jesus being greeted by the wise men; and it was also Jesus, it seems, who, at the age of seven, argued with the Scribes and bested them.

Such stories are particularly numerous in the gospel of Nicodemus. But this gospel is apocryphal.

Mayakovsky described the day of his birth as follows:

> In the sky of my Bethlehem
> no special stars were shining,
> nobody disturbed
> the tomb-sleep
> of the curly-haired wise men.
> It was a day absolutely like everyday—
> repulsive in its sameness—
> the day
> of my descent to you.[1]

Ilya Muromets [2] has no childhood. His story starts with some wanderers paying him a visit. Until then, Ilya Muromets had been lying on the stove, feeling bored.

Don Quixote in Cervantes' *Don Quixote* has no childhood. At the very end we learn that his name is Alonzo the Good.

Don Quixote begins with the reading of novels and with old Don Quixote going into the world to carry out heroic deeds.

It begins with dedication, with a vocation.

Saul the peasant went to search for the asses and met Samuel. He came to Samuel, the seer, in order to learn where the asses were. Samuel answered:

"Go up before me to the high place; as for your asses that were lost three days ago, do not set your mind on them, for they have been found."

Saul had a change of heart and began to prophesy. Later on, he slaughtered his oxen and sent chunks of meat to all the villages to show what he would do to those who did not heed his call. That is called vocation.

Pushkin wrote about that.

Inspiration overcame the poet in the desert.

It overcomes like death, it arouses like a wound.

It revives lips and sets the heart on fire.

Now, let us think about when the call came to Mayakovsky.

We won't write about his childhood. He had a father who wore a forester's coat. He loved his mother. He had beloved sisters [who resembled him very much].

With his father, Mayakovsky rode in the mountains through the wooded passes where the far mountain wind blows.

Chapter **2**

The Landscape

Still, let us write about the place where Mayakovsky was born.

Southeast of the ancient town of Kutaisi lies the village of Bagdad or Bagdadi. It stands on the right bank of the river Khanis-Tskhali where the river emerges from a gorge.

There is a bridge. To the right of the bridge, at the foot of the mountain, stands a house made of chestnut logs. In the house are three rooms with pointed windows.

The house stands on a rather high foundation. The staircase is of stone. A spring flows down from the mountain.

It is here that Mayakovsky was born.

He was born into the family of a forester, Vladimir Konstantinovich Mayakovsky.

This is a heavily forested area, though at that time, boards for crates were brought to Batum from Austria.

This is beautiful country. In spring, the mountains are covered with gray grass, and flowers cover the trees like smoke.

The grapevines lying on the red soil look like springs that have been cut to pieces.

And the leaves on the grapevines have not yet unfurled their wings.

There, farther on, snow covers the mountain passes, and beyond the passes—Russia.

This is Georgia, Imeretiya. Turkeys wander in the large courtyards covered with short tight green grass.

In the middle of these courtyards are nut trees, decorated with burls.

The river rushes out of the gorge, ruffled and whirling. Diverted to one side, the water spurts right onto the wheels of a water-mill.

The river is bubbly, full of foamy air and mountain muddiness.

Vladimir Vladimirovich Mayakovsky was born in Bagdadi in the Kuchukhidze house by the bridge.

But he grew up in a different house, a little farther down the river. A fortress stands there, a big, high bulwark faced with stone, and the stone is overgrown with a braiding of brushwood roots.

In the fortress there are cannon mounts. This fortress protects three roads: one leads to the eastern part of Imeretiya; the second one goes to Guriya and Mingreliya. There is a house in the fortress, somewhat larger than the Kuchukhidze house. The third road leads to Kutaisi.

From Bagdadi, Mayakovsky went to study in Kutaisi. They travelled, if my memory does not betray me, in a small one-horse diligence. I still saw such diligences back in Kutaisi. They are greenish-blue.

The road from Bagdadi to Kutaisi passes through groves of oak trees. Some trees are pink when in bloom. The houses are covered with a blue foam of blooming shrubs as though a vat of lilacs had boiled over and covered the entire town with caps of foam.

The Rion in Kutaisi is still a mountain stream.

The rushing waves carry tree trunks, battered and ragged from beating against the rocks.

The tree trunks come from the mountains.

This is a stream on which one cannot return.

Tired buffaloes lie up to their eyes in the water.

A mountain rises above the town; on the mountain are

ruins, the immense capitals of the temple of Bagrat III. This temple was built a thousand years ago.

The capitals are so heavy that it is hard to imagine them lifted on top of columns.

Ivy covers these fallen stones, which, through a millenium, still adhere together.

On the river bank stands a small two-story house. This is the palace of the former tsars of Imeretiya.

This house stands at an angle to a large building, the *gymnasium*.

Between the large *gymnasium* and the small palace grows a tree as tremendous as an epic poem. Not far above the ground, the tree divides into several enormous trunks.

It is larger than that tree in which Paganel and Robert Grant [1] lived.

Under such a tree, nations can be judged and armies gathered. Probably, this tree was the true palace of the tsars of Imeretiya, and the palace near the tree was just a guardhouse.

In town, balconies overhang the stream, the houses are decorated with small arches.

All around, on the mountain slopes, are gardens and vineyards.

Then his father died. The Rion flowed on, carrying the same large tree trunks, battered and ragged from beating against the rocks. The houses were covered with lilac foam.

The books about Indians had not yet been read, nor had he finished the revolutionary leaflets published in Rostov, and there was still shooting in the Caucasus.

He was at home here, but the family had to leave; there was nothing to live on. There were three rubles in the house. They had to go somewhere. They went to Moscow. Moscow was big. Something would have to happen there.

"After Tiflis, strange sights began: sand—first, plain, then desert-like, without any soil and, finally, oily and black. Beyond the desert was the sea, leaving a spittle of white salt on the shore. At the edge of the shore were brownish camels, tearing out leafless bushes as they walked. At night, fantastic structures emerged, as though black well-holes had been lifted up and quickly covered with boards. These structures blotted out the entire horizon, they ran toward us, then climbed the mountains, then receded and clustered together."

At the railroad stations, iron towers. To escape the mosquitoes, they say. Mosquitoes don't fly that high.

Desert—even the water is brought in tanks.

And farther on, white huts, and geese in the fields.

The geese in the fields looked like scattered and torn pieces of paper. On the horizon were windmills, and then the uniform Russian forests began.

Moscow appeared.

As a child, Vladimir Mayakovsky saw a lot and he had much to remember.

There is a fairy-tale about the peasant who made his own weather and forgot the wind, but the wind is needed when rye is in bloom.

The Caucasus had kept Mayakovsky whole; the Caucasus gave him Russia new and fresh; even the sounds of native Russian speech were new.

Let's be grateful to the wind of the mountain passes.

Chapter 3

Moscow Was Rusty

David Copperfield, a book about childhood, may be the best book Dickens ever wrote.

This is because the wound inflicted upon Dickens, the wound he kept licking all his life, was a childhood wound.

It was then that he saw the quiet girl, the insulted boy, and Micawber, the happiest of all ne'er-do-wells. Because this particular ne'er-do-well was eloquent.

Inspired by his childhood, Dickens lived in his novels.

That is why *David Copperfield* is a wonderful book.

The *Years of Childhood of Bagrov, the Grandson,* by Aksakov, tells about the joy of discovering the world, about how a river flows into the consciousness, and how water reveals its transparency.

My son came to me many years ago and said:

"You know, Papa, horses have no horns."

That is how a child discovers life.

He discovers a butterfly, the color of a fir tree, and the gloomy, sinister turmoil of a crossing on rafts.

Children are born alike; poets emerge in various ways. The biographies published by Pavlenkov were actually footnotes to the work of Mikhaylovsky and the other Populists. These books, all of the same format, are based on the assumption that history is made by heroes, and that heroes are born.

Gorky's book, as well as Dickens' book, is not a monologue. These are books about men who found their vocation in early childhood.

The call to be a poet came to Vladimir Vladimirovich Mayakovsky in Moscow after the Butyrki [1]—that was the year 1910.

The poet's vocation begins with anguish.

You know of this spiritual thirst, this withdrawal from life. Of that new way of seeing and hearing.

A great poet is born out of the contradictions of his time. He is preceded by the inequality of things, their dislocations, the course of their changes. Others do not yet know about the day after tomorrow. The poet defines it, writes and receives no recognition.

[Pertsov's article about Mayakovsky in the Butyrki is a good article. Facts have been collected. Of course, one should enter cell number 103,[2] to see what Mayakovsky saw from his window.]

People remember Mayakovsky as a conquerer. They talk about how he resisted in prison, and that is true. Vladimir Mayakovsky was an exceedingly strong man.

He was, however, sixteen years old.

The boy was kept in solitary for five months. He came out of prison shattered.

He read voraciously in prison—so much that it could be grasped only later.

He came out knowing what it means to think, and how a man is responsible for his convictions.

In prison, Mayakovsky learned to be a comrade and, at the same time, he learned to withdraw.

He was a very secretive man who knew how to be silent.

Mayakovsky left the Butyrki in winter without an overcoat: his overcoat had been pawned. He came home to his small apartment. Easter eggs had to be painted again for the Datsiaro Store and for other stores; at that time, the Böhm illustrations of Russian proverbs were in fashion. Girls and boys with blond hair, all pink and white, in Russian shirts, kissing, with inscriptions of various wise folk sayings underneath. This was a combination of the quasi-national and the quasi-popular.

He was paid fifteen kopeks for the whole lot: the folklore, the nationalism, and the innocence.

A great deal had to be produced. Thin, broad-shouldered and flat-chested, Vladimir Mayakovsky was always an energetic worker.

He burned out designs, painted and polished one thing after the other.

It was almost warm in the room. [His sisters also worked "in art."]

In a story by Wells, an impoverished couple, living at the edge of town, join the Salvation Army and dress in a blue canvas that can be removed only with one's skin. They do metal relief work, raising some designs on thin metal sheets with an instrument similar to a thimble.

People from large cities like handicraft and mechanize the artist.

One of my friends in LEF,[3] a man of strange and unexpected knowledge, told me the theory of selling ties.

Several boxes of ties are offered to the customer. Among them is one tie different from all the others. It is called "original." The customer tries to decide for a long time what would gratify his soul. He chooses the "original" tie.

Only "original" ties are mass-produced by the factory.

The rest of the ties, the non-originals, exist only to lead him on. In the same way, beaters drive the bear to the guns.

For originality, at that time, one needed handicraft.

Manual, mechanical, applied. But the quality was mediocre, though the product was described as "art."

Mayakovsky, who knew the Caucasus and loved the swift Rion; Mayakovsky, who read Marx and believed in revolution—was condemned to manufacture "Böhms."

He had lost all his friends.

He was not a student; he had no schoolmates; he was not

working in a factory. The people from his revolutionary group had been arrested.

He was alone in the city.

He was not homeless. He had a home, an apartment, and a family. But in his poetry, and even in the reminiscences of his friends of that time, he seems homeless.

It is the homelessness of a young man breaking away from home and seeking a destiny of his own.

Fast, roomy and expensive streetcars were running in the streets of Moscow. On the Sadovayas,[4] the trees were rustling.

Moscow was completely circular and confusing; it was full of signboards—gaudy signboards and black signboards with golden letters. All of Moscow was paved with the skulls of cobblestones. Mayakovsky, in his black velvet jacket, with his black hair brushed back, roamed this circular Moscow. Foremen of printing shops were dressed like that. But their shirts were of sateen. A shirt like that was called a "bubble," and a person wearing one an "Italian."

He walked the boulevards. Above Moscow ran wires, cutting across the slim necks of the belltowers. The narrow Sobolevka, the prostitutes' quarter, merged with the ring of the Sadovayas. Above it, the streetcar wires crossed their sparks. Moscow nights are long.

In the morning light, Red Square seems to be strewn with bones. The cobblestones look like skulls and ribs.

The morning pavement may look like a lake, covered with ripples, with an unwieldly ship of shopping arcades moored at its shore.

There are puddles on the pavement. The puddles reflect, in fragments, the five cupolas of the temple of Vasily Blazhenny. Pigeons walk among the glittering fragments of sky, walls and churches.

A woman with a basket strolls in the square. Her basket contains various grains.

The pigeons follow her in a crowd, pushing one another and stepping on the stones and fragments of the sky.

This woman feeds the pigeons from money given by passers-by.

Early morning. The sun rises, a warm wind blows.

Steep Tverskaya Street. The low wall of the Strastnoy Monastery.

Hat in hand, tall among the low buildings, washed by the rain, Pushkin stands, gleaming in his bronze cloak.

Facing him stands a tall boy, only recently grown up, in a black shirt.

On Strastnaya Square stands Mayakovsky, not yet born, the word not yet found.

On the Pushkin monument, on the pedestal, a falsified inscription.[5]

But, anyhow it was spring.

> Moscow
> choked me
> in the embracing ring of her endless Sadovayas.
> Into hearts,
> into tiny watches,
> mistresses are ticking.
> In ecstasy the partners share their lovers' bed.
> I catch
> the wild heartbeat of the capitals,
> spread out like Strastnaya Square.
> Opened-up—
> my heart almost bared—
> I expose myself to the sun and the puddle.[6]

Chapter 4

Painting Reinterpreted

Vladimir Mayakovsky studied painting with Zhukovsky. There he painted still-lifes composed of objects already beautiful in themselves: silver with silk or with velvet. After a year, he realized that he was learning craftsmanship, not art. He went to the painter Kelin.

Subsequently, Vladimir Vladimirovich was to respect Kelin a great deal; and he made a point of expressing his respect. So passed the year 1910. In 1911, Mayakovsky was accepted as a regular student in the School of Painting, Sculpture and Architecture. He disliked this school. At that time, artists went to study in Paris and Munich. Of all the foreign artists abroad, fifty per cent were Russian. All innovation came from there.

The School of Painting, Sculpture and Architecture was located across the street from the Main Post Office. Mayakovsky used to say that only this saved it from getting lost in Moscow.

This was the way of fixing its address.

It still stands there. And it still has the same rounded, worn corner.

It was the kind of school in which students could wear uniforms with gold shoulder straps.

Almost nobody, however, dressed like that. The large classroom held about forty people. One had to fight for seats. It seemed that some angles of foreshortening were more desirable. People would come late at night and wait for seats as they waited for Chaliapin tickets.

They drew neither heads, nor nature, but half-nature.

Women or men, half-dressed.

The idea was to teach people to draw little by little. First the head, then the bust, then add to that the stomach and legs. It was assumed that the student would later combine what he had learned and be able to draw a whole man.

Mayakovsky had done good work at Kelin's school, but here in the large studio of the School of Painting, Sculpture and Architecture, he did not do so well.

The student body was very mixed. One of the students even had bangs, shoulder straps and a plummet.

The student with bangs viewed the model through the thin line of his plummet. He wanted to find the best stance. He aligned his plummet with the point where the collarbones come together. The man with the bangs asserted that the plummet was a great discovery and that it would enable him to avoid the influence of Cézanne.

Everybody talked about Cézanne.

The man with the bangs did not like Cézanne. He believed that Cézanne did not know how to draw vertical lines.

In the dining hall, people ate sandwiches with sausage, drank beer and argued a lot. Mayakovsky argued more than anybody else, but he ate no sandwiches. He stood at the counter. In the pockets of his black velvet jacket, he had matches and cheap cigarettes. A writing pad. A book. His pockets bulged. His neck was strong, not thin. His hair, brushed back, was brown but looked black to the superficial observer. His hands red from the cold. His trousers narrow, black, dusty. About sixteen of his teeth were decayed. Healthy teeth were not for him. Just like sausage sandwiches, they cost money to be fixed.

His lips were full and already in the habit of articulating distinctly.

The man with the bangs drew diligently, and because of his diligence he was even excused from the nature class. Later on, he made it to the AKhRR,[1] having learned how to draw, nicely, glass ink wells and how to combine figures out of the various parts in such a way that, if they did not look alive, at least they looked copied from something worthwhile.

Mayakovsky, though, did not make any effort. This was a period in painting when the ice suddenly began to move and everything became confused.

Jules Verne, in his writings, tells of such a case: some people, hunting for furs on the wooded shore of the North Sea, built a factory.

The land on which they had settled turned out to be an ice floe. The ice floe broke off and floated along the same route that was later taken by the Soviet Arctic explorers. The ice floe floated along, carrying its lakes, its forests.

The sun would rise from one side, then from the other. There were no tides at the shores because the ice floe rose with the tidal waves.

There was a lot of talk on the ice floe about astronomy and geography.

In the smoking room of the School of Painting, Sculpture and Architecture, there was talk about the Impressionists. This ice floe had been floating along for some years. Some time before, French artists, fighting the brown disease of academic painting, had left their studios, their customers, their subjects, and had begun to draw the naked body on the grass, having realized that shadow too has color.

They were shifting from paints to color. They destroyed knowledge of an object in order to perceive the truth of an object.

The effort was difficult and bitter. At their exhibitions, people laughed and stuck umbrellas into their pictures. Later on, fame came to the dead, whose pictures had already been bought up. But the ice floe floated on.

Soon Impressionism itself was questioned. The goal now was to create real space in paintings, to circumvent the retina and to create a world of space that would not be an illusion, not only visual, but accessible to muscular cognition. They created space not by light, but by color.

Those who remained with the Impressionists gave up their brush strokes and replaced them with colored dots. Others began to learn from the Japanese and Chinese. Sculptors, disenchanted with Phidias, began to appreciate archaic Greek sculptors. Later still, Negro sculpture came into fashion.

Paris became *the* city of painting. People from everywhere gathered there as they had once gathered in Italy. They came together to ride the fast-thawing ice floe toward the land of the sun where there is no fixed sunrise.

Paris became the capital of the Spaniard Picasso. People no longer believed in color in their urge to understand space. They began to examine the object, to dismember it, trying to represent it not only as they saw it, but as they knew it.

Paris resounded with people speaking to one another in unintelligible languages. A similar case happened once during the construction of a certain tall building in Babylon.

Chapter 5

David Burlyuk

In his poem "Burlyuk," V. Khlebnikov described this period as follows:

> Russia is an enlarged continent
> that amplified enormously the voice of the West
> as though transmitting the scream of a
> monster thousands of times louder.
> You, fat giant, your laughter has rung through all of Russia.
> And the stem of the Dniepr estuary smothered you in its fist,
> fighter for the right of the people to an art of titans,
> you gave to Russia's soul an outlet to the sea.
> Strange break-up of painted worlds,
> precursor of freedom, liberation from chains.

Burlyuk was not alone.

Goncharova and Larionov displayed pictures painted under the influence of Russian folk painting and the Russian icons. Poster art was being discussed.

In reputable Leningrad [1] galleries, which displayed the competent, insipid but respectable nature paintings of Aleksandr Benois of *The World of Art*,[2] and where quiet people who knew how to copy were exhibited—there, suddenly, appeared Goncharova, Larionov, Chagall.

Rooms of the *Fauves* began to be opened at the exhibitions. The paintings in these rooms seemed to shriek. People began talking in whispers at these exhibitions. The customer was lost.

Now people began to say that a transitional period in art is art itself.

Since olden times, the sculptor and artist creating form reduced it to basic geometrical shapes. And then, later, from this fused form, they moved to the dismembered form. It was now assumed that the second stage was not necessary.

For a long time already, painters had seen paintings as a relationship of colors. To the poet, verses came as rhythmic impulses and dark sounds, not yet expressed in words.

This was a generation destined to see war and revolution.

For Russia, it was a generation destined to see the end of the old world.

And this generation was already renouncing it.

In the smoking room, there was talk about painting, about Cubism, about Goncharova, Cézanne, about the Russian icon.

One of Mayakovsky's friends was Vasily Chekrygin, a very young, handsome painter with a high forehead.

The frescoes of the Therapont Monastery had recently been restored.[3] Under the first layers appeared contours of figures in strange movements, looking like the grain of a sawed-off tree-stump. The frescoes of the Therapont Monastery—filled with tension, constraint and tightness—were frightening and people did not believe them. They decided that the restorers had tricked the archeologists. The frescoes were covered again, painted over. Vasily Chekrygin knew these frescoes and had faith in the unknown artist who had been extinguished once more.

Chekrygin and young Lev Shekhtel were friends. And then, one day, David Burlyuk arrived, heavy-set, one-eyed, no longer very young. Burlyuk had studied in Kazan and later in Odessa. He had been abroad. His drawings were powerful and he knew anatomy to perfection.

Burlyuk was about thirty years old. He had gone through

a phase of admiring Nekrasov. He had read extensively, he had many skills, and he no longer knew how one ought to draw. Skill had deprived academic drawing of any authority for him. He could draw better than any professor and, now, had become indifferent to academic drawing.

He heard a great deal, saw many things; his ears were used to noise, his eyes to constant irritation. Artists, at that time, were eloquent. Pictures had begun to appear with prefaces. Artists argued with themselves. David arrived through paintings shown first at the exhibition with the modest name "The Wreath" [4] and, then, at the exhibition called "The Donkey's Tail." [5]

The donkey of the exhibition was not related to the asses of Saul.

In 1910, the flaming manifesto of the "Excessivists" was published. The manifesto was signed by the resounding but hitherto unknown name of Joachim-Raphael Boronali and read as follows:

"Extremism in everything—that is force, the only force! The sun can never be too hot, the sky too green, the distant ocean too red, the dusk too black. . . . Let's exterminate the senseless museums! Let's do away with the shameful routine of artisans who produce candy boxes instead of pictures! Down with lines, design, craftsmanship! Welcome dazzling fantasy and imagination!"

[A painting by an unknown artist was called "Sunset over the Adriatic." This painting, as was certified later by a notary, was drawn by a donkey, using his tail.

New Time [6] and *Niva* [7] reproduced this drawing, this ass's feat.

The donkey's tail, which was ridiculed, became a banner. This banner meant that we did not want your recognition and that we would flick you away by any means. Let a stream of contempt flow between us and the past. We will mobilize all resources of purely abstract expression.]

Colors no longer sufficed. Objects began to be introduced

into pictures. At one exhibition, Larionov put some objects and paints around a ventilator. The ventilator was electric; it was switched on, started running, and the artist stood in fascination before a painting which had absorbed movement.

David Burlyuk had grown up in the Steppe. His father managed a large estate near the Crimean peninsula. The family had little money, but lots of food. David, his brothers and his sister all painted. They even had their own sculpture gallery: a Scythian idol, found in a burial mound. When David's father subsequently lost his position, the family took this idol to Moscow. Further transportation of the family treasure proved beyond their means, however.

This Scythian idol, which had travelled to Moscow by mistake, somehow came to rest on Nastasyinsky Lane, near a barn where students of the art school gathered.

One-eyed David Burlyuk brought news with him. He had many friends in the provinces. He knew Khlebnikov, a man from Astrakhan who was a poet and philosopher; he knew an aviator from the Kama River—Vasily Kamensky. He knew Guro, the prose writer.

They published a booklet, printed on wallpaper, with the slightly puzzling name, *A Hatchery of Judges.*[8]

Viktor Khlebnikov called himself Velimir. He was acquainted with Vyacheslav Ivanov and visited him at his home in Petersburg. He was in touch with the Guild of Poets.[9] There, his poetry was read, but scarcely noticed.

To foretell the future is difficult. Marco Polo lived in China a long time and assimilated its ways at a time when there were no printing presses, gun powder or compasses in Europe. Later, he brought back to Persia not only a Chinese princess, but Chinese paper money with which, apparently, he caused a rebellion. When Marco Polo wrote about China for the Italians, he told them that in China there were burning stones and coachmen. But he did not mention printing presses.

If, tomorrow, we were propelled fifty years forward, many of us would bring back from the future our past.

Khlebnikov was neglected by our literature even though he was an accomplished master; his entire being pulsated with the future.

The future lives within us hidden under its contradictions. It lives within us by the way we flow toward it or ascend to it.

Khlebnikov judged his time; he analyzed the literature of his day and wrote that although Artsybashev, Merezhkovsky, Andreyev, Sologub and Remizov said that our life was a horror, the folksong said that life was beauty. He wrote that Sologub was a gravedigger and Artsybashev and Andreyev preached death. But the folksong was life.

Khlebnikov said that the Russian book and the Russian song were now in different camps.

Khlebnikov sensed the future. He wrote about the future war and future destruction of the state, naming 1917 as the year of the cataclysm.[10] He spoke about the rebellion of things; he said that chimneys with the years imprinted on them and with the smoke over them would invade the city; that the Tuchkov Bridge would fall off the shore; that the railroad tracks would tear themselves off the roads, and that in our life, as in soft flesh, new seeds had ripened. A new rebellion was beginning, a new flood, on which a crazed child, clutching a pillow to its chest, would float along.

It would float as Mayakovsky, in his poem *About That,* was to float like a white polar bear on an ice floe, propelling himself with a paw through the decades.

In Burlyuk's world, the world of the painter, everything was adrift.

In springtime, when the water is going down and the rafts are running aground, the willow branches that tie the logs together are cut apart.

Loose tree trunks, racing one another, jostling one another, drenched by the waves, take off from the sandbanks and float toward the sea.

One-eyed Burlyuk had set everything in his pictures adrift long ago. This is what he brought to Moscow. He was sensible and wanted to elbow his way through. He wanted to obtain a better diploma and graduated in a very short time from the School of Painting, Sculpture and Architecture.

At first, he provoked fights with Mayakovsky, taunting him and Chekrygin. But later they became friends.

They walked the circular boulevards of this enormous Moscow. Moscow was like dough which had been whipped up with a giant beater.

Moscow rang with the sound of its autumn boulevards. Moscow flaunted its rusty signboards and golden letters. It looked as it never had looked in any painting. It looked as it had never been seen before.

Mayakovsky knew it well. He had felt the evening dampness a thousand times, and he knew the long nights when the black cape, worn out by the touch of his large hands, no longer warmed him, and when the cap on his head was getting damp.

Now Mayakovsky had finally found a friend for his night walks.

Burlyuk had read a lot; he knew not only Khlebnikov, but Arthur Rimbaud in translation; he knew the poetry of the "poètes maudits"; he knew other voices, other names for things. In the pictures of the artists of that period lived not only objects but letters—big signboard letters.

Mayakovsky knew them all.

He saw the moon not as a glittering path across the sea. He saw a lunar herring and thought that it would be good to have some bread with this herring.

Already, unwritten verses lived within him. He saw the letters O and a French S skipping on the rooftops advertising watches. He saw the signboards and read those iron-backed books. He admired the china teapots and the flying rolls pictured on tavern shutters.

Chapter 6

Neighbors

Symbolism [1] wanted to be more than a school of art.

It lived by intersecting with other systems and, above all, it attempted to live through religion.

It lived through the substitution of one meaning for another and often by the rustle of analogies.

At times, this led to obscurity and false profundity.

Vyacheslav Ivanov's art relied entirely on substitution of one series for another.[2] He was a religious poet. Blok's religiosity was ironical.

Beyond Blok's symbolism, a second theme arose, a theme not of religion, but of everyday life.[3]

There were echoes of Fet, Yakov Polonsky; the gypsy romance re-emerged. Before his death, Blok was recording in his diary one gypsy romance after another. At our meetings, I talked to him about these romances, although at the time, I did not yet know that he was writing them down. He used to agree with me then.

The gypsy romance is no small matter. It lives through the voice of Pushkin and through the voice of our best lyrical poets. Gypsy romances are numerous; Blok wrote down twenty of them to remember.

"Misty Morning, Silver-Haired Morning," wrote Turgenev and, later, Blok used these words for the title of a book.

"Wild Nights, Sleepless Nights," wrote Apukhtin. But Blok wrote:

> You were more radiant, truer, and lovelier than all.
> So, do not curse me, do not curse!
> My train is flying like a gypsy song, like those
> Days which will never return. . . .[4]

In these pre-war years the gypsy romance had already made its appearance in Blok's poetry.[5]

The gypsy song is, indeed, no small matter. I heard gypsies sing their romances only after the Revolution.

In the house of Sofiya Andreyevna Tolstoy, Tolstoy's granddaughter, old gypsies were playing guitars whose sounding-boards were almost worn out from use.

They played and reminisced about Lev Nikolayevich Tolstoy.

The old man loved romances. He had loved the romance "Do Not Call Me to a Sensible Life," and he used to say, "this is poetry."

When he listened to a record of Varya Panina, he would turn the horn of the record player toward the peasants, who waited for him, so that they too could hear her.

The romance is a street song, but it is not as yet the song of the street. [Here, too, the Symbolists failed to find the simple musicality of words.]

At that time, Blok was interested in wrestling and read the novels of Breshko-Breshkovsky. In those days, everything outside the sphere of pure art gained new importance. Blok used to say that a real work of art could be born only if an artist had a direct, rather than an intellectual, relationship with the world.

Kuzmin demanded that words be precise and unequivocal. Poets searched for new masters, they remembered Rabelais and Villon; they struggled against the fluidity of words.

An it was then that Akhmatova appeared.

[We know her, but while knowing her, we have already

partly forgotten her; and that is why it is hard to understand her.]

She restored the concrete gesture of love to poetry. In her poems, the woman has feathers on her hat and the feathers brush against the top of her carriage. At that time, the first automobiles appeared and they, too, were built with a raised roof to allow for ladies' feathers.

Akhmatova is as concrete as a limousine builder:

> He touched my knees again
> With an almost steady hand.[6]

Akhmatova wrote:

> The music in the garden
> Sounded with such inexpressible sorrow.
> Fresh and sharp, smelling of ocean, lie
> The oysters in ice on the platter.
>
> He said to me: "I am a loyal friend!"
> And touched my dress.
> How unlike an embrace
> Is the touch of those hands.[7]

Poetry was thirsting for concreteness.

Similies and metaphors withdrew into the depth of the verse line.

Music is here juxtaposed to the smell of oysters, and oysters give us back the sea.

Blok contrasts a restaurant to love. Here they are side by side.

The metaphoric expression becomes complex.

Akhmatova wrote:

> High in the sky a small cloud looked gray,
> like the stretched-out skin of a squirrel.
> He said to me: "Never mind that your body
> will melt in March, delicate Snow White!"
>
> In my fluffy muff, my hands are getting cold,
> I feel frightened, I feel somehow uneasy.

> Oh, how to call them back, those swift weeks
> of his love, so aerial and so fleeting.[8]

Snow White belongs to literary series; these two lines are bad.

But love, aerial and fleeting, is associated with the dissolving cloud. The concrete cloud and the tiny squirrel skin became the banner of Acmeism.[9]

Acmeism, however, could not warm the world with a muff. Its concreteness was narrow. Zenkevich attempted to make coarseness and primitiveness concrete. Sergey Gorodetsky attempted to introduce archaic elements into the language and to mate poetry with the Russian song.

Never was poetry more open to invasion. A civil war between forms was being waged in poetry. And then, it was invaded by painting.

Chapter 7

More Neighbors

In the School of Painting, people had other interests.

They even made mistakes differently.

Chekrygin talked about the resurrection of the dead, echoing Fyodorov, the old bibliographer of the Rumyantsev Museum.

He was painting angels, when Mayakovsky wanted him to paint a fly.

Through the long nights, Burlyuk and Mayakovsky walked among the humps of the dark boulevards, past the crosses of Moscow churches.

Burlyuk talked about words, about rejuvenated painting, the coarse, shell-like, splintery brush-stroke, the word as such and objects in rebellion.

The poet received his initiation into art from Burlyuk—a man without direction, an artist who had lost himself in experimentation, an eternal wanderer.

Mayakovsky walked with Burlyuk and they discussed Khlebnikov, paintings, words and even letters entangled in paint. They discussed the Rayonism [1] of Larionov and their old friend, the donkey.

In Burlyuk's apartment, there was no table, no chairs either, nor even beds. Two mattresses lay on the floor, and by

the wall a board lay across two trestles. He put Mayakovsky
up at his place. Vladimir was painting a portrait.

The portrait, on a background of blue-gray, was painted in
dark blue and dark green. It was the portrait of a woman
with arms bent, wearing a large hat. Her elbows were raised.
The portrait was neither avant-garde nor very interesting.
Burlyuk went everywhere, preaching his gospel.

Open discussions were organized. Burlyuk would show
Raphael's Dresden "Madonna" next to photographs of curly-
haired boys. Mayakovsky made speeches. He still spoke as a
polemicist, claiming that each period had its own art. They
went to the furnished rooms where the art school students
lived, and preached.

Outside the window lay Moscow, large and blue. That particular section was called Basmannaya.

On the table was a fat copper samovar and, next to it, rolls
and *baranki*.[2] Mayakovsky stood at the window. The side of
the samovar was blue, reflecting the Moscow night outside
the curtainless window. Beyond the windowpane, snowflakes
swam like fish in an aquarium, leaving the blue of the night
undisturbed. Mayakovsky said that it was time to exchange
camel-words, words heavily burdened, for free words, expressing a new rhythm.

Disputes were heated. "The Jack of Diamonds"[3] invited
them to give a lecture. Maksimilian Voloshin asserted that
graves do not open in vain. If Byzantine and Russian icon
painting were being resurrected now, it was because the Greek
Apollo had died. A new swarthy, bowlegged Apollo was
creating a new Gothic art.

At the lecture, a short, gaunt young man yawned noisily,
like a cat opening its small mouth. He was wearing a uniform
cap with an emblem. It was Aleksey Kruchyonykh.

Vladimir Mayakovsky descended the unfamiliar steps of
the Polytechnical Museum and, at the low rostrum, said:
"Artists, Jacks of Diamonds, remember Kuzma Prutkov!"

He recited a poem, changing it thus:

> If the worm of doubt has crawled up your neck,
> Squash it yourself, and do not let the valet do it.

"If you have doubts about the new art, why did you challenge the Symbolists?"

This was in winter.

At one time, Valery Bryusov wrote a drama about future mankind.[4] That mankind left the sun and lived underground. A great traveller of the time roamed around the building and discovered the sun through the glass. He went to the people and told them they would be happier if they raised the roofs and lived under the sun. A wise elder knew the secret; there was no air above the roofs.

The sun shone in a gaping void.

Mankind, however, had grown tired. In its midst arose a sect of assassins who wanted to hasten the end of cave life. Mankind had weakened. Zinaida Gippius called the people of that time ants—those were the cave dwellers. The "Moon Ants" of Wells perished easily; when struck, they disintegrated like mushrooms.

But let's go back to the story left by the wayside, covered with snow.

The elder decided to lift the roofs. The long unused machinery was found with great effort. The counterweights creaked as they were lowered and the roofs were raised.

And the sun, enormous, with the flaming trumpet of the last angel of the Last Judgment, rose above the crowd as it perished from lack of air.

The Symbolists believed neither in the world nor the air, and hid themselves under the roofs of their correspondences.

Andrey Bely went off to the West, to join the Anthroposophists, and concealed his enormous ability, his talent and the words already found in *Ashes*, under the arches of the wooden temple that Rudolf Steiner was building in Switzerland. Mayakovsky knew that air exists.

Mayakovsky, already inspired, but still silent, moved among people. He read *The Satyricon* [5] writers.

There was Sasha Chyorny.

Sasha Chyorny wrote verse for *The Satyricon. The Satyricon* was a strange place. Its God was a one-eyed man who knew how to make people laugh—Averchenko, a man with no conscience who had learned long before how to enjoy the comforts of life: he was stout; he loved turkey with chestnuts and he knew how to work. He was already an entrepreneur.

Not lacking in self-confidence, Averchenko used his widely read "Mailbox" column to mock a poor telegraph operator named Nadkin,[6] who sent in poems that kept getting better and better.

The telegraph operator—a downtrodden, insignificant person—was one of the attractions of *The Satyricon.*

The pale, one-eyed Averchenko, with his fondness for turkey with chestnuts, pretended that he was being harassed by the police. He even pictured *The Satyricon* itself as a sort of satyr grown fat on sweet rolls—a faun that gnaws at the censor's red pencils and cannot break out.[7]

Even if this faun, overstuffed as he was on sweet rolls, had managed to break the pencils, he would not have run very far.

Sasha Chyorny, Pyotr Potyomkin and Valentin Goryansky published their poetry in this *Satyricon,* or, as it was called after 1912, *The New Satyricon.* Mayakovsky loved their poems.

"The street lamps shine like wall eyes," wrote Sasha Chyorny.

"The puddles glitter like the bald skulls of dead old men."

That sounds like Mayakovsky:

And then—crumpling the blanket of street lights—
night, obscene and drunk, was exhausted from lovemaking
and beyond the suns of streets, somewhat hobbled
the flaccid moon, unwanted.[8]

Pyotr Potyomkin appeared on the same pages.

Both Chyorny and Potyomkin resemble the Symbolists. Sasha Chyorny's pseudonym [Black] parallels Andrey Bely's [White].

They are Symbolists without the correspondences. In their poetry, they also use the street and the tavern, and they gave a second reinterpretation of all that.

In the "Unknown Lady," Blok describes the landscape beautifully:

> Far away above the dust of the lanes,
> Above the boredom of suburban *dachas,*
> The gilded bakery sign shines faintly
> And a child is heard crying.
>
> And every evening, beyond the city barriers,
> Experienced crack-wits,
> Their bowler hats cocked,
> Stroll with their ladies among the ditches.
>
> Over the lake the ear-locks creak,
> And women are shrieking,
> And in the sky the moon's disk,
> Bored by it all, grimaces senselessly.

This is Ozerki, a country suburb of Petersburg.

The Unknown Lady enters this landscape.

With Sasha Chyorny nobody enters, nothing happens, there is no eve, and no violet color. This color was for Blok the light of his inspiration.

This was after the 1905 Revolution and before the war.

Old recollections of the Romantics and the Symbolists, parodies of stylization and of simplicity—all this is in Potyomkin.

His hero is in love with a doll in a beauty parlor's window display:

> Every evening at the usual hour I go to the corner
> Where, by the sign "Municipal Pawn Shop"
> I can press my face against the glass
> *   *   *   *
> And there, in the window, wrapped in silk,
> Standing on a thin leg, cold,

> With her back to the display shelves,
> She is beckoning to me.[9]

Potyomkin used unexpected rhymes and varied metrics. Mayakovsky knew also Valentin Goryansky and many other writers whose names may be forgotten by now. Many of them strongly resemble Mayakovsky in their writings, but they began resembling him only later on.

All these people spoke with one voice, a voice that proclaimed that there will be nothing or there will be nonsense.

Their drawings were terrifying. One, for instance, presents a student family; the husband, his ugly wife, and on the floor a child knawing at the bone of a human leg.

This is terrifying nonsense.

Chapter 8

David Burlyuk Finds a Poet

It was in this milieu that Mayakovsky moved. Time passed. Mayakovsky talked with everyone: with people in the streets, with friends, with cabdrivers.

He lived, read poetry and wandered through the streets. At one time, Mayakovsky admired Viktor Gofman, who wrote of beauty and was not untalented as a poet, but of limited scope. Gofman's poems tormented Mayakovsky as he walked the Moscow streets. Now, he walked with Burlyuk. Burlyuk tried to convince Volodya[1] that he was a young Jack London.

And so, one night, as Burlyuk walked with Mayakovsky along the Sretensky Boulevard, Vladimir recited verses to him, fragments about the city, odd pieces that Mayakovsky later did not publish:

"One of my friends wrote that."

David stopped and said:

"You wrote it yourself. But you're a genius!"

[The hazel-eyed Army doctor Nikolay Kulbin used to say: "All people are capable of walking a tightrope because of the way their ear labyrinths are built. But they don't realize that."

Geniuses can write poetry, but they don't know they can. They try too hard and break their stride.]

Mayakovsky left. Burlyuk met him the next morning and introduced him to someone with the following words:

"Don't you know him? This is my friend, the genius, the famous poet, Mayakovsky."

Volodya nudged him, but Burlyak drew him aside and said:

"Volodya, now you'd better write or you'll make me look like a fool. Don't be afraid of anything. I'll give you 50 kopeks a day. As of today, you are a man of means."

Mayakovsky wrote his poems, Burlyuk looked over his shoulder, grabbed the still warm lines and rearranged them. His first poem began like this:

> Purple and white were discarded and crumpled,
> handfuls of ducats they threw at the green,
> and into the black palms of crowded windows
> they dealt burning yellow cards.

> It was not strange for the boulevards and squares
> to see the blue togas on the buildings.
> Those who arrived first received from the lights
> bracelets to ring their feet like yellow wounds.[2]

He entered the realm of poetry without changing. With him he brought maps, paintings—his own and Burlyuk's—innumerable declarations, and fragmentary, dislocated and distorted images.

He thrust image into image. In his poetry, he used the methods of contemporary painting.

> A grim rain slanted its eyes.
> and behind
> the grill
> of clearcut
> wires of iron thought—
> a featherbed.
> And on
> it
> rest lightly
> the feet of rising stars.
> But the death
> of the streetlights,

> tsars
> with crowns of gas,
> made it more painful
> to behold
> the hostile bouquet of street prostitutes.[3]

Burlyuk had not much skill, but he saw Khlebnikov. Falling from heaven without breaking his neck, Vasily Kamensky,[4] not a minor poet, had also recently joined him. Essentially, Burlyuk was a theoretician who knew the techniques of experimentation; his skill was limited, but now he could see another accomplish what he, Burlyuk, was unable to do.

Poems were born.

There would, however, have been no Mayakovsky without cell number 103. Mayakovsky was an inmate and read books in that cell. As a boy, he had distributed revolutionary leaflets, and read them, but he had lost contact with those comrades long before. But Mayakovsky had his own—however schematic—map of the world and a scheme of history.

He became neither a Potyomkin, nor a Valentin Goryansky, nor even a David Burlyuk, but a man who felt responsible for the world—a man who had known bakers' meetings and Party discussions before he knew the disputes at the Polytechnical Museum—a man who realized well that one pays for words with prison and exile.

The Symbolists wrote about Dionysus, the "Eternal Feminine," and Demeter. In a Moscow, embroidered all over with crosses, Mayakovsky, seeking the simplest, most accessible mythology and fresh images, adopted religious images which he destroyed in the process. The number of such religious passages in his first volume is astounding.

I will not quote them all. His second poem ends like this:

> Beyond the turmoil
> and the horror,
> to look
> is pleasing to the eye:
> slave

of suffering-quietly-indifferent
crosses,
coffins
of brothels
the Orient threw them all into one flaming vase.[5]

Mayakovsky sees policemen crucified by crossroads. In the morning, slush is seen kissing the tunic of the icon Christ. He cries out to the sun in the same way as, in the gospel, Christ on the cross spoke to God who had forsaken him.

Sun!
Father mine!
Have mercy, at least thou, and do not torture me!
It is my blood, spilled by thee, gushing on this far-away road.
It is my soul
in shreds of torn cloud
in a burnt-out sky
on the rusty cross of the belfry! [6]

In the tragedy *Vladimir Mayakovsky,* the old man with the cats says:

And I see—in you on a cross of laughter
a tortured scream is crucified.[7]

And the people said:

Let's go,
where for his saintliness
they crucified the prophet. . . .[8]

Mayakovsky spoke like a prophet and when people attacked him, barely protected as he was by his yellow blouse, he wrote down the following:

This led to my Golgothas
in the auditoriums of Petersburg, Moscow, Odessa and Kiev,
and there was not one
who
would not shout:
"Crucify,
crucify, him!" [9]

This image is exact, it is a quote. He knew that when Christ faced Pilate, the crowd did not free Him, but Barabbas, the sycophant and bandit.

> See—again
> Barabbas is preferred to
> the spat-upon Golgothian? [10]

He wanted to call his book *A Cloud in Pants, The Thirteenth Apostle*. In the book *Man*, he called his love his "thousand-leafed gospel" and he divided the poem into chapters entitled "Birth," "Passions" and "Ascension."

It would be ridiculous to try to prove what is clear to everyone, namely that this tortured man in a black velvet jacket, this man with large hands, this passionate gambler who was still almost a boy, was not religious. But, these simple images are universally understood, and they existed side by side with the lower literature, a literature reminiscent of Sasha Chyorny. These lines are not religious, but blasphemous. These lines attack an existing foe and rob him of the emotions with which he is associated.

Only much later did the Revolution teach Mayakovsky to examine the former God under a magnifying glass like a noxious bacillus.

Mayakovsky had just learned to write poetry. His throat was clear, the words he spoke were new and he was getting ready to join them into a sentence.

He had found his voice; he had learned to write as others learn to swim. He discovered that he could float on water. Later, he learned how bitter that water was.

Impassioned by his work, impassioned by his words, the poet is joyous when he speaks of grief. But, though exalted, grief remains grief. The poet tames grief to come and go at his beck and call. It does not have to be leashed.

And so, Mayakovsky became a poet.

David Burlyuk gave him 50 kopeks a day. That was a lot of money. Dostoyevsky's Raskolnikov,[11] to prove that he did not

The house where Vladimir Mayakovsky was born in Bagdadi (now re-named Mayakovsky), Soviet Georgia.

Vladimir Mayakovsky, at the age of 3, with his sister Olga.

Mayakovsky, in high school uniform, with his family.

Vladimir Mayakovsky in Moscow, 1911.

In 1913–1914 the poet travelled across Russia to spread his Futurist ideas on poetry and society. He is shown in Kiev in 1913.

Group of Futurists in 1913, from left to right: Kruchyonykh, David Burlyuk, Mayakovsky, Nikolay Burlyuk and Livshits. (*Leonard Hutton Galleries*)

Anna Akhmatova, considered one of the greatest Russian poets of the twentieth century.

Aleksandr Blok, the great Russian lyric poet, with Korney Chukovsky, the writer and critic.

ABOVE: Viktor Shklovsky, circa 1914. Drawing by the famous Russian painter Repin.

Velimir Khlebnikov, leading Futurist poet. Sketch by Mayakovsky.

David Burlyuk, dressed and made up in a typically Futurist manner. (*Sarah Bodine, Leonard Hutton Galleries*)

ОКНО САТИРЫ РОСТА №70.

1) ТОВАРИЩИ, НЕ ПОДДАВАЙ-
ТЕСЬ ПАНИКЕ, ОНА
ДЕЛАЕТ ОБЫКНОВЕННО
ИЗ МУХИ СЛОНА.

2) И ВОТ СЛЕДСТ-
ВИЕ ЭТОГО

3) НО И ВОСТРО ДЕРЖАТЬ
УХО,
ЧТОБ ИЗ СЛОНА НЕ
ПОЛУЧИЛАСЬ МУХА.

4) СЛЕДСТВИЕ
ЭТОГО ТАКОЕ.

5) БЕЗ ВСЯКОЙ ПАНИКИ, НО И НЕ ЗРЯ РЕЗВО
ИДИТЕ НА ФРОНТ ХЛАДНОКРОВНО И ТРЕЗВО.

Propaganda posters drawn by Mayakovsky during the Civil War.

Mayakovsky (seated) with Lily Brik, Boris Pasternak (left) and Sergey Eisenstein when they were all connected with *LEF,* the central organ of avant-garde art. (*Herbert Marshall from his book,* Mayakovsky, *published by Hill and Wang, New York*)

Mayakovsky is photographed in Mexico in 1925. From there he travelled to the United States.

Group of Mayakovsky's friends, from left to right: V. Mayakovsky, O. Brik, B. Pasternak, S. Tretyakov, V. Shklovsky, E. Triolet, L. Brik, R. Kushner.

Mayakovsky (standing at left) during rehearsal for his play, *The Bedbug*.

Mayakovsky reading his play, *The Bath-House,* a satire of Soviet bureaucracy, on the radio in 1929.

Mayakovsky's room on Lubyansky Passage, where he shot himself.

Mayakovsky's funeral, April 17, 1930 in Moscow.

Statue of Vladimir Mayakovsky on Mayakovsky Square in Moscow.

murder because he was starving, said that he was paid up to a half a ruble a lesson. Later on, Pisarev wrote about this half a ruble.

And so, he was not hungry, or almost not. There were public appearances. He gave lectures, spoke about black cats. They were black cats, dry cats, which may be stroked to produce electricity.

These black cats were discussed in his lectures and he wrote about them in the tragedy *Vladimir Mayakovsky*. Their meaning is the following: electricity can be obtained from a cat. The Egyptians did it that way. But it is more efficient to produce electricity industrially and not have to bother with cats. We believed then that the old art obtained its artistic effects the way Egyptians obtained electricity, but we wanted to have pure electricity, pure art.

Lectures were based on such themes. To be printed was out of the question, but one could always make a speech. However, one needed catchwords to announce these speeches. Nikolay Kulbin taught us how to make up these slogans, powerful slogans, as though the Turks had taken the city and were announcing it with drum beats. This was when Mayakovsky put on his yellow blouse. He had two blouses: the first one was yellow. Yellow was considered the color of Futurism. The blouse was wide at the bottom, with a soft collar; the material was not heavy so that through the yellow blouse—which was rather long—his black trousers could be seen.

His second blouse was striped: yellow and black.

His blouse had more success than the cats. It was easier to write about it. A journalist, then, had to be given easily accessible entrance doors. He did not venture farther than the door.

Chapter 9

Women

Shakespeare said about one of his characters that Cupid had patted him on the shoulder, but had not touched his heart.

So it was with Vladimir Mayakovsky. The tragedy had not yet been written.

There were women and there were poems about women. It was all long ago. So permit me to call some witnesses to explain what happened.

Mayakovsky is the first to speak. The poem is entitled "After a Woman."

> The tin in the copper alloy of houses,
> the tremors of the streets are scarcely contained,
> teased by the red cover of lust,
> the smoke columns pierce the sky with their horns.
>
> Volcano tights under the ice of their dresses,
> the full-eared breasts are ripe for harvest.
> With a thief's smirk blunt arrows soar jealously
> from the sidewalks.[1]

Gleb Uspensky speaks second.

This is a passage from a piece entitled "New Times, New Concerns," from the chapter headed "In the Old Homestead." A man finds himself in the position of not receiving any mail: there has been some confusion about his name. Now, he sits and reads Rocambole.[2] He likes Rocambole.

"Please, gentlemen writers, when you write for the lonely working-class reader, do use stronger, coarser colors in your novels than you have up to now. . . . Beat your drums, strike your cymbals with all your might. Try to picture love as a searing flame that would actually burn through your nerves, so that they would be consumed as they are in life, by the real, true fire. . . . Also, use a style as disproportionate and unrealistic in describing all other human relationships. Feminine beauty should be depicted especially incongruously: breasts should be described without fail as being gorgeous, verging on indecency, and compared to two fire-spitting mountain tops, to the columns of Hercules, or to the Egyptian pyramids. . . . Only with such absurd exaggerations can you convey to a person, abandoned in the dead-end darkness of loneliness, an approximate idea of what is accessible to others in the real artless form of genuine beauty." [3]

Mayakovsky's attitude toward women was of the kind described by Gleb Uspensky, with the same exaggeration of the most elementary femininity. This was still youth speaking.

As a boy, Pushkin drew skirts, feet and skirts; the woman was not seen.

Mayakovsky hungered for life. And there were all kinds of women. The Italian Futurists wrote about women, and this was a subject they knew something about. Marinetti wrote:

"The degradation of love (as emotion or lust) is due to the growing freedom of women and their resulting accessibility. The degradation of love is due also to the generally exaggerated emphasis on feminine luxury. Stated more clearly: women, nowadays, prefer luxury to love. Men hardly ever love women deprived of luxury. Lovers have lost all prestige. Love has lost its absolute value." [4]

Clearly, Mayakovsky's attitude to women differed from Marinetti's.

Marinetti's woman is a very real, bourgeois, and in her own way progressive woman—a woman who does not love. Her love is overshadowed by what formerly used to complement love or be caused by love. Now love itself is overshadowed by these tertiary characteristics of love.

Mayakovsky's woman, as he describes her, is unreal. She is the woman of his first desires.

She is described naively, in a simplified manner, and still this is a woman.

There was a certain circle in those days. Today, its building on Dimitrovka houses the office of the Public Prosecutor, but it is unrecognizable: a new story has been added. It was the Society for Free Aesthetics at one time. Andrey Bely and Balmont read their poetry there; dress coats and elegant dresses were worn—it has all been described by Andrey Bely. I, personally, was never there. Bunin used to go there; so did the young, long-faced, curly-haired Aleksey Tolstoy, wearing a scarf instead of a necktie. At one time, they were planning a revolution in art there, they talked about abysses, quarreled about the nature of this abyss and about whose residence, in point of fact, this abyss was.

They quarreled and Chulkov was noisily expelled. Later, the abyss became very livable, bluish-grayish drapes probably hung there, scandals were rare. Bely left and many lawyers attended.[5]

This was the center of Moscow; this was the new assembly hall.

Downstairs was a billiards room which Mayakovsky frequented.

He was admitted; after all, he was an event, one of the landmarks of Moscow. And it was a good billiards table.

He played billiards with utter involvement and integrity, losing again and again, creating his own rules; he never paid, for instance, for the last game and never asked others to. This was a rule he valued greatly.

It was here that he met Elsa K.[6] and wrote verses to her:

> There stands a house,
> it's full of windows,
> to the right of Pyatnitskaya.

And that meany witch
lives
there and doesn't write to me.

Mayakovsky had already gone through a great deal, had suffered frequent toothaches and even had a collection of drawings of giraffes. The giraffe was Mayakovsky himself. And, now, the giraffe in his drawings wore a bandage for its toothache.

The giraffe—handsome, golden-black—wore nature's own Futurist blouse.

Chapter 10

Already About the Briks
and More About the Circle

By 1910, Symbolism had spread to the magazines, made itself at home, and become domesticated.

It had expected to conquer the country, but instead it became a mercenary army like the Barbarian mercenaries who served Rome. Bryusov wrote for *The Russian Thought*.[1] Symbolists were even published in the family magazine *Niva*. Only Blok was writing little. Balmont, a genuine poet, had lost his driving force, lost his resistance.

He translated from all languages, read a tremendous amount, drank wine and wrote poetry.

Balmont was a real poet, even a warrior, but disarmed. Having settled down in his quarters, he ran around in a sheepskin coat or in some Roman sandals taken from his host. He lived with the wife of his host who treated him like a landmark and he would set up the samovar and, over tea, tell about the campaigns, about Denmark.

A celebration was given in honor of the venerable Balmont. Everything was done according to the rules. There were academic speeches, poetry recitations, words of welcome, and then Balmont would read his poetry slurring his Rs. And then Mayakovsky spoke, too. He was isolated, weary, tragic, cheerful and loud.

He spoke about Balmont and recited Balmont's poems splendidly, much better than Balmont himself.

He recited as though he were swimming with broad strokes in a wide, familiar sea. He spoke about Balmont's verse with its recurring lines. There was a recurring line:

> With my reveries I was catching the departing shadows
> The departing shadows of the dying day. . . .

and further on:

> I climbed the tower and the steps were shaking
> And the steps were shaking under my feet.[2]

Mayakovsky said that all this was passé: the steps were passé, the repetitions were passé, and the alliterations were passé.

Actually, it was all very proper. But his voice, the force of his speech, and his thorough knowledge of Balmont supplanted the jubilee. It was as though they were preparing to give an old man a warm bath and an elephant had shown up; he put his foot into the bathtub and when he took it out, the water was gone and the tub was dry. The gathering was brought to an end with some effort.

Balmont was far from being an untalented man. Later he came to Petersburg. He had already been recognized by the gray-bearded Semyon Afanasyevich Vengerov and in university circles. They forgave him everything because he translated from the Spanish. Besides, at the University, they understood that literature must go on.

The University had a long corridor that extended from the Neva to the Small Nevka. Unfortunately, this corridor has now been shortened.

The University stands at an angle to the Neva. The University has twelve roofs which used to shelter the twelve Petrine Collegia. The University corridor used to connect all twelve institutions. As one walked down the corridor, one could sometimes see a student way down at the other end of the hall, and he looked very small.

They led Balmont through this corridor to the auditorium. In front of the auditorium was a dark room. Then, in the large auditorium, students in heavy jackets read their own poems to Balmont.

A lecture was delivered in which Balmont was called the grandfather of Russian poetry.

[When the poetry reading was over, Balmont stood up and threw out an envenomed *R:*

"I'm an ungrrrateful grandfather. I don't accept my grandchildren. This is bookish, erudite, but poetry is over there, in the street," and he pointed to the window.]

There was snow outside the window. The street was empty, poorly lit; across the street stood the Otto Clinic; farther on was the wide, blue, snowy, deserted Neva.

Balmont, of course, understood Mayakovsky.

Osip Brik had finished law school and was married to a very beautiful young woman with large hazel-brown eyes.

["Osya" Brik was not a writer and despised literature. Still, at the University, he started out by planning with some friends to publish a Pinkerton detective series. But Osya was very bright and he despised the Pinkerton series as much as poetry. He did not publish it for personal satisfaction, but with some imagined simpleton in mind. The readers, however, did not appreciate Osya's Pinkerton and his wrestlers.]

Brik read a great deal. He did not like the Symbolists. [He travelled all over Russia with his wife, but did not travel to Venice. He visited Buryato-Mongolia and there he witnessed a fire in a pagoda. Its top was enveloped in flames.

Brik, however, left before seeing the end of the fire.

Years later, or perhaps only a half-year later, he saw a newsreel in a movie house: there, he saw that same pagoda, ablaze. It burned, then the fire died down, and the roof collapsed.

This taught him another lesson: curiosity does not pay.]

He visited Central Asia; he saw catamites and the desert. He even took along a poet whom he supported and the poet wrote a book entitled something like *The Desert and the Petals.*

Because of his self-control, Brik himself was never tactless. Now, he looked at Mayakovsky, but did not approach him.

A book was published with a coarse linen cover. It was called *A Slap in the Face of Public Taste.* In it appeared David Burlyuk and the other Burlyuk—Nikolay—and Kruchyonykh, Kandinsky, Mayakovsky and Khlebnikov.

Again the book ended with a warning. Khlebnikov wrote: "A Look at the Year 1917," which listed the dates of the downfall of the great powers, 22 dates in all, without any commentaries. It ended with the words "Someone, 1917."

PART TWO

Composed of six chapters. In these chapters, the author gets to know Mayakovsky. Contemporary critics, art
theoreticians, and "The Stray Dog" [1] are discussed. Also, how
that generation faced the war and what the poet Vasily
Kamensky had to say about it. How we loved and how we
made mistakes. These chapters also deal with the Revolution
and tell how the poet turned cheerful and came to love the
world.

Chapter **11**

Petersburg

It was the year 1912.

I met Khlebnikov in Petersburg. The discussion had just ended, people had left, it was dark and the chairs were already being stacked. The blond Khlebnikov stood, slightly hunched, as always. He wore a long, black coat, all buttoned up. His hand touched his lips.

I approached him and said:

"1917—is that the fall of the Russian Empire?"

"You have understood," he said in a very low voice, but no lower than usual, and added: "Can you let me have twenty kopeks?"

He borrowed rarely, and usually less than a ruble.

That was already in 1913 in Petersburg.

Debates were organized everywhere. Much was being said about them, not all of it accurate.

The debates were not always noisy. Once, Kazimir Malevich spoke at the Troitsky Theater.

Stocky, not very tall, he lectured in a quiet voice and said things inconceivable to the audience. Before the lecture, Malevich had exhibited a picture: on a red background, women in black and white, shaped like truncated cones. This was a powerful work, not an accidental find. Malevich did not intend to shock anyone, he simply wanted to explain what it was all about. The audience felt like laughing.

Malevich spoke quietly:

"Serov, that mediocre dauber. . . ."

The audience began to clamor joyfully. Malevich looked up and calmly said:

"I was not teasing anyone, that is what I believe."

He continued his lecture.

Usually, officers sat in the first row, elegantly dressed, their uniforms so gaudy that they differed from ladies' dresses mainly by the absence of décolletés and the heavy texture of the fabric.

And in the back were students—men and women.

Burlyuk lectured.

The first-row spectators looked at his worn and frayed trousers with hostile pity.

Nikolay Kulbin came out, spoke in a very quiet, matter-of-fact manner. With his laterna magica, David Burlyuk showed new pictures, and the audience reacted noisily.

The exhibitions of the young were rather empty. Unsold pictures hung in unpaid galleries.

In the two-kopek press, there was a lot of fuss.

These were experienced newspapers, cautiously pornographic.

The Speech,[1] in which Aleksandr Benois gave his sermons on the mount about art, tried to avoid mentioning Mayakovsky.

Apollon,[2] a square-shaped journal, printed on fine quality paper, tried not to notice the Futurists. Later on, Redko wrote about them in *The Russian Wealth*,[3] and Bryusov, very briefly, in *The Russian Thought*.

But their books were published. It is true that Burlyuk and Kruchyonykh published these books in a nervous manner, repeating the same things.

Kruchyonykh used to wear a civil service cap and his books looked like a series of pictures. Olga Rozanova was responsible for their production, coloring and make-up. The word was used as an ornament in the picture. In the art of that period, painting and literature had not yet separated.

Mayakovsky wanted to get into the theater.

In the tragedy *Vladimir Mayakovsky,* the poet is alone.

He is surrounded by people, but they are not three-dimensional. They are screens, painted shields from which words come forth.

This is the cast:

His woman-friend ("he" is Vladimir Mayakovsky). She is described as 15-20 feet tall. She does not speak.

An old man with dry, black cats (several thousand years old). Then come the Mayakovskys.

A Man without an Eye and a Leg, a Man without an Ear, a Headless Man, a Man with a Stretched Face, a Man with Two Kisses, and an ordinary Young Man who loves his family. Then come the women, all with tears. They offer their tears to the poet.

The poet himself is the theme of his poetry.

The poet dissects himself on stage, holding himself between his fingers as a gambler holds his cards. This is a Mayakovsky Deuce, a Trey, a Jack, a King. The stake of the game is love. The game is lost. The Man with the Stretched Face says:

> You can also use my soul
> to make
> such dressy skirts.[4]

This is Mayakovsky's theme.

Mayakovsky has nowhere to go. He is surrounded by his own unhappy Mayakovskys and by kisses.

What can one do with kisses? The poet even looked for a frame for them.

As for the leading woman, this is what happened:

Mayakovsky tore off her veil and, under the veil was a doll, a huge woman, who later was hoisted up and carried away.

This case is familiar to us.

There was Blok's play *The Puppet Show.*

There was the novel [5] in which Blok's rival called himself "Red Domino" and danced, probably as a harlequin.

In the *Fiery Angel,*[6] the conflict is between Bryusov, a mercenary and a false sorcerer, the woman Renata and Bely.

Pierrot and Harlequin are in love with the same woman.

They are surrounded by the dolls of the Ethnographical Museum. Columbine is made out of cardboard. Pierrot sings:

> In no way did he offend her,
> But the beloved fell into the snow!
> She could not hold up, sitting.
> I could not hold back my laughter.
>
> And to the dance of the frozen needles,
> Around my cardboard beloved,
> He jingled and jumped high.
> I danced behind him around the sleigh!
>
> And we sang on the sleepy street:
> "Oh, what trouble has come upon us."
> And high above my cardboard beloved—
> A star shone green and high.[7]

The fact that the beloved is made out of cardboard is indicated in all the stage directions; the distant horizon turns out to have been painted on paper. The people, and even Pierrot himself, bleed cranberry juice.

The world of the poem *Vladimir Mayakovsky,* despite its similarity to the world of *Puppet Show,* is very different.

For Blok, still a Symbolist then, people, that is the characters of his play, are chess figures or stylized silhouettes of roles flickering like live ones.

Now, they're real, now they aren't. The meaning of the play is that the world is transparent, dematerialized, and that everything keeps repeating itself: the girl becomes death, the scythe of death changes into the girl's braid. But in Mayakovsky's drama, Mayakovsky himself is utterly real. His boots have holes, very real, oval-shaped holes.

Vladimir Vladimirovich knew well how boots wear out. And, even the poet's laurel wreath was real. Mayakovsky wanted to wear a real laurel wreath on his head.

The real woman still stands there. But he hasn't broken through to her. The poet tests the world and turns it upside down; he leaves for the street, for the square, which he so stubbornly calls a "tambourine."

The world itself can be used as an instrument to produce bass sounds. Even fame is real and has to be won.

This poem or drama was played in Leningrad on Ofitserskaya Street. Blok lived nearby. He came to the performance and watched it very intently.

A stagehand had written the word "Futurists" on the iron door. Mayakovsky did not erase the inscription. That was not the issue. In any case, that too became part of the tragedy.

Filonov painted the decorative shields. Filonov was a painter inspired by the repudiated school of Russian icon painting, by those same frescoes of the Therapont Monastery. Distorted figures were solidly outlined, coated with splendid paints and shaped into decorative shields. There was also a large, very handsome cock which Filonov painted over several times. Mayakovsky was overjoyed by the performance.

The Thousand-Year-Old-Man was sketched and pasted over with down feathers. The woman really was fifteen feet tall.

The poet was gratified that these things and people existed outside himself and that one could look at them.

The other Mayakovskys, modest student actors, spoke with shy voices.

The audience was amused at times and, then again, it went along with the poet.

The audience believed that it was playing with the poet, that the whole thing was a joke and that, later, they would go home and everything would be as usual.

That same year, a lithographically produced book by Maya-kovsky was published in Moscow with the title *I*. Half the book was made up of drawings. The drawings were by Che-krygin and Lev Shekhtel. The drawings had nothing to do with the text; they even had personal signatures, in mirror writing.

Chapter 12

On Criticism

Aleksandr Benois was a highly cultured man who wrote articles competently. His drawings were rigid, not precise; his paintings were better. He knew how to copy and combine beautiful things created by others. This man wrote methodical sermons on art in *The Speech*. Seemingly, these sermons made no specific point—not even the necessity of establishing responsible government in Russia while retaining property qualifications; they never mentioned the Dardanelles; they only dealt with art. At that time, encyclopedic dictionaries listed all the problems and overwhelmed the reader with an extraordinary number of names. Biographical dictionaries listed such detailed biographies that they usually went no further than the third letter of the alphabet. Great people were written up completely without bias and even with compassionate disrespect.

The point was made that these people were basically just like us.

The Speech considered itself the guardian of Russian culture. It defined good and evil, and determined the beauty and melodiousness of poetry. Benois reviewed art exhibitions broadly and with restraint. For him, Repin was already dated, Larionov and Goncharova, savages. The truth was to be

found in *The World of Art.* He accepted Petrov-Vodkin in
order to worry Repin.

Aleksandr Benois wrote about Cubism and, somewhat losing his composure, entitled his article "Cubism or Don't
Give a Damnism."

But when Larionov contributed pictures to *The World of
Art,* he was discussed with restraint and maybe even with
respect.

The argument was about hegemony in art. Benois personally liked the dark brown, competent paintings of academic
epigones who used subjects from antiquity. Benois was less of
a figure than Diaghilev; he did not succeed in gaining the
world market for his goods.

However, he certainly deserved his journalistic position. He
was a hypocrite of a high order. His talent itself, minor as it
was, made him more qualified for this sort of pastorship.

Benois also wrote about Russian art. He did not understand
icon painting, but sympathized with it. He praised Russian
architecture and extolled Russian painters of the eighteenth
century, although neither Borovikovsky, nor Levitsky have
anything in common with *The World of Art.*

Broadmindedly, Benois discussed all world art as slowly
progressing toward *The World of Art.*

Presumably, there would be no time. There would be a
bloc of right-thinking people; thus humanity, developing
correctly, on the whole, would attain at last the ability to wear
ties, read the morning papers and be concerned about responsible government.

It was assumed that everything was developing correctly
and normally although somewhat slowly, perhaps. Did not the
mollusk achieve the honor of becoming the forefather of
Aleksandr Benois, who maybe would write the history of
painting. The picture was slightly spoiled by Lev Tolstoy;
one could not declare him uneducated, a mediocrity, nor even
behind his time.

The Speech very much wanted to use Lev Tolstoy to take on the look of a nationwide opposition.

Of course, *The Speech* had nothing in common with either Tolstoy's conception of God, or his criticism of existing society.

Nor was it concerned with literature. And that is why it kept many from understanding literature.

Kuokkala was two kilometers from the border. The *dacha* of Korney Ivanovich Chukovsky was on the outskirts of Kuokkala. Next to his house was a high stone wall. His was the last *dacha* with a beach front.

The beach was stony, gritty. The *dacha* faced the sea with a narrow, unpainted fence. Inland the plot widened. The *dacha* was built on the bank of a small river.

It was a two-story house, somewhat reminiscent of an English cottage. Korney Ivanovich worked a lot for the paper; at that time he was not yet writing for children. But he had a great deal of work. His nerves suffered and, like Leonid Andreyev, he lived in his *dacha* during the winter. Nearby was a summer theater, bought by Repin, and called "The Prometheus." It was an enormous barn with beams of painted imitation marble supporting the roof. Amateur performances and sometimes balls were held there.

A military brass band or the local Finnish amateur band played. The military one came from Beloostrov and had yellow trumpets; the Finns had nickelplated trumpets.

In the evening, orchestral music.

The vast sea, though only a bay there, washes over the sand in waves; the sand is as porous as cloth, and the sound of the waves is muffled.

Clouds, like flowing curdled milk, float through the sky day and night.

There were summer residents: Nikolay Ivanovich Kulbin rented a *dacha;* Nikolay Yevreinov, too. His hair was combed back—a well-groomed, very handsome, official sadist, and the author of a book, *The History of Corporal Punishment in Russia.*

When one visited him, he would clap his hands and a maid, young and plump, would appear. Yevreinov would say:

"Serve the pheasants!"

The maid replied:

"The pheasants have all been eaten."

"Then, give us tea."

This is called "theater for oneself." [1] There is a book about it. And here, too, was young Lev Nikulin, who loved Sasha Chyorny.

Korney Ivanovich had a studio on the upper floor of his *dacha.* Even in winter, writers would come to visit him. He wrote for *The Speech.* But at *The Speech,* he was disliked and only tolerated for his talent.

I was young and wore cheap short trousers and a sailor blouse. I boated from the end of the *dacha* area, called Ollilo, to Korney Ivanovich's.

[We had probably met through Pyast. Pyast was a friend of Blok's. He met with grief, swallowed hot coals instead of poison, then changed his mind and drank some ink in order to coat the wounds of his esophagus; he threw himself under a train, but the grill of the locomotive pushed him aside.

Pyast remained alive.

He wrote some poems, one in "ninths." The "ninth" is an extended octave. Pyast used to frequent "The Stray Dog" cellar.

At the Tenishev College, Pyast and I lectured on Futurism. Previously, I had spoken at "The Stray Dog."

Actually, Korney Ivanovich liked Mayakovsky's poetry, but he was limited by *The Speech* and by his own enormous self-respect. How could he stake such a capital—his literary reno-mée—on a risky card? Better to write so that it would appear this-a-way and that-a-way and, finally, none-a-way. And thus the reader, whether in Moscow or in Zhmerinka, would leave content with the feeling that everything remained, so to say, as usual.

Korney Ivanovich only respected translations from English —Oscar Wilde, Walt Whitman.]

In the spring, birds fly over Kuokkala. It is a major migratory route for birds. In the spring, there are white nights, and the migration of birds never ceases. Fir trees, sand, swamps among the sands, pink hues on the horizon and deep blue above. The sun passes at the edge of the earth, its head slightly bowed. And the birds fly back to their homeland, far away.

They have a homeland.

Chukovsky mentioned the rebellious verse of the young Mayakovsky in the almanac *Hedgerose* [2] of 1914.

He had met Mayakovsky earlier, also in Kuokkala. He talked about him, made up a lecture, and travelled with it to all the provincial towns, trying to explain Futurism. Korney Ivanovich was a universal man who tried to understand everything:

"A critic must behave this way, or else what is criticism for? And, if he cannot, for example, become Tolstoy or Chekhov for at least an hour, what can he know about them! I swear that in my lifetime I have already been Sologub, Blok, and even Semyon Yushkevich. One must become the person one is writing about; one must be infected by his lyrics, by his soul. Thus, from this very moment on, I am no longer me but Burlyuk. Or rather—Aleksandr Kruchyonykh!"

"Sorcha, krocha, buga na vikhrol!" [3]

[Unfortunately, Korney Ivanovich transformed all of art so that it would not disturb anyone. He himself once said about Osip Dymov that he was a man completely adjusted so as not to disturb.

Blok and Bely, Gorky, and all the Acmeists, Yesenin and Bagritsky—the great Russian literature in its supreme moment—bypassed Korney Chukovsky.

Nothing could astonish a man who could turn into Yushkevich. Gifted and sensitive to literature, he understood Mayakovsky in his own way; he crumpled him up and rephrased him in a way that would not disturb the public. That was the task of criticism. If great criticism offers a general interpretation of a work of art, enhances the impression it produces or, at least, enjoys it, then Chukovsky wasted all of his talented life before the Revolution, smothering art in pillows, choking it, reducing everything to anecdotes, and rendering it all in the angelic voice of a parodist. Everything lost its terror and could be shown to the public, who could then go home for tea, contentedly.]

Toward Mayakovsky, Chukovsky was condescending.

"Of course, I like Mayakovsky—these convulsions of his, spasms, crazy drunken sobbings about bald cupolas, about evil roofs, about bouquets of street walkers, about urban mirages and nightmares; but, confidentially, let me tell you: Mayakovsky is an illusionist, a visionary; Mayakovsky is an Impressionist and is utterly alien to the Futurists; he is among them by accident; even Kruchyonykh himself is sometimes not unwilling to snicker at him. Moreover, for him the city is not a delight or an intoxicating joy, but a crucifixion, a Golgotha, a crown of thorns, and each urban vision is for him a nail driven into his heart. He cries and he thrashes in hysterics:

> At bricks I shout,
> thrusting the dagger of frenzied words
> into the pulp of the swollen sky! [4]

And one would like to take him by the hand and lead him away like a child, away from this prison of bricks, somewhere to daisies and cornflowers. What urbanist or glorifier of the city is he, if the city is a torture chamber, an agony, for him? Poor fellow, he cannot even merge with the crowds of the city, and this makes him cry even more bitterly." [5]

This is only the beginning. The critic pursues his belittling:

"There is Nikolay Burlyuk, anemic, shy, and meek; there is Mayakovsky, who simulates madness and ardor, but is actually (should I reveal the secret?) a perfectionist who carefully polishes the images he pastes together into mosaics—another epigone of modernism; there is Khlebnikov who, completely drained by his first poem, now lives only off the interests of this large capital. . . ." [6]

At the time when Chukovsky was writing, Khlebnikov had already published his poems; "Menagerie" had been well-known for some time; but for the reader it was more amusing and more convenient to have everyone small-sized.

Chukovsky gave his lecture everywhere. The Futurists debated. The lecture at the Tenishev College went well.

Mayakovsky calmly mounted the rostrum.

Kruchyonykh recited with despair and shook the audience.

His head thrown back, Igor Severyanin purred. Khlebnikov did not perform.

Korney Ivanovich went up to him. Khlebnikov cursed him soundlessly, only moving his lips.

Ledentu and Ilya Zdanevich also came to the lecture.

Both had their faces painted, not without coquetry.

Very politely, pleased with the audience's full sympathy, the police officer escorted them out.

Chapter 13

Kulbin/
"The Stray Dog"/
Debates

At that time I was a Futurist.

I studied at the University; I had already taken up sculpturing in the *gymnasium*. I never became a sculptor. Through sculpture, I came to understand painting, and I was connected with the Union of Youth.[1]

I was not associated with the Moscow Futurists. I was acquainted with the physician Nikolay Ivanovich Kulbin.

He was a gifted man, with a fine mind, but as a painter he was an amateur. His paintings were strongly influenced by the Impressionists; he loved Blok and Sudeykin. He believed in the influence of sunspots on the Revolution and believed that a stone falls to the ground because of its love for it.

He drew multi-legged women to show them dancing. He was highly intelligent.

I went to see him. He promised me that I would be a genius, gave me money and kept it up every month. He ordered me to sleep no less than ten hours a day, and to eat cheese with butter and without bread.

Kulbin was one of the many people who wanted peace in art. He began his attempts to establish peace just before the war. Kulbin said that a new muse had made its appearance—the muse Tekhnè.

She was the muse of craftsmanship and professional skills elevated to art.

This was in opposition to the Symbolists.

It was serious.

Blok used to come to Kulbin for talks.

Tekhnè grew; she had presentiments of a struggle for new craftsmanship. It all ended, however, in the crimes of the epigones. About ten years later, Shengeli made his appearance and began to write his books like *How To Write Articles, Poems, and Stories.*

These books were advertised alongside textbooks like *How To Repair Galoshes,* but they were cheaper and sold for only 90 kopeks.

Still cheaper was *How To Feed Canaries,* 50 kopeks.

That is how low Tekhnè sank.

However, this technique was not the technique of Tekhnè. This was the conceit of people who did not understand change in art.

For them Kulbin, for instance, was an amateur.

And he really was an amateur, but Herzen had also called himself an amateur.

This word has various meanings.

Kulbin wanted to publish a review in which Blok, Yevreinov and the Futurists would appear side by side.

[His personal life was unhappy; he did not get along with his wife.

He painted the decorative columns of the sideboard in his room blue and hung up a poster with the words: "I thirst for lone . . . lone . . . loneliness."]

He had disciples, he was a teacher of life. According to his words, a certain B.[2] was a Judas towards him.

What was then sold by B.—and to whom—I do not recall. This man was a poet and a publisher. Mediocre poets of this type sought out other people to be published with. Similarly, Jews in Odessa used to pay for ten Russian boys, to have their sons admitted to the Commercial School.

No, B. was no Judas. He was simply a fifth wheel, a spare, but a spare with no tire.

"The Stray Dog" was located on Mikhaylovskaya Square in a rear courtyard. It would have been all right to come in through the street entrance, but it was essential to meet in a basement, and the basement had to be in a rear courtyard. This was the center of the city. Steps down and arches; the arches decorated by Sudeykin. A fireplace and the windows were blocked by furniture. This was where people met. It had been a theatrical organization. Originally, they had, in all likelihood, wanted to revolutionize the theater, but they ended up drinking wine.

At the head was Boris Pronin, a man who probably never slept nights [and does not look his age even now, though he is sixty.

He has not aged at all; but on stage he already plays old men, mimicking them, leaning against a wall.

Obviously, there is no way to avoid aging; there are only different ways of aging.

Basically, Pronin was a director.] At "The Stray Dog," he presided for many years over evening and night performances of writers and artists.

Kuzmin went there, with his hair combed back over his naked skull, with his bevelled cheeks. He looked like an old woman, suddenly aged. There was Georgy Ivanov, probably handsome and slick, as though painted in majolica; and the old Tsibulsky and Pyast, and Radakov from *The Satyricon;* and, once, even Nagrodskaya stopped by.

Verbitskaya did not dare to come in.

Khlebnikov whispered his poetry here. In the second room, the one with no fireplace, Anna Andreyevna Akhmatova sat in a black dress.

> We are all drinking companions, lascivious women
> How sad we are together!
> On the walls—flowers and birds
> Are languishing on clouds.

* * * *

The windows are boarded up forever.
What is out there—frost or storm?
Your eyes look like
The eyes of a cautious cat.[3]

Mayakovsky loved Akhmatova, the poet. He loved Blok.

Burlyuk asserted that he was driving Blok out of Mayakovsky with a club. He never succeeded, of course.

Khlebnikov liked Kuzmin and refused to have Kuzmin's name mentioned in a certain disrespectful Futurist manifesto. His name was added after Khlebnikov left.

This was not out of friendship, but out of an awareness that art is a common cause.

This does not mean that there were no Futurists.

Pushkin called Romanticism "Parnassian Atheism"; he defined it negatively but, still, Romanticism did exist.

Mayakovsky was aware of his ties with art, with Balmont, with Blok, and with *The Satyricon* writers, but at the same time, he was not one of them.

These memoirs are not about me, and if I seem to take a lot of space, it is because one remembers most about oneself. So, I have to write this way. I had my own theory, my own window on the world, as Baudoin de Courtenay said. I believed that art was not a method of thinking, but a method of restoring sense perception of the world; I believed that art forms change in order to preserve the perceptibility of life. I studied the philosophy of change, first using architectural and, later, linguistic material. I gave a lecture at "The Stray Dog." Few people came; the arguments were heated, and my opponent was the famous specialist on Sumero-Akkadian language, the poet Shileyko.

In his apartment, Shileyko had tables of cuniform characters, that looked like cheap cookies, lying on his desk. For him, Assyria was already modern times. His special field was a language already dead in Babylonian times. Shileyko contradicted me passionately.

Here are the main points of my lecture "The Place of Futurism in the History of Language":

"The attitude of critics toward the new trend. The word as an elementary form of poetry. The word-image and its petrification. The epithet as a means of rejuvenating the word. 'The history of the epithet as the history of poetic style' (A. Veselovsky). The fate of the works of bygone artists of the word is the same as the fate of the word itself: both shed light on the path from poetry to prose; both become coated with the glass armor of the familiar. 'Commercial Art' as proof of the death of the old art. The death of objects. Strangeness as a means of fighting the familiar. The theory of shift. The task of Futurism is to resurrect objects, to restore to man his ability to sense the world. 'The tight language' of Kruchyonykh and 'the polished surface' of Vladimir Korolenko. Abusive and tender words as words which have been changed and distorted. The connection between Futurist devices and devices pertaining to the verbal thought process, in general. The half-intelligible language of ancient poetry. The language of the Futurists. The scale of vowels. The resurrection of objects."

We went to the Bestuzhev Institute where Korney Ivanovich was lecturing. He finished with exclamations about science and democracy.

"The Futurists will fail! Even if they bite off their own heads," he sang out in a nasal twang that suggested the precious twang of an ancient viola da gamba.

Mayakovsky recited poems. Kruchyonykh spoke, but first he read some parody poems that were not very good and not at all transrational. I remember one rhyme:

"Gaudy, talky, sit the Futurists."

He was a success. Some Acmeists read poetry and, later, one of the Futurists said that Korolenko's style was dull.

The audience decided to beat us up.

Mayakovsky made his way through the crowd like a red-hot

iron through snow. Kruchyonykh walked out screeching and beating off attackers with his galoshes to defend himself.

He was feeling the pinch of science and democracy.

I advanced, pushing away heads right and left with my hands; I was strong—and got through.

But Korney Ivanovich took his lecture elsewhere. Then, the war came. No one believed in it. War could not be! Even a war that lasted three months was inconceivable!

But, then, the war did come and many of us enlisted. Pyast joined and couldn't take it—he wound up in an insane asylum. Pasternak was rejected—I don't remember why. They did not dare to take Mayakovsky.

"The first battle. The horror of war stared us in the face. War is loathsome. The home front is still more loathsome. To speak about the war, one has to see it. I went to enlist. Rejected. (Politically) unreliable." [4]

There was no doubt about that.

After all, no one published Mayakovsky.

Only the Burlyuks published him, but these Burlyuk books sold as curiosities. Once, Yasny promised to publish him. Mayakovsky even put a book together. It was called *Blouse of a Dandy.*

The last date on the page proofs was the year 1918. But even then the book was not published.

It was a small book, subdivided into sections entitled "The Orange Blouse," "The Blue Blouse," etc.

This was a soul in various garments.

At that time, Mayakovsky was sporting a top hat and, with the first money he got, he bought himself a fine orange scarf. In general, he wanted to dress well.

Merezhkovsky spoke out against the Futurists. [He is still upbraiding them today somewhere in the *Encyclopaedia Britannica.*]

Concerning the Futurists, they remembered Merezhkovsky's old warning: at the time of the 1905 Revolution, he had spoken of the "Coming Boor." Mayakovsky replied to this in his lecture "Arrived Himself." It was a report on the new Russian literature.

Subsequently, V. Khlebnikov, in his poem "Confession" (subtitled "Rough Style"), commented on this report.

He said that the word "kham" (boor) could be formed from the initials *Kh* and *M:*

> Boor!
> Let us both be proud
> Of the stern destiny of sound.
> We will stand, both of us, at the tree of silence
> And get drenched in whistle.
> We will chase the Turks of doubt
> As Jan Sobiesky did from Vienna.
> Iron tsars,
> We will heavily place on your heads
> Iron crowns of the boor,
> And—out come the swords!
> Out of the sheaths of the past—let them shine, let them shine!
> Days of peace, go to sleep!
> Shush!
> Ancient lamentations sleep like Merezhkovsky:
> He wailed as the daddy of our tenderness.
> Sounds are instigators of life.
> We will proudly reply with a wild song
> Into the face of Heavens.
> Yes, but he who came is no boor, but himself—
> We will build up rough logs
> Over the swarm of humanity.

Chapter 14

The War—The Years
1914 and 1915

In October, 1914, Gregory Ivanov published an article in the
Apollon, "The Test of Fire." Among other things, this is
what he wrote:

"Strange as it may seem, the reaction of the Futurists to
the war, which they glorified in peace time in every way, has
been weaker than that of all the others. In one Moscow publication, some tortured and unappealing poems by Mayakovsky,
V. Shershenevich, and others, have appeared."

Mayakovsky's poem, which failed to gain the approbation
of *Apollon,* was "War is Declared."

The streets were crowded with men trying to wear black
and to tuck their trousers into high boots. They were being
mobilized and walked in large groups. A policeman, carrying
a heavy ledger, marched at their side.

Then there were the large military barracks. People were
crowded into them, but there were no uniforms provided for
them. The barracks smelled of army soup—a soup generously
salted with laurel leaves—of bread and of soldiers' greatcoats.

I enlisted and requested service at the front. I had no right
to promotion. I was in the Army, but the Army had little use
for me. Shortly afterward, I returned to Petersburg and became an instructor in an armored division.

On the eve of my mobilization, Blok and I walked

through the streets of Petersburg for a long time. He said to
me:

"In time of war no one should think of himself."

He was not happy about the war, but accepted it as a stage
of history, unaware of what would follow. In his poetry, this
is clearer:

> People born in stagnant years—
> Do not remember their way.
> We—children of Russia's awesome years—
> Are unable to forget anything.
>
> Years which reduce us to ashes!
> Is it madness or hope that you bring?
> From days of war, from days of freedom—
> A blood red light reflects on the faces.
>
> Muteness reigns—the deep noise of the tocsin has
> Sealed lips.
> In hearts which have known ecstasy,
> There is a fateful emptiness.[1]

To understand how this poem differs from other war
poems, one has to take a look at the others. There were poems
on St. George the Dragonkiller, stories of valor, with references to Lvov.[2]

Or there were poems skillfully avoiding the issue.

Vladislav Khodasevich appeared in *Apollon* with a piece
entitled "From Mice Verse." I am quoting two stanzas.

> People are waging war. But to our underground
> Its bloody noise will not reach.
> In our circle—there is eternal praying,
> In our world—the calm abundance
> Of beneficial and humble thoughts.
>
> * * * *
>
> France! In the midst of your landscape
> The sword whistles, destroying your vineyards,
> Birthplace of beloved freedom!
> He is no mouse who has not loved you!

"He is no mouse" is a parody of the phrase: "He is no man."

But it may also be a parody of the Nekrasov verse:

> He is no Russian who will look without love
> Upon that muse, pale and bloodied,
> Whipped by the knout.[3]

Of course, we no longer worry about Khodasevich. Let him be dead.

Still, his "underground" was an attempt to dodge the issue, not to join the others in glorification.

Mayakovsky had not been drafted yet.

Mayakovsky met Gorky.

Mayakovsky read his poems to Gorky in Mustamyaki. Aleksey Maksimovich told me that he was stunned and that even a little gray bird hopping on the path ruffled its feathers, cocked its head and still could not bring itself to fly away: very interesting!

Mayakovsky was writing *Cloud in Pants*.

Excerpts from *Cloud in Pants* were published in the first issue of *The Archer*[4] in 1915.

Kulbin's project was realized: a book came out which included Blok, Kuzmin and a long article by Kulbin himself; verses by Kamensky and Mayakovsky, and some prose by Remizov. Kulbin's article was divided into many chapters, the last chapter was entitled "Ends of Ends." It was an explanatory article, and it said that Cubism was ending and that Futurism was beginning.

It turned out that war does not destroy *dachas* at once. Life went on in the *dachas;* Petersburg was not being shelled. In May, 1915, after winning 65 rubles, Mayakovsky went to Kuokkala. He used to have dinner at Chukovsky's, Yevreinov's or Repin's. Repin's wife had a double name, Severova-Nordman. She tried to solve all social problems by keeping living expenses down; she wore a coat lined with fine wood shavings and ate fried cabbage stumps.

In Kuokkala, Mayakovsky lived according to the "seven-friends system," which he called, in parentheses, "the seven-crops rotation system." On Sundays, he ate at Chukovsky's, on Mondays, at Yevreinov's; Repin and the cabbage stumps fell on Thursday. And, in the evening, he strolled on the beach.

The Briks lived in Leningrad. Osip Maksimovich had been drafted and assigned to an automobile company. Later on, it was decided that a Jew ought not to be in an automobile company, and all the others were assembled and sent to the front. Brik went home.

At first, he went out in his uniform; then he started wearing civilian clothes. They forgot about him. Two years went by. He would have been torn to pieces, but for that, they had to find him, to work up enough interest. Brik was living on Zhukovskaya Street, number 7, and dozens of people came to see him. There was only one thing he could not do: move to another apartment. That would have made him a moving target and he would have had to register. He could, however, enlarge the house he lived in by adding three stories and not be noticed.

Going for walks was no simple matter for him. There might suddenly be a roundup!

He built, on top of the piano, a theater the size of at least one cubic meter, and an automobile made out of cards. Lili Brik was delighted with his constructions.

The Briks loved literature. They even had a bookplate of their own. This is a thing of the past; at that time, bookplates were more numerous than libraries. But the Briks' bookplate was special.

It pictured an Italian youth and girl kissing, and the inscription read: "And that day we read no more." [5]

With a bookplate like that, who needed a library?

Lili's sister Elsa arrived. Mayakovsky dropped by to see her. They said to Elsa: "Don't ask him to recite."

Elsa, however, disobeyed. Volodya recited his poetry. Osya picked up the notebook and started to read.

Brik was impressed by Mayakovsky. He decided to publish him, and, in general, to go into publishing. This took courage on the part of a man who was living without a passport.

Brik is a cat, that very Kipling cat, that walked over the roofs all by itself at a time when there were no roofs yet.

Mayakovsky decided to introduce me to the Briks. I lived on Nadezhdinskaya Street and he lived across the street. It has now been five years since the street was renamed after Mayakovsky.

Volodya came by and left me a note: "Come over to the volunteer Brik." And I happened to know a volunteer with the same name in the automobile company. Once, this man had started a car and the car shot forward, lurched and demolished the door in front. The volunteer went into reverse, the car careened sideways and backward, and demolished another door in back. I wanted to have a look at Brik. I went to the indicated address: Zhukovskaya Street, number 7, apartment 42. A wrought iron lamp post grew out of the cobblestones. It was a tall building, with a stable that sported a sculptured mare's head in front of it.

I opened the door. On the other side of the door was Brik, but not the one I knew.

It was a second Brik.

This second Brik stood by the piano—young, his hair cropped short. On top of the piano was the automobile made of cards.

The apartment was very small. The foyer led straight to a corridor, to the left of which were two rooms, but the bedroom was off the foyer. The apartment was modest, though the beds were covered with quilts. In the first room also off the foyer, not the corridor, was the aforementioned piano. On the walls were Japanese fans and a big oil painting, under glass, by Boris Grigoryev; it was the mistress of the house, reclining in a dress.

A poor painting. Later, Lili sold it.

Farther on, a narrow dining room. That was where Mayakovsky recited his poetry.

Mayakovsky had found a haven.

"Haven" is an old Russian word; a port used to be called
a "haven for ships."

For a long time, Mayakovsky had been buffeted and tossed
around. He knew how to use his elbows; he would send his
photograph to a magazine and write an article as though saying: "Look, that's me!"

He made fun of the "roundup." Enclosing a photograph,
he wrote:

Dear Ladies and dear Gentlemen:

I—am an impudent fellow who knows no greater pleasure than
to throw on a yellow blouse and crash a party of respectable
people protecting modesty and dignity under their proper coats,
jackets and formal evening dress.

I—am a cynic—one glance from me will provide your attire with
permanent grease spots roughly the size of a dessert plate.

I—am a cabby who no sooner gains entrance to a drawing room,
than the air is filled with words as heavy as axes, words of a pro-
fession little equipped for salon dialectics.

I—am a publicity seeker who feverishly scrutinizes all the newspapers every day in the hope of finding my name.

I—am....[6]

Great—isn't it? But when this was printed in a journal in
1915, a photograph was included—Mayakovsky wearing a cap.
But the journal—it was called *The Journal of Journals* [7]—
added an insult saying: "All in all, you are an uninteresting
young man and an epigone."

As to the photograph, this is what happeed: it was reproduced, over and over, and retouched each time. Mayakovsky
kept changing; in particular, his coat and necktie kept im-
proving. Evidently, this process is unavoidable.

Excerpts from *Cloud in Pants* had already appeared in
The Journal of Journals, the same that maligned Mayakovsky, and in *The Archer,* No. 1.

Cloud in Pants is a beautiful poem in which the poet has already found his own voice. A world was already defined. Igor Severyanin, dancing through his verses as gray as a quail, and the one-eyed beloved poet-painter David Burlyuk who can climb out of himself just to say: "Good."

Mayakovsky's path was paved with blood—millions of drops. So much blood and poetry that all of it may shine in the sky like the Milky Way, its pink made invisible by the distance.

Everyone shoved the poet, everyone wounded him—and these were the people for whom he lived.

There will even be no vengeance against them. And why should I paraphrase Mayakovsky?

But now, finally, he had a home and a contract with Brik: half a ruble per line, forever, and tomorrow he would publish. Brik published *Cloud in Pants* as a simple little book, a book with no illustrations.

Chapter 15

About Love and Man

L. Brik made Mayakovsky cut his hair, [ordered him to wash,] changed his clothes. He started using a heavy walking stick.

He had already written a lot about love.

He searched for love. He wanted to heal wounds with flowers.

> As a matter of fact,
> one time I found her—
> the soul.
> She came out
> in a blue housecoat
> and said:
> "Sit down!
> I waited a long time for you.
> Won't you have a glass of tea?" [1]

In mechanics, there is such a term as "linkage weight." That is the weight of a locomotive on the front wheels.

The friction of the front wheels is fifty times greater than the friction of the rolling wheels. Without linkage weight, movement is impossible, and man is linked to life through love.

Love is heavy with useful weight.

And so he fell in love with her at first sight, and, actually, forever—till the very loss of weight. So he began writing verses for her.

Her eyes are hazel-brown. She has a large head; she is beautiful, red-haired, graceful and wants to be a dancer.

Her friends are wealthy ladies.[2]

Even bankers. Actually, bankers are people without a homeland; they live in apartments that look like oriental bath houses; they collect china and, once in a while, even say something witty. They are not stupid and, in their own way, are international. They bring along actresses who do not have many acting engagements, and who have heard a bit about Symbolism and, perhaps, about Freud. Pre-revolutionary, pre-war society, reinforced by the war. War makes enterprises thrive and money cheap. L. Brik did not respect these people at all, but still, she mingled with them. They ate some unbelievable pears that almost had coats of arms and pedigrees attached to their stems. That was also curious.

But, of course, the most curious of all was Osip Brik, who [did not believe in anything and] did not visit all those bankers.

He was the one who upheld Mayakovsky's fame in the house.

L. Brik loved things—earrings in the shape of golden flies and antique Russian earrings. She had a rope of pearls and was full of lovely nonsense, very old and very familiar to mankind. She knew how to be sad, feminine, capricious, proud, shallow, fickle, in love, clever and any way you like. Thus Shakespeare described woman in his comedy.

But Mayakovsky was a Plebeian. He said:

> I,
> made fun of by today's people,
> like a long
> dirty joke,
> I see him who crosses the mountains of time,
> whom no one sees.

> Where man's short vision breaks off,
> at the head of hungry hordes,
> in a thorny crown of revolution
> the year 1916 is emerging.[3]

But she said to him:

"I want to go to Finland, but Jews can't register there."

And she cried. And he said, embarrassed, like a person in a small room who cannot make the appropriate gesture:

"All this will be taken care of when the time comes. We shouldn't think about petty matters. We have to speak in the factories about revolution."

I witnessed this conversation. Perhaps I am not quoting it accurately. He said:

"We have to go to the suburbs and make speeches and not about registration."

He loved her as long as he lived; he wrote about her and kept seeing her. What else could he do? He had no home. He was Jack London before success. Money, love, passion. He thought he would somehow manage. But he didn't.

> She'll remain yours.
> Have a lot of clothes made for her,
> so that her shy wings will grow fat in silks.
> See that she does not drift away.
> Like a stone 'round your wife's neck
> hang necklaces of pearls.[4]

Nothing to be done. Nothing helped, neither the voice, nor the charm of a genius, nor the fact that everyone looked at you, and that rivals knew you were better.

Once, Mayakovsky was reading his poems in the apartment of the artist Lyubavina on Basseynaya Street. Aleksey Maksimovich Gorky came—tall, slightly stooped, with a crew cut, in a long frockcoat. Aleksandr Nikolayevich Tikhonov followed him. Mayakovsky began with a lecture. He muttered about the poets of the past who wrote on their country estates and had vellum paper. He spoke, referred to me, and then he began to cry and went into the adjoining room.

He cried, then returned, and read his poetry.

Gorky liked him then. A bit later, he said that *The Back-bone Flute* was the music of the backbone, the very meaning of world lyrics, the lyrics of the spinal cord.

We used to meet at the Briks'; all kinds of people came. At that time, Lenin was writing a letter to Inessa Armand. Inessa Armand wanted to write a book about free love. Lenin wrote her a letter:

[Dear friend:] [5] I strongly suggest that you outline your pamphlet in greater detail. Otherwise, too much is unclear.

There is one point I would like to make right now.

I advise you to completely remove No. 3—demand (by women) for free love.

This really is not a proletarian, but a bourgeois demand.

Actually, what do you mean by it? What can it mean?

1. Freedom from material (financial) considerations in matters of love?

2. Freedom also from material worries?

3. From religious prejudice?

4. From daddy's interdictions, etc.?

5. From social prejudices?

6. From the narrow environment of the (peasant, petty bourgeois or intellectual middleclass) milieu?

7. From the fetters of the law, courts and the police?

8. From the seriousness in love?

9. From child bearing?

10. Freedom to commit adultery? And so on and so forth.

I have listed here many nuances of meaning (but not all, of course). Of course, you do not have Nos. 8-10 in mind, but rather Nos. 1-7 or something close to them.

For Nos. 1-7, however, one should choose a different name, since "Free Love" does not express this idea accurately.

And the public, the readers of the pamphlet, will inevitably understand "Free Love" to be something like Nos. 8-10, whatever your intentions.

Precisely because in contemporary society, the most vociferous, the loudest and the most conspicuous classes understand "Free

Love" to be Nos. 8-10, precisely because of this, it is not a proletarian, but a bourgeois demand.

The most important points for the proletariat are 1-2, and then
1-7, but this is not actually "Free Love."

The issue is not what you subjectively "want it to mean." The
issue is the objective logic of class relations in matters of love.

[Friendly shake hands! W.L.][6]

What Lenin was writing then was unknown to all of us.

It was written to a good progressive woman—a woman who
studied theory—but it had to be explained even to her.

The ethics Lenin was writing about were only being created
or, rather, were only coming into consciousness.

The instability of the new ethics and the rejection of the
old ethics were typical of the period before the war.

Both men and women denied what should not have been
denied, asserted what should not have been asserted.

Enjoying the despair of our aunties, we sometimes drove
ourselves to despair; and not only ourselves.

How did the Briks' old friends get along with the new ones?

We were gradually squeezing them out.

I remember there was one fellow, Krichevsky, who was
probably a manufacturer. I met him many times.

At first, I was intimidated in Lili's apartment, so I would
shove the silk cushions into the back of the big low sofa—
very carefully, tightly.

Whenever I met Krichevsky, I always said to him: "Viktor
Shklovsky."

The short, well dressed man finally got annoyed and
replied:

"We have been introduced many times. When will you
learn to recognize me?"

I replied:

"If you tie a handkerchief around your arm, I will always
recognize you."

Mayakovsky's book was already out; Lili had it bound in
purple Elizabethan brocade, and Osya put up a shelf of un-

painted wood and, on that shelf, were all the books of the Futurists.

And on the wall, they hung a roll of paper on which everybody could write whatever they wanted to.

Burlyuk pasted on some kind of pyramids, and I drew small horses which looked like nipples.

[In 1915, at the seashore in Ollilo, I met Velimir Khlebnikov. I told him that the woman he loved had married someone else.

We were at the seashore. Far off on the horizon, in three or four places, the port lights were shining like dots and dashes of an uncoded cable.

I told Khlebnikov that the girl from the house where the furniture was of Karelian birch, and where Izabella Grinevskaya was considered a poetess, the girl from this generally "intelligent" house had married an architect.

The waves were simple from Kuokkala—they did not come from afar; in the darkness stood the small bath houses where one undressed before swimming.

Khlebnikov said to me:

"Do you know that you've wounded me?"

I knew.

"Tell me, what do they need, what do women ask of us, what do they want? I would have done anything; I would have written differently. Maybe they want fame?"

Nadezhda Aleksandrovna, are you still alive? As I am writing now, is your husband alive? Are Viktor Khlebnikov's letters to you safe? No, it was not your fault at all.

It is not your fault if the letters were lost, if they remained unread—you are not to be blamed either. You are not to blame and Korney Ivanovich Chukovsky is not to be blamed either.

Those letters and Mayakovsky's poems were not understood, like cables written in dots; words had not yet filled those signs for you. The poet brought the crown of a kingdom which did not exist yet.

It is easy to be cruel in love: one merely has not to love.]

In a revolution, the very core of man's inner life has to be transformed. Then, sometimes in the future, and only then, when seven rivers will have been crossed, there will be a new love.

Only in verses, protected by rhymes, do we dare to speak about love. What is most important is elevated by art beyond shame.

In art, man fights for the poetry of his heart, for his happiness.

Mayakovsky had linked the destiny of the world to the destiny of his love, to the fight for the only happiness.

He stretched fame as a bridge across the Neva, a bridge to the future, and he took his stand on that bridge.

Neither he, nor Mark Twain, needed a heaven without a heart.

Happiness is needed right here, and it was not for himself that he was going toward that happiness through the revolution.

I did not sleep last night, though I did dream. I dreamt of large rivers eroding the river banks, and of Mayakovsky standing on the bank.

I awoke: on the table were lying books of poems, marked up.

"Oh garden, zoological garden!" [7]—wrote Khlebnikov, describing many animals.

There are many animals in this world, but not that many poems. Poems are like the different roots of a single complex equation.

We will find, together with mankind, the only simple and happy answer.

This was the way they lived on Zhukovskaya Street 7. The war went on, dragging us along.

People returned from the war. Each of us was linked to the war in his own way. Thus came the year 1916.

The visitors to the Briks were dressed differently. There was a tall, elegant man by the name of Schieman.

He was an artist from Munich, a leftist, probably of the Kandinsky school. He did not know music but, at home, he had a harmonium. He was not an improviser but, sitting at his harmonium, he produced with its help some concordant musical wails.

One should not assume that this was theoretically meaningless music. It was harmonium as such. He painted in the same way. Color by itself. He lived in a large, very clean room.

On a small table, covered with white silk, stood a small nickel-plated coffee pot on an almost invisible alcohol flame.

Europe, as they saw it at that time.

The artist was rather well off. He painted designs on scarves. Colorful wails and mutterings were transformed into things suitable to adorn ladies.

The paint was dissolved in a clean tub. The scarf was covered with hot wax, and the wax was spread into Kandinsky-type designs. The parts of the scarf that had no wax were imbued with color. The wax was then removed with an iron. Then wax was spread again over the already dyed parts, and the scarf was again immersed in the tub.

Then, worn silver fox fur was cut up, and the strips were sewn to the scarf. The entire thing sold very well.

The money he made was sometimes lost gambling with Mayakovsky.

It was a contest between the calm, patient, industrious willpower of the German artist and Mayakovsky's willpower.

Why do I describe this at such length? Because all the transrational language of painting was adapted with frightening ease to serve commercial art. At the time, this method of dyeing technique was called Javanese; now, it is called batik.

In those days, the artist was easily manipulated.

He would be corrected and told: "This design would go for fabrics and that one for cigarettes."

One such transrational artist from Tiflis, a talented man, got to Paris, where he is now making or had been making designs for modern fabrics.

The one-eyed Averchenko hated Mayakovsky. Averchenko had already become owner of the *New Satyricon*.

He already had monuments to himself—small, portable ones. He used the journal *Argus* [8] for this. On its cover were printed Averchenko's broad face and the crown of a straw hat. A piece of cardboard, shaped like the rim of a straw hat, was enclosed in each copy of the journal. The journal would be rolled up, the rim slipped on and the cylinder-shaped monument, a paper monument, to Averchenko would stand at each street corner, at each newsstand.

Sasha Chyorny had gone abroad.

Radakov and Potyomkin remained with *The Satyricon*. All in all, *The Satyricon* was not just Averchenko. At the same time, the best of the *Satyricon* writers had their own logic: that talented fellow, Mayakovsky, could be put to good use. People were laughing at his poetry; therefore, he could turn out humorous poetry.

And so, Mayakovsky was invited to join *The Satyricon*, and he did join because one needs to eat, as he himself put it. But his pieces did not blend in with *The Satyricon*, they disrupted this magazine.

Mayakovsky was writing *The Backbone Flute* during that period.

He was often in "The Stray Dog." Officially, at that time, wine was not served at the "Dog." Presumably, they drank coffee. It was crowded, and more and more outsiders came. At the "Dog," they were called "pharmacists." Special evenings were even organized for the "pharmacists."

People who profited from the war were buying up old collections, the houses and wives of the collectors included. This was their kind of love.

Once, the basement of "The Stray Dog" was completely reserved for a dancer. [9] The entire basement was filled with flowers; the lady danced on a mirror with a little girl dressed up as Cupid.

The Ego-Futurists [10] were already on their way out. Ignatyev had cut his throat, and the son of Fofanov—a pale young man, with combed back hair and thin wrists—had vanished from the scene. He had called himself Olimpov.

People in *zem-gusar* [11] uniforms made their appearance.

At "The Stray Dog" the mood was patriotic. When Mayakovsky recited his poem:

> For you who only love women and food,
> should I give my life for your pleasure?!
> I'd rather serve pineapple juice
> To the whores at the bar.[12]

What a squeal went up!

This was the bar. Wine was prohibited and they served pineapple drinks.

Women cried a great deal.

And then the year 1916 came.

We used to meet at the Briks'. Pasternak was already coming there. He came with Mariya Sinyakova. His verses moved with extraordinary power; gaps in meaning were bridged by the momentum of the rhythm; dissimilar elements grew closer, and words changed their meaning through musicality.

At that time, Khlebnikov was with some mangy detachment on the Volga.

Many of us felt that revolution was imminent, but many of us thought that we were outside space; that we had established our own kingdom of time, and that we were not expected to know which millenium it was outside.

New Year's Eve. We dragged a Christmas tree into a corner of the room. Candles for the tree were placed on small paper saucers. The hostess had draped a shiny, silk scarf around her bare shoulders. On the tree hung small, black pants filled with a cotton cloud. The hostess' sister had her hair done up high with peacock feathers. And the hostess wore a Scottish plaid skirt, short red stockings, a silk scarf instead of a blouse and the white wig of a marquise.

I was dressed in a sailor's blouse and my lips were painted. Brik was a Neapolitan. Vasily Kamensky's jacket was trimmed with a broad strip of colorful fabric; one of his eyebrows was made to look higher than the other, and a little bird was painted on his cheek.

This make-up was already dated; it was the make-up of the early Futurists.

The blond Vasya was handsome by candlelight. He raised his glass and said:

"Cursed be this war! We are guilty of not understanding it and ashamed of having held onto the tail of General Skobolev's horse."

Vasily Kamensky was a very talented man who had greatly contributed to Russian poetry. Of course, he sometimes suffered from rhyme disease, "Rhymatism," as he used to call it.

And the war went on. Mayakovsky was drafted.

We were then working for Gorky's journal *The Chronicle*.[13] Mayakovsky's poems were being published. Brik and I wrote reviews.

Through friends, Gorky got Mayakovsky into an automobile company as a draftsman. Volodya was shielded from the war.

Many issues arose in poetry, many of them complex. It seemed as though *Cloud in Pants* had won a complete and acknowledged victory. But *Cloud in Pants* is entirely based on metaphors, on the "how," on similes. *Cloud in Pants* deals with a world which is unthinkable for Anna Akhmatova. Akhmatova's world is narrow as a ray of light entering a dark room.

Narrower than the edge of a knife.

There is evening. An awakening, a separation.

It is a world captured by stabs.

Much as a telescope stabs the sky, picking out stars and depriving the universe of its breadth.

Kuzmin's world, with its exact designation of previously non-poetic objects, was so narrow that it had to be broadened by novels and stories from the stylized past, attached to it like balconies.

A new world was needed, but Mayakovsky's old world already had its summer visitors, they were the Imaginists,[14] but let's not include Yesenin among them here.

Mayakovsky's images, as Khlebnikov said to me, praising Vladimir—are clumsy, not fully consistent; they make noise, shift levels. His metaphors are contradictory, and the currents in his poetry are of differing temperatures.

Shershenevich, already present on the scene, was happy in the discovery that things may sometimes be similar; associative ties based on similarities were already declared to be the master key to the gates of art.

The Imaginists equipped the game of "how" like a billiards room—with six tables.

Mayakovsky and Pasternak led verse down the path of association and contiguity.

Lyrical movement and a syntax which places things side by side according to their inner relationship were created by the new verse.

The short breath of the Akhmatova line and the sequences of similes were being overcome in Mayakovsky's new verse.

The thematics of the Ego-Futurists descended into the popular song, lower than the romance—the conventional, narrow, melancholy purring song of Vertinsky.

But Mayakovsky moved forward like an icebreaker, cleaving himself a path into the new.

In the winter of 1916, we published collections on the theory of poetic language. The publishing house was OMB, meaning Osip Maksimovich Brik.

And Volodya wore a ring with initials, a present from Lili. He gave Lili a signet ring on which he had the letters L. Yu. B. engraved. The letters formed a circle, so the monogram could be read *lyublyu*—"I love."

A tired buffalo retreats into the water.

An elephant, perhaps, really warms himself in the sand. But he had no place; there was no sun for him, and his love was a heavy load.

But spring was coming.

Sunup! Sunup! The stones were turning gray.

Even bluish, and somewhere far away in Petersburg, wheels were already clattering on the pavement.

The sky was already turning red.

Clouds were passing over puddles.

The stiff leaves of the poplar trees rustled in the morning air. They grew between Spassky and Artilleriysky Boulevards on Nadezhdinskaya Street.

Volodya and I were exploring Petersburg. The sun was rising; low trees rustled near a red house.

The sky had already opened up; the clouds were beginning to turn pink and blue. The houses looked empty; darkened clouds floated on the window panes.

Mayakovsky walked along, his usual self, almost calm; he recited verses—somber verses about unrequited love, at first for many women, later for one.

This was a love without a haven.

The kind of love you can never eat away, drink away or write away with poems.

I think we were walking down the middle of the street. A spacious world, quiet houses. Above us—the sky.

"Look," said Vladimir, "it's a Zhukovsky sky."

And yet, we had full confidence, [as an important school,] that we would conquer life and build a new art. There was the review *Took*,[15] one issue—one issue with a printing of 500 copies.

We were preparing a collection of essays on the theory of poetic language. Also in 500 copies.

There was almost recognition.

There were Pasternak's poems and young Aseyev with his

verse moving from word to word with his finely constructed, solid verseline.

We lived in the grip of war, neither understanding nor fearing it any more.

The review *Took* was published by Brik. Poems by Mayakovsky were included, also poems by Pasternak and Aseyev, a somewhat rhetorical article of mine and a few very bad poems.

The review was printed on expensive paper and with a brown wrapping paper cover.

The word "Took" was set in the kind of wooden type used in posters.

The cover contained tiny grains and splinters; the wooden letters were off kilter and, later, we hand painted them over with Chinese ink.

Burlyuk also appeared in the review with his [already academic] drawing of multilegged horses.

However, poetic inventiveness, as well as innovations in rhythm and verse, abounded in *Took*.

Mayakovsky claimed that he knew nothing at all about verse meters anyway and that the following phrase was probably a trochee:

"Store and workshop, paints and brushes."

And this was an iambic:

> The orchestra offers its music
> on Tuesdays and Thursdays, as well.

He built his verse on intonation.

Took published Aseyev's poems. Here are some of his commentaries on these poems:

"I remember walking down the street once when a sign over a hay market caught my eye: 'Sale of oats and hay' *(prodazha ovsa i sena)*. The closeness of this phrase in sound and structure to the hackneyed prayer phrase 'In the name of the Father and the Son' *(vo imya otsa i syna)* inspired my imagination to form a parody stanza consisting of these two phonetically close colloquial word groups. I wrote down the following:

> "I would prohibit the 'sale of oats and hay . . .'
> for does it not hint at the killing
> of father and son?
> And if my heart
> should remain deaf
> to the anxieties of the streets,
> then, cut off, you roar,
> cut off my stupid,
> deaf ear!

"I remember how pleased I was with the harmony of the sound waves, woven for the first time in an intonational-rhythmic consistency unfettered by rules of meter. The irony of the mutually echoing sound patterns of the first two lines brings out the contrast of the emotional impact of the following two." [16]

Mayakovsky had firmly entered poetry.

Valery Bryusov understood Mayakovsky, but could not renounce his own work.

Those who renounce are not always the best.

It was Salieri who changed everything in his life and in his art when he heard the new music:

> . . . . When the great Glück
> Appeared and revealed to us new mysteries,
> (deep, enthralling mysteries)
> Did I not then discard all that I had known before,
> All that I had loved so much,
> All that I had so fervently believed in?
> And did I not follow him readily,
> Unquestioning like one who had lost his way
> And is sent by a passerby into a different direction? [17]

It was also Salieri who killed Mozart because he could not

be a fellow traveller of Mozart's. Yet, Salieri did not dare call Mozart a fellow traveller, as Mayakovsky was called.

Bryusov was not a Salieri.

He said about Mayakovsky, shielding himself in semi-recognition:

"I am afraid that Mayakovsky will not amount to much."

Vladimir Vladimirovich made a very funny imitation of Bryusov waking up in the middle of the night, howling:

"I'm afraid, I'm afraid!"

"Afraid of what?"

"Afraid that Mayakovsky won't amount to much."

Mayakovsky's usual method is revealed in this witticism: the transference of emphasis onto a secondary word, the reinterpretation of that word, and the destruction of a familiar meaning.

The result was the truth. Bryusov was afraid.

Man was finished just before the February Revolution of 1917.

Mark Twain loved his double, Huck Finn; he loved him more than himself. Huck Finn was luckier—he managed to sail away with his Negro friend.

The King and the Duke were not friends but, on the whole, they were harmless charlatans. Huck Finn floated on the wide river reinterpreting American life.

There are really only two things by Mark Twain which were not changed by his wife and daughters: this boy, a relative of Diogenes, and *Captain Stormfield's Visit to Heaven*.

This captain examined the sad variety that heaven had to offer, lost his way and finally arrived in the American heaven, where he received wings and a prayer book, both of which he threw away.

In Mark Twain's heaven, the greatest writer is not Shakespeare, but a shoemaker who had never been published. He died just when he was being mocked and crowned with cabbage leaves.

So glorified was this shoemaker that the posthumous cele-
brations attracted the attention even of the other heavens.

Mayakovsky, like the old pilot of the American river, knew
this heaven of disappointed Plebeians.

But he introduced into the poem a poet's perception;
proudly, he ascended to a dull heaven.

Love led him away from life.

The heart yearns for a shot, the throat craves a razor.

The Neva, the embankments.

An old song Tatlin sang when they were still in the School
of Sculpture and Architecture:

> A pharmacy stands on the corner,
> Love gnaws at man.

And here are the verses:

> Pharmacist!
> Pharmacist!
> Pharmacist,
> where
> will the heart come to
> the end of its pain?
> In the vast fields of heaven,
> in the delirium of the Saharas,
> in the demented heat of the deserts,
> is there a haven for the jealous?
> Many are the mysteries behind the jars' glass walls.
> You understand the higher laws of justice.
> Pharmacist,
> let me lead
> my soul
> painlessly
> out into the spaces.[18]

[Instead, the poet soared, flew up to heaven—such as they
had dressed him up in Petersburg: in an American jacket,
shiny yellow shoes.] Mayakovsky had now written his celestial
memoirs. And even in heaven, he did not betray his love, but

returned from heaven, back to the Neva, to Zhukovskaya
Street which, by then, was named after him.

His prediction was wrong: they gave his name to Nadezhdinskaya Street.

The river is cold, shining, calm, alien—eery.

> There was that shine.
> And it was
> then
> called Neva. [19]

Mayakovsky was saved by the October Revolution.
He enjoyed the Revolution physically.
He needed it very badly.

Chapter 16

February—
The Years 1917-1918

During the February Revolution, Mayakovsky was in the automobile company. He wrote about it in his "Chronicle." I was in an armored division. The streets rapidly had become bumpy from the spring snows. Some homely birds, left over from the winter, were screeching loudly. Snow hung from the roofs and the armored cars swayed. They were shooting in the training detachment of the engineers' battalion. They were shooting in Lesnoi.

Searching for Mayakovsky, I dropped in at the Briks'.

The air in the room was thick with smoke, and new clouds of smoke were spreading through the air.

Mayakovsky was not there. Nor do I remember seeing Brik. Kuzmin was there and many others. They were playing *Tyotka* [1] for the second straight day; nobody had gone home.

The Revolution began with bread lines, with the indignation of the soldiers.

It began the way clouds or wind arise in the mountains.

I don't play cards, so I went back out on the street.

In the streets, the wind was blowing. Spring was arriving precipitously; the roads were getting bad; everyone was shouting, and everyone was running around, armed. Nikolay Kulbin organized a militia and died on the first day.

Mayakovsky entered the Revolution as he would his own home.

He went right in and began opening windows in his home.

He needed more than the February Revolution; in its day, he was already talking about the great heresy of Socialism that was coming into being.

He wanted to transform the streets; the streets had to find their own language.

The Revolution gave Mayakovsky new strength and peace of mind.

I saw Mayakovsky cheerful.

The Field of Mars was not green yet. . . .

And Suvorov's statue stood as ever with his back to the parade ground, looking at the Neva. Behind his back, they were dynamiting holes for the Tomb of the Victims of The Revolution.

"The Stray Dog" was closed and renamed "Comedians' Shelter." It was moved, decorated and turned into a kind of basement theater.

We dropped into this basement by chance. Mayakovsky was there with a woman; they soon left.

A few minutes later, Mayakovsky came running back. His hair was cut short; it seemed black, and he looked altogether like a boy. He ran in, dragging into the dark basement what seemed like a whole chunk of spring.

The Neva was young and good; her bridges were cheerful— not those he later described in *Man,* nor those bridges we know from the verses of *About That.* It was almost a Caucasian spring. The Neva, blue like the blooming foam of wisteria in Kutaisi, flowed between the gray and cheerful embankments.

[In that room sat a blond girl [2] who was probably in love with Mayakovsky.

She looked at him, squinting her eyes as if looking into the sun and said with pain in her voice:

"Now, you have found your handbag in life and will go on carrying it."

"Yes, I'll carry it in my teeth," he answered meekly.]

The Neva, a mild wind blowing, passed by the cheerful Peter and Paul Fortress. This was a revolution for all time. Its flames were spreading.

> October blew,
> > as always,
> > > its winds.
> Their rails
> > snaking over the bridge,
> streetcars continued
> > their
> > > race,
> already—
> > under Socialism.[3]

Mayakovsky was in Moscow.

He played in a film entitled *Not for Money Born.*

It was a film based on Jack London—Jack London, as understood by Mayakovsky.[4]

Ivan Nov saved the brother of a beautiful woman.

Then he fell in love with this woman. But the woman did not love the tramp. Then, the tramp became a great poet and frequented the Café of the Futurists.

All this was filmed by the "Neptune" company, whose owner was Antik.

There was hardly any light; that is why, in the Café of the Futurists, the backdrop was almost touching the screen. It was not a large backdrop; it had a ten-legged horse painted on it. Burlyuk, with his painted cheek, and Vasily Kamensky were in the café.

Ivan Nov recited verses to Burlyuk:

> Beat on the squares the tramp of revolt!
> Up higher the ridge of proud heads!
> With the tide of the second flood
> we will wash over the cities of the world.

The bull of days is piebald
Slow is the cart of years.
Speed is our God.
The heart is our drum.[5]

Burlyuk said to Ivan Nov what he had once said to Mayakovsky on the boulevard:

"But, you're a poet of genius."

And fame began, and the woman came to the poet. The
poet wore a cape and a top hat. He put the top hat on a
skeleton, wrapped the skeleton in the cape and placed the
whole thing next to an open safe.

The safe was so stuffed with gold from his royalties that it
was disgusting. The woman approached the skeleton and
said:

"What a stupid joke."

And the poet left. He left for the roof and wanted to jump
off.

Later, the poet played with a revolver, a small Spanish
Browning, probably the very same one whose bullet ended
his life.[6]

Then, Ivan Nov wandered off down the road.

Mayakovsky played in a film entitled *Teacher for Workers,* in which he was a hooligan, who reformed, fell in love
and then died under a cross.

He acted without make-up, and Antik was not very pleased
with him. When the producer argued with him, Mayakovsky
would answer coolly:

"You know, if worst comes to worst, I can always write
poetry."

He frolicked like a boy; he frolicked like a redskin at a
wedding. He finally published *War and the Universe* in its
entirety and *Cloud in Pants* without censorship deletions. He
also published *Man,* a sad book about a poet who cannot
achieve genuine love.

PART THREE

This part begins with recollections about the great lyricist Aleksandr Blok. Theoretical discussions follow, at times rather dry and overburdened with quotations. This part has to be read if one wants to know about the theoreticians, Mayakovsky's neighbors, people who used his poetic experience to reinterpret the art of the past. There are four chapters to this part, and they are long.

Chapter 17

On Blok

[Lili wanted to own a book autographed by Aleksandr Blok. Mayakovsky went to see Blok. Blok received him in the way one poet welcomes another and wanted to have a long talk with him. But Mayakovsky had no time; he was in a hurry. Having gotten his autograph, he left. Blok didn't even have time to think up an inscription. He wanted to talk with the poet. A real talk came much later.]

The bridges on the Neva were raised. It was dusk; there were lights in the windows, street lamps were not lit. In the large and ungainly opera building on the Kronverksky Prospect, on the right bank of the Neva, Chaliapin was finishing a performance of the opera *Demon.*

The house was sold out. Chaliapin sang; the audience sat. *Demon* was being performed.

Military detachments in Petersburg, bonfires in Petersburg. Mayakovsky roamed the streets. At that time, he walked always in the streets—arguing and taking part in those small, movable, easily dissolving meetings.

At a bonfire, he met Aleksandr Blok in the uniform of a military functionary. That night, perhaps, he was not wearing his shoulder straps.

At that time, Blok often used to walk the streets and enter movie houses.

In those days, a movie theater was called a cinematograph. Singers sang popular ditties in small, stuffy halls.

On the wide, empty Neva, the *Aurora* [1] was anchored, its guns practically at the temples of the Winter Palace. The entire city was ready for its sailing; only on the Petersburg side, the *Demon* was sung, undisturbed.

They walked down the streets, those two poets, speaking about the Revolution, about what is most important to poets.

Later, I saw Blok with Mayakovsky a few more times.

Mayakovsky read *Mystery Bouffe* in the Miniature Theater on Liteynaya Street.

Aleksandr Blok was tall, blue-eyed and fair. He always spoke in a low, calm voice.

He read poetry as though it were written out in front of him, but not in large letters. He read very attentively.

Blok had found a new voice in the Revolution.

The wind of the Revolution breaking through a poet whistles through him as through a bridge. It passes through him like breath between lips.

Blok wrote *The Twelve* and when he was asked about Christ marching in front of the Red Army soldiers, he answered in a quiet voice:

"I look closely and see that it is really so."

Blok never recited *The Twelve*. He could not find the strength for it, could not repeat it.

He worked in the theater; he read other people's plays; he staged *King Lear*. Once, he and his wife performed *Hamlet* in the country for peasants, and the audience laughed a lot.

Sailors laughed on seeing Othello strangle Desdemona, not because they didn't understand Othello's jealousy, but because by their laughter they showed that they understood the conventions of the stage; their laughter protected them somewhat from horror.

It was a time when spectators at the theater wondered if Khlestakov [2] would succeed in safely escaping from the Mayor.

Whenever the actor in Schiller's *The Robbers* said the

lines, "bullets are our amnesty," the audience would burst into applause.

Blok saw and heard the new music of that time; he isolated himself from his friends; he used to say: "Unfortunately, the majority of mankind are Rightwing Socialist Revolutionaries." [3] He had already isolated himself from that part of mankind he knew when he walked with the man Mayakovsky.

Mayakovsky recited in the Miniature Theater.

Blok said:

"We were very talented, but we were not geniuses. Now, you are abolishing us. I understand it, but I'm not happy about it. And, besides, I'm sorry that you're rhyming 'bulkoyu' (by a roll) with 'bulyaka' (gurgling). I'm sorry for both of us that a roll makes us happy." [4]

He belonged to the new mankind which had inspired *The Twelve* and *The Scythians*. He was not abolished. Because art does not pass.

[He lived.

His wife was fond of the circus and took him to see the shows of a clown by the strange name of Anyuta Dosvidanya (Annie Goodby).

Blok died, suffocated.

Shortly before his death, he drew up plans for a new bookshelf for his library; the library, however, had been sold. At his funeral, only a few people followed the casket, no more than usual.

People in the street asked:

"Whose funeral is it?"

"Blok's."

"Genrikh Blok?"

Genrikh Blok had been a banker who also sold typewriters. He advertised a lot and hanged himself in his office. People remembered this so well that they were ready to bury him a second time.

And so died Aleksandr Blok.]

Chapter 18

I Continue

Petersburg was sunny because no smoke rose from the chimneys.

There was no grass on Nadezhdinskaya Street, but Manezhny Lane was all overgrown with grass and a horse roamed about on it. Grass also grew next to the Alexander Column on Palace Square. People came to graze their rabbits, which they brought with them in baskets. In front of the Hermitage they played skittles; it was a wood block pavement there.

In the Summer Garden, people swam in the pond.

Blok was still alive and worked in the Theater Section, the TEO.[1] Brik published the journal *Art of the Commune*.[2]

He worked in the Commissariat for Art. IZO,[3] the Section of Visual Arts had its office on St. Isaac's Square, in the beautiful Myatlev house.

It is a well built, highly artistic dwelling.

Not a palace. Better. Intelligent rooms.

Here were David Sterenberg and the flat faced Natan Altman; Vladimir Kozlinsky and Vladimir Mayakovsky came. They played billiards together.

Brik was Commissar of the Academy of Fine Arts and called himself the doorman of the Revolution; he said that he opened the door for it. The Briks still lived at 7 Zhukovskaya Street, on the same stairway, but they had a larger apartment. In winter, the apartment was very cold.

Everyone kept his coat on but Mayakovsky, who removed his to boost the morale.

Nikolay Punin came regularly. He had worked for *Apollon*, but now he was a Futurist who lectured painting instructors on Cubism with snobbish, academic assurance.

On the table was a cake made of nuts and carrots. It contained nothing rationed. All of it could have been bought in good conscience.

In the city, a lot of things were being sold sporadically and in small quantities; now, a second-hand store selling china on commission was opened; then again, chocolate was being sold on street corners.

The chocolate was called "Chocolate made by George Borman's workers." When mixed with finely ground rice, it became fancy "Mignon" chocolate. The whole thing can be explained by the fact that, in the city, cocoabeans and butter were still available.

Small rye cakes were being sold; all from hand to hand.

Art of the Commune propagated the idea of new art; Futurism wanted to conquer the country. Lunacharsky objected on the grounds that the workers did not like Futurism, although they appreciated Mayakovsky.

Mayakovsky said that things ought to be explained.

Articles about signboards were published in *Art of the Commune*. I stood apart; I was arguing that we should not participate in these matters. I was against the *Art of the Commune* and, politically, among the Futurists, I was on the right wing.

On the square, opposite the Ciniselli circus, there was a corner bookstore, quite appropriately called "The Book Corner." It sold old books and new manuscripts; Kuzmin and Sologub were writing books in longhand.

In the same building, on an upper floor—the sixth floor of the walk-up—there were empty rooms where Futurist paintings hung quietly. There were small stools that no one was using. This was IMO.[4]

IMO stands for Art of the Young. Mayakovsky, Brik and I. We published books. On Leshtukovy Lane, we found a printing press with very poor paper. The paper could only be used on one side; it was very thin, but it held the print and was waterproof.

That is where Mayakovsky published *Mystery Bouffe*.

It was set in one night, but we hadn't alerted the typesetter, so he put a capital letter at the beginning of each line. Mayakovsky kept his temper and said that it was his fault. This is also where the large volume *All of Mayakovsky* and the collection *Poetics* were set and published.

Poetics has 165 pages of exceedingly tight print with wide lines.

It contains writings by Brik, Yakubinsky and me.

Lili worked at home on counter-reliefs.

Counter-reliefs originated in paintings into which iron and plaster had been introduced.

First, the painting was raised, then the flat surface of the picture disappeared and several intersecting metal planes, variously bent, were suspended in the air.

An immense exhibition opened at the Winter Palace; it occupied all the rooms. Repin was there, and Chagall, with a corpse sitting on a roof and candles with flames blowing in different directions, a quiet herring on the table of David Petrovich Sterenberg—the colorful ascetic—as well as a counter-relief by Lili Brik.

On the circular Kronverksky Prospect stands a house, built before the war in northern Finno-Swedish style.

On the ground floor was an antique shop where no one ever went. It was called "The Merry Native."

On entering the house, one went through a service stairway and a kitchen to get to Gorky's apartment. It was a big apartment. Aleksey Maksimovich's room was not big and had a small library, almost completely made up of books about folklore. It had a single window from which one saw a semi-circular park, the People's House and that very same theater

in which Chaliapin sang the *Demon*—also the spire of the
Peter and Paul Fortress.

[Next to Gorky's room was a large room in which Ivan
Nikolayevich Rakitsky lived. In this room were green cloth
drapes, a Petrine cupboard, two Siamese enamel elephants
and a large, low sofa on which lay a large fur coat used as a
cover. Chaliapin visited Aleksey Maksimovich from time to
time; the artist Valentina Khodasevich and her husband
stayed with him; she wore green felt boots. Aleksey Maksimovich's son, Maksim, lived there; young, still single. Maksim
wore a moth-eaten sweater, gaily darned in red.]

A relatively short time before, Volodya had still been very
close to Gorky. Gorky played cards at the Briks'; he played
Tyotka. *Tyotka* is the kind of game in which whoever gets
the most tricks loses.

Aleksey Maksimovich stayed home, writing his recollections
of Tolstoy and a circus piece.

[He wore a Chinese bathrobe and Chinese slippers with
multilayered paper soles. He had scurvy, and rinsed his mouth
regularly with an oak bark infusion.]

In the dining room it was fairly warm—the fire was fed
with wooden crates. There were always people at Gorky's
house.

[Once, an actor—Borisov, I believe—lost his son. The actor
came to Gorky. Chaliapin was also there. A harmonist by the
name of Dymsha, I believe, came too.

We sang all night, outsinging one another.]

It was a large, complex house, from which roads went in
different directions.

[Here already appeared Pyotr Kryuchkov, who was exposed
only twenty years later—red headed, his hands covered with
coarse hair.

Gorky was being kept away from people.]

It was impossible to alienate Gorky and Mayakovsky on
literary grounds. Gorky had said that *150,000,000* was a
titanic work.

[The person who caused the discord between Gorky and Mayakovsky was evidently around his house for a long time because even by the year of Mayakovsky's death, Gorky had not changed his condemnation of the poet. This means that someone in the house kept the poisonous infection active.

I am convinced that this person was Pyotr Kryuchkov.

When he was very young, Mayakovsky had written some imitative poems close to the poetry of the "poètes maudits."

Those poems, long forgotten, served as evidence against the poet.]

And then we found out that someone had told Gorky that Volodya had wronged a woman.

I arrived at Aleksey Maksimovich's with L. Brik.

Of course, this conversation was not pleasant for Gorky. He drummed the table with his fingers and said: "I don't know, I don't know, I was told this by a very reliable comrade. I'll tell you his name; they'll give it to me."

L. Brik looked at Gorky, smiling furiously.

Aleksey Maksimovich was not given the name of the comrade, and he wrote a few words to L. Brik on the back of her letter to him, promising that he would find out who said it.[5]

Aleksey Maksimovich didn't get mad at me for meddling.

Apparently, he was not completely convinced that he was right. Slander, pure and simple, was used in this affair [and later on, the two of them were destroyed, one at a time].

Gorky considered Mayakovsky a genius. He passionately admired the poems "A Good Attitude to Horses" and *The Backbone Flute.*

Had they been together [not in museums but in life], both would have been happier, [and the course of the history of Soviet literature would have been different].

Mayakovsky asked me to stay with Gorky.

Everyone expected them to reach an understanding, to come to terms.

But no understanding was reached.

Chapter 19

OPOYAZ[1]

Mayakovsky was already living in Moscow. During the publication of *Poetics,* he came to Leningrad only occasionally.

Brik used to come too. The first conference of OPOYAZ took place in the kitchen of the abandoned apartment on Zhukovskaya Street. We used books to make a fire, but it was cold and Pyast kept his feet in the oven.

In the University which we attended at that time, little attention was given to literary theory. A. Veselovsky had died long before. He had followers, but they were already gray haired and still did not know what to do or what to write about.

Veselovsky's vast research, his broad understanding of art, his juxtaposition and evaluation of facts according to their functional role and artistic significance—not limited to their causal connection—were not understood by his followers.

The theory of Potebnya, who regarded the image as the changeable predicate of a constant subject [2]—the theory which essentially stated that art was a method of thinking (a method of simplifying the thinking process), and that images were rings linking various kinds of keys—had degenerated.

On one hand, Potebnya's theory had degenerated into the doctrine of Sumtsov and his conception of art as the memory of an ancient poetic language, while on the other hand,

Potebnya's followers had integrated Mach's theory of the economy of life forces. It was assumed that a work of poetry provided a means to an easier assimilation of reality; poetry was viewed as the shortest way in life.

In general terms, Potebnya's theory was the theory of Symbolism. Potebnya pointed out that in naming an object, one chooses an already existing word; the content of that word (its meaning) has to have something in common with one of the properties of the object to be named. Therefore, the meaning of the word is broadened by the image; yet the image, as Potebnya understood it, belongs exclusively to poetry; hence the symbolism of a word equals its poetic quality. "The symbolism of language," said Potebnya, "may evidently be termed its poetic quality; inversely, the neglect of inner form may appear to us as the prose quality of the word. If this comparison holds true, then the problem of the changing inner form of the word is identical with the problem of the relation of language to prose and poetry, that is, to literary form in general." This is the scheme Potebnya used to analyze artistic phenomena.

What, then, is the value we look for in art and, specifically, in poetry? It is that its images are symbolic and have multiple meanings. In these images "coexist contradictory properties, determinable and infinite in their contours." Thus, the objective of art is to create symbols that, in their formula, unite a diversity of things.

This was the formulation of poetic theory presented by Potebnya in his book *Thought and Language*.

This theory was being altered and vulgarized.

Collections of writings by Potebnya's last pupils were being published. They were entitled *Problems of the Theory and Psychology of Art*.

In these collections, direct references were made to Avenarius. Avenarius and Mach dominated the minds of those days. This is what Avenarius wrote on the principle of economy:

"If the soul had inexhaustible power, then, of course, the quantity spent from this inexhaustible source would hardly matter—except perhaps in terms of the time necessarily spent. But since its power is limited, one must assume that the soul will strive to carry out its apperceptive processes in the most expedient manner, that is, with a relatively minimal effort or, in other words, with a relatively maximal result." [3]

Our hostile neighbors were the Symbolists and the Machists.

I began my polemical career by polemics with Filosofov.

We knew and learned again that, in prose speech, the phenomenon of the economy of forces does generally take place, and the dissimilation of identical consonants does occur. In poetic language, however, a phenomenon occurs loosely described as "orchestration," that is, an orientation toward the phonetic aspect, toward pronunciation, a tendency to accumulate identical sounds.

The Symbolists had observed this too. But they had interpreted it either in an illustrative sense, believing that in verse sounds are onomatopoeic; or in a mystical sense speaking about poetry as sorcery, as magic through sounds.

But we said: "Magic? Fine."

But then let's study the question of magic as ethnographers do; let's examine the law of invocations—how they are organized, what they resemble.

Whereas Symbolism saw the word and art as intersecting with religious systems, we saw the word as sound.

Lev Yakubinsky made a distinction between prose language and poetic language; he said that language follows different patterns of development according to its diverse functions.

In opposition to the Symbolists, the poets Khlebnikov, Mayakovsky and Vasily Kamensky put forward a different kind of poetics.

They required of a thing not so much multiple meaning as perceptibility. They created unexpected images and revealed the unexpected phonetic aspect of a thing. They mastered in poetry what had previously been called "dissonance." Mayakovsky wrote

"There are some good letters left: *R, Sh, Shch.*" [4]

This was broadening the perception of the world. Mayakovsky had previously written that such words as "scoundrel" and "borscht" were the last words left to the street.

Part of the work of OPOYAZ was connected with this new poetics. The theory of "defamiliarization" was put forward in its name.

This theory originated from an analysis of Tolstoy's realistic art. In Mayakovsky's own poetics, there was something that suggested to us the search in that direction.

Once, Tolstoy had written:

"I was dusting my room and, going around the room, I went up to the sofa and could not remember whether I had dusted it or not. Since these movements are habitual and unconscious, I was unable to remember, and I felt that I would not be able to remember. Therefore, had I dusted and forgotten it, that is acted unconsciously then it was as though it had never happened. If someone had witnessed it consciously, it could have been reconstructed. If, however, nobody saw it, or if someone saw it, but unconsciously, if the entire life of many people is lived unconsciously, then that life, in effect, did not exist." [5]

Tolstoy restored the perception of everyday reality by describing it in newly found words as though destroying the habitual logic of associations he distrusted.

This new attitude to objects in which, in the last analysis, the object becomes more perceptible, is that artificiality which, in our opinion, creates art.

A phenomenon, perceived many times, and no longer perceivable, or rather, the method of such dimmed perception, is what I called "recognition" as opposed to "seeing." The aim of imagery, the aim of creating new art is to return the object from "recognition" to "seeing." In terms of contemporary physiology, we deal with inhibitions and stimulation. A signal given many times produces drowsiness and inhibition. That the views I expressed at the time coincided with Pavlov's work, was pointed out to me by Lev Gumilevsky.

This is what Pavlov writes:

"At the human stage in the development of the animal world, the load on the mechanisms of nervous activity was greatly increased. For animals, reality is signaled almost exclusively through stimuli and their traces in the large cerebral hemispheres; they are transmitted directly to the special visual and aural cells and cells of other organs of perception. This is what man, too, has as impressions, sensations, conceptions of the surrounding environment, both in its general forms and in its forms peculiar to us—with the exception of the word, seen and heard. That is the primary signal system of reality common to us and animals. Nevertheless, a second, specifically human system of signals for reality was created by the word, it being a signal for primary signals. On one hand, the numerous stimuli by the word have moved us farther away from reality, and we must always remember this in order not to distort our relation to reality; on the other hand, it is the word that has made us human, a fact which, of course, we need not elaborate on here. There is, however, no doubt that the basic laws which rule the work of the primary system of signals must also direct the secondary one, because it functions through the same nervous tissue." [6]

In 1919, I wrote:

"In analyzing poetic language for its phonetic and lexical structure, for its syntax and its semantics, as well as for its characteristic distribution of words and in the characteristic thought structures compounded from its words, we will always encounter the same property of the artistic: that it is created expressly to liberate perception from automatism and that the aim of the artist is the 'seeing'; it is 'artfully' created in such a way as to hold perception and bring it to its highest possible intensity and longest duration, while the object is perceived not in its spatial aspect but, so to speak,

in its continuity. 'Poetic Language' meets just these require-
ments."

The preceding quotation doesn't prove that OPOYAZ was
right. Nor does it prove that Pavlov was right. These were
ideas of the time. Pavlov partly moved away from them. It is
well known that Pavlov prohibited the use of the word
"psychology" in his laboratory and even instituted a fine
against its use. Later on, he worked on the higher cerebral
activity of man. Once, he came to the laboratory and, with
a grim laugh, said:

"Always reflexes and more reflexes. The time has come to
invent a new term for all these reflexes, as for instance 'psychology.' "

Well, we failed to invent such a term.

Signals, but signals of what? Actually, in the final analysis,
examining all my writings on plot, we can see that art aims
at restoring sensory perception.

Sensory perception of what?

And here, I began to argue that art develops on its own, in-
dependently.

Thus, while I was empirically right and right in my opposition to Symbolism and Machism, while I was right about the
physiological basis of the phenomena, I mistook the temporal
connection in the change of dissimilar art forms for a causal
connection.

Mayakovsky, at the time, was patiently working to get our
things published. We used to go to Lunacharsky together.
Mayakovsky got money for us and drew us into LEF, but he
had his own poetics, and his liberation from automatism was
his own.

Let's examine Lenin's views as reported by Gorky:

"It so happened that we had a free evening in London, and
a small group of us went to a music hall, a small democratic
theater. Vladimir Ilyich laughed easily and infectiously on
watching the clowns and vaudeville acts, but he was only
mildly interested in the rest. He watched with special interest

as workers from British Columbia felled trees. The small stage represented a lumber yard, and in front, two hefty fellows within a minute chopped down a tree of about one meter circumference.

" 'Well, of course, this is only for the audience. They can't really work that fast,' said Ilyich. 'But, it's obvious that they do work with axes there, too, making worthless chips out of the bulk of the tree. Here you have your cultured Englishmen!'

"He started talking about the anarchy of production under capitalism and ended by expressing regret that nobody had yet thought of writing a book on the subject. I didn't quite follow this line of reasoning, but I had no time to question Vladimir Ilyich because he switched to an interesting discussion on 'eccentrism' as a special form of theater art.

" 'There is a certain satyrical and skeptical attitude to the conventional, an urge to turn it inside out, to distort it slightly in order to show the illogic of the usual. Intricate but interesting.'

"In Capri, about two years later in a conversation with A. A. Bogdanov-Malinovsky on the utopian novel, he said to him:

" 'Well, you should write a novel for workers on how the predatory capitalists have despoiled the earth and wasted all its oil, iron, lumber and coal. That would be a very useful book, Mister Machist.' " [7]

Let's analyze this extremely important excerpt:

1. Lenin is interested in eccentrics.
2. Lenin is watching the demonstration of real work.
3. He evaluates first class work as senseless and wasteful; he talks about the anarchy of production and the necessity to write about it.
4. Lenin talks about eccentrism in art, a skeptical attitude toward the conventional, and the illogic of the usual.

The transition which Gorky missed is that the wastefulness and, so to speak, the absurdity of the capitalist world could be shown through methods of eccentric art with its skeptical attitude toward the conventional.

Finally, Gorky himself ties this talk in with the suggestion that it would be interesting to write a novel about the wastefulness of capitalism.

Summing up: Lenin became interested in "eccentric" art and immediately broadened its field of application.

He began talking about the area of applied eccentrism as found in the works of the great Realists like Tolstoy, for instance.

Tolstoy's Realism is based on a skeptical attitude toward the conventional; he re-described life with different, nonautomized words.

Thus, "eccentric" art can be realistic art.

The issue of the tendentiousness of all art arises.

In the passage preceding the section quoted, Gorky said:

"It is difficult to convey or to depict the naturalness and flexibility with which all his (V. I. Lenin) impressions flowed into one channel.

"Like a compass, his thought always turned its needle toward the class interests of the working people." [8]

Innovation enters art by revolution. Reality reveals itself in art in much the same way as gravity reveals itself when a ceiling collapses on its owner's head.

New art searches for the new word, the new expression. The poet suffers in attempts to break down the barrier between the word and reality. We can already feel the new word on his lips, but tradition puts forward the old concept.

> And it turns out—
> that before the song rises,
> one has to walk for a long time getting corns from wandering,
> and the stupid fish of imagination
> flounders quietly in the mire of the heart.
> While, scraping rhymes, they boil down
> some infusion of loves and nightingales,
> the street writhes tongueless—

it has nothing to shout with, nothing to speak with.
In our pride, we are building again
Babylonian towers of cities;
But God
crashes
cities on the field
confusing the word.[9]

The old art tells lies with its melodrama, with its rhymes,
if it is not reinterpreted.

Chapter 20

Mayakovsky's Verse

The work of the theoreticians of that time connected with Mayakovsky was incomplete. Mayakovsky valued this work very highly; he and I tried to persuade Anatoly Vasilyevich Lunacharsky to give us the opportunity of publishing our books. But we published little. Our talks were more interesting.

My basic studies were on plot and did not deal directly with verse. Brik's writings on rhythmics were never finished. I hope that he will finish them now.[1]

Now, it's easier for me to write about rhymes. Let's begin with the attitude of the Symbolists toward rhymes.

They wanted to attribute a precise symbolic value, a direct meaning, to sounds.

It is a property of the Russian language that its unstressed syllables are very weakly realized.

"In Blok's pronunciation," Bely wrote, "the ending 'yi' and a simple 'y' would sound identical, and the consonance 'obmanom-tumannye' (by fraud-misty) would pass for a rhyme."[2]

Turgenev called Aleksey Tolstoy's rhymes "lame."

Tolstoy retorted in a letter:

"It seems to me that vowels at the end of a rhyme, if unstressed, are inconsequential and of no significance. Only the consonants count and form the rhyme. 'Bezmolvno-volny' (wordlessly-waves) to my mind, rhyme far better than 'shalost-mladost' (prank-youth), or 'gruzno-druzhno' (heavily-all-together) in which the vowels fully correspond." [3]

Turgenev sees rhymes, but Aleksey Tolstoy, being more sensitive to Russian verse, hears them.

Lomonosov had already rhymed "kichlivy-pravdivy" (conceited-truthful), and Sumarokov had bitterly reproached him in his important article, "On the Structure of Poetic Meter."

Syllabo-tonic verse knew stressed and unstressed syllables, but it did not know a reduced, unrealized syllable.

The Symbolists gave sound a mystical interpretation and they interpreted the trends of the development of language as the rudiments of mystical words.

Andrey Bely has the following to say about Merezhkovsky: "He at times caustically mocks Blok's poetry: 'Blok is inarticulate; he rhymes "granits-tsaritsu" (frontiers-queen).'

"His small eyes darted glances at me and at Filosofov, as if throwing balls.

" 'In Lev Tolstoy's novel, when Anatol's leg is being amputated, he cries out: "Ooo!" But in his death agony, Tolstoy's Ivan Ilyich cries: "I do not want to-o-o . . ." But in Blok it is: "Tsaritsuuu?" *Uuu* is like a little tail; like the train on the dress of his suspicious "lady"; don't get caught in that train, Borya!' " [4]

That tidbit on "tsaritsu" is very typical of Symbolist poetics. The Symbolists studied the sounds of the language, but attributed emotive and even mystical meanings to the sounds themselves.

Mayakovsky's rhymes are structured on sound, not graphic similarity. He gave his rhymes a phonetic transcription, inasmuch as it can be done by means of an approximate orthography.

Trenin, in the book *In the Workshop of Mayakovsky's Verse,* writes:

"Mayakovsky's notes and drafts contain numerous entries of such tentative rhymes:

Nevo-Nevoy (him-by the Neva); pleska-zheleska (splash-irontool); kak te-kagtey (like those-of claws); samak-dama (selfmade man-lady); aparat-para (apparatus-couple), etc.

I have never run into this type of note with any other poet but Mayakovsky.

The peculiar characteristic of these notes is that Mayakovsky decidedly rejects the traditional orthographic word form and attempts to fix each word approximately as it is pronounced (that is, he creates something resembling a scientific phonetic transcription)." [5]

As early as 1916, we published collections dealing with the theory of poetic language and in the first book, we printed translations of Grammont and Nyrop. They were French and Danish scholars who demonstrated fairly accurately that sound as such has no fixed emotional value but is variously emotional. We thus cleaned the table on which we were going to work.

Our neighbors and friends were Lev Yakubinsky and Sergey Bernstein.

We knew that the "u" in the word "tsaritsu" and the groan of Ivan Ilyich were two different phenomena.

Degenerating Symbolism tied meaning to the little tail. To the "u." The poem furnished an address.

The address turned out to be in the other world.

Mayakovsky's verse is organized throughout.

In its development, Mayakovsky's verse solved a great many issues in the history of Russian versification.

Mayakovsky renounced syllabo-tonic verse and the counting of syllables.

Pushkin had already believed that the future of Russian verse lay in Russian folk poetry.

In this connection, he referred to Radishchev, Tredyakovsky and Vostokov.

Radishchev and Tredyakovsky were revolutionary thinkers, and revolutionaries in the field of poetry as well.

Aleksandr Sergeyevich Pushkin later solved both, the problem of metrics and the problem of rhyme:

"Radishchev, an innovator at heart, endeavored to change the structure of Russian verse as well. His study of the 'Telemachid' is remarkable. He was the first among us to write in ancient lyric meters. His poetry is superior to his prose. Read his 'Eighteenth Century,' his 'Sapphic Stanzas,' and his fable, or rather elegy 'The Cranes'—they all have merit. The chapter from which I took the passage quoted above includes his famous 'Ode to Liberty.' It contains many powerful lines.

"I am now turning to Russian versification. I believe that, in time, we will turn to blank verse. There are too few rhymes in the Russian language. One rhyme demands another. 'Plamen' (flame) unavoidably drags in 'kamen' (stone). 'Iskusstvo' (art) inevitably peeks out from behind 'chuvstvo' (feeling). And, who is not tired of 'lyubov-krov' (love-blood), 'trudny-chudny' (difficult-wonderful), 'vernoy-litsemernoy' (loyal-hypocritical), etc.?

"A lot has been said about genuine Russian verse. A. Kh. Vostokov defined it with great erudition and wit. Probably, our epic poet of the future will adopt it and make it national."

It was already known that a definite rhyme scheme and the very emphasis on rhyme lends a new quality to a verse, adding irony. Ostolopov, in his *Dictionary of Ancient and Modern Poetry,* wrote:

"Sometimes it is customary to have in verse several rhymes in series or in combination; this occurs mostly in free verse, and, generally, in verse describing trivial matters."

He cited an example from Pushkin:

> Learn, Ruslan: your enemy
> is the dread magician Chernomor,

of old abductor of beautiful maidens,
master of midnight mountains.

No glance has as yet penetrated into his abode;
but you, destroyer of evil schemes,
you will enter it, and the villain
will perish by your hand.[6]

In modern Russian verse, the rhyme proved victorious. Vostokov's predictions were not fulfilled; he had said: "We would perceive the delight of rhymes still more sharply if they were used less frequently, and only in certain types of poetry, and if they were intelligently selected, and used only in certain cases to enhance the charm and harmony."

Vostokov thought that, with the trend toward folk poetry, our verse would lose its rhyme, but this, too, proved wrong.

The search was on a wide scale. One should not think that Pushkin completely solved the problem of rhyme. He declared several times that our rhymes had been exhausted, but at the same time Vyazemsky claimed that Pushkin had quarreled with him for speaking disrespectfully about rhymes.

Here is that curious remark of Vyazemsky's:

"It is up to Pushkin; I am not defending the euphony of my verses, but even now I do not hear a cacophony in those verses. The real issue is the following. Pushkin was angered and chagrined by another one of my lines in the same epistle, namely the one in which I had said that our language is poor in rhymes. 'How could you dare admit such a thing,' he said to me. He took the insult to the Russian language as a very personal affront. In a sense, he was justified, since he is one of the highest, if not *the* highest, representative of that language. That is so. But I am also right. As proof, may I refer to Pushkin himself, and to Zhukovsky, for later on both began writing more and more in blank verse. Even in the poetry of these two giants, Russian rhyme had become worn and forlorn." [7]

Pushkin himself wrote as though negating rhyme, but

Pushkin was publishing *The Contemporary*.[8] *The Contemporary* was in the fullest sense an editor's review. The articles in *The Contemporary* were ordered, outlined, and specified by Pushkin. Each issue was thoroughly organized. In the first volume, following the official section, there appeared an article on rhyme by Baron Rozen. I believe that that article was written after lengthy discussions. Rozen wrote:

"Aside from *The Song of Igor's Campaign*,[9] the ancient poems collected by Kirsha Danilov already show the extent to which our folk poetry, especially that of an epic nature, is alien to rhyme. We consider it unnecessary to bring in more evidence to prove that rhyme is suited only to the Russian joke; we could point to light and gay songs, and specifically the song 'The Titmouse beyond the Sea' which is filled with harmony. We hope, however, that the reader will not demand more convincing arguments." [10]

Thus, in the first issue of Pushkin's review a statement is made by a man of very minor importance. Rozen devotedly loved the Russian language, but had a very slim understanding of Russian literature.

His opinion is very interesting by the fact of its mentioning the sphere of usage for the rhyme, and also because it was printed in Pushkin's review. Rhyme could have been revived in our language as punning rhyme.

At the end of his article, Rozen wrote: "The last refuge of the rhyme will be the drinking song or, surely, the family album." [11]

That actually occurred in the quasi-album verse of Minayev.

From there came the punning rhyme.

Mayakovsky annihilated syllabo-tonic verse and created a new Russian verse. Blok's deviations from syllabo-tonic versification cannot be put side by side with Mayakovsky's system.

Art does not change little by little. New phenomena accumulate without being perceived, later they are perceived in a revolutionary way.

Blok's contractions, his lines, which for an instant seem to disconnect the general laws of the old Russian verse, are similar to a skier's descent from a mountain. After all, this is a skier, not a bird. Part of the curve of his descent is made without touching the snow, but he lands again on the slope.

Mayakovsky's verse has wings.

The rhyme, however, had to be newly reinforced, because now the rhyme determined the limits of the rhythmical units.

The rhyme was reborn in the form in which it had existed in the folksong and the proverb.

This kind of rhyming endows the rhymed word with greater power. In that same essay, Mayakovsky described how he searched for a rhyme:

"Perhaps it can be left unrhymed? Impossible. Why? Because without a rhyme (in the broad sense of the word), the verse will fall apart.

"Rhyme takes you back to the preceding line, forces you to remember it, forces all the lines forming one single idea to hang together." [12]

That is why a new theory of rhyme was needed.

Rhyme drastically reinforced allowed the definitive transformation of verse; it was now possible to graphically break the line, set off the main word and contrast that word to the entire phrase.

Verse did not become prosaic, though Mayakovsky's verse, when read aloud, is closer to prose speech than Pushkin's, since it does not demand the restoration of what has been lost in the language.

It is oratorical verse and, hence, non-melodic.

Mayakovsky's verse is also extremely innovative in its vocabulary.

He changed the adjective, and into his lowered verse with punning rhyme, he introduced the hyperbolic complex epithets: either simply unexpected ones like "bareheaded church," or complicated ones like "lump-meaty bull-faced crowd." He changed the relation between modifier and the modified, treating the inanimate object as animate, for instance: "Violins' speeches," "Blankets' quilting." He inverted sentences, changed prepositions and completely twisted them around; he shifted the order of important and neutral auxiliary words in the sentence.

Mayakovsky changed poetic language by substituting almost everywhere parallel instead of coordinate sentence structure.

That is the difference between Mayakovsky's verse and that of his imitators.

Mayakovsky rearranged words in the Russian language and changed their semantic value.

Poets had concentrated all their efforts on minor changes in shades of meaning; they had already worked with rhythmico-syntactical segments which they kept transposing. All this was destroyed by Mayakovsky, who broke through the solid ice field of words and built a new, perceptible poetry based on Khlebnikov's vast experience, on folksong and on oratory.

He could do that because he had a "sail."

Blok once told me that when he listened to me, he heard the truth about verse for the first time, but that it was dangerous for a poet to know what I said.

It was dangerous because it was not the whole truth. There was no "sail."

The whole truth would have been useful for the poet.

But, why do I evoke a sail? Viktor Khlebnikov once wrote to Kruchyonykh: "A long poem combines poor lines with a passionate and concise understanding of our time."

Further on, crossed-out words: "In it there is a hint of the wind, the impact of a storm. Hence the ship can move on if the necessary word sails are hoisted."

A poem can be born by impulse, by something like Fet's presentiment of a song, a presentiment not yet knowing what form it will take.

Speaking of Ukrainian songs, Gogol said: "Then, abandon

reflection and vigilance! Their entire mysterious make-up requires sounds and sounds only. That is what makes poetry in songs elusive, fascinating, gracious, like music."

The poetry of ideas is more accessible to everyone than the poetry of sounds or, rather, the poetry of poetry. The latter can be understood only by the chosen one, the one who is a true poet in his heart. That is why the most beautiful song often remains unnoticed, while a mediocre one will succeed owing to its content.

In Pushkin's fragment "Autumn," it sounds like this:

> And I forget the worlds, and in sweet stillness
> I am sweetly lulled by my imagination,
> And poetry awakes in me.
> My soul contracts in lyrical excitement,
> It throbs, resounds, and tries as in sleep
> To pour out, at last, in a free expression.

Pushkin goes on about old and familiar fantasy encounters, images belonging to a poet and, at last, the image of the sail arises:

> Another moment and the verses will flow freely.
> Thus a still ship dozes in still waters,
> But, hark! The sailors rush suddenly to the masts,
> Up and down—the sails billow, filled with wind;
> The giant moves and cleaves the waves.
> It sails. But whither shall we sail?

Mayakovsky's verses were born out of rhythm, but rhythm with him originated in a basic word—the task.

"I walk, swinging my arms, and mumbling still almost wordlessly; now, I slow down so as not to interrupt my mumbling; now, I mumble more rapidly to keep in tune with my steps.

"So the rhythm is trimmed and shaped, for it is the basis of all poetry and runs through it like a roar. Gradually, out of this roar, one starts to pick out separate words.

"Some words simply jump off and never return, others linger, turning over and inside out dozens of times, until one feels that the word is in place; this feeling, which grows with experience, is what is called talent. The first word to emerge is usually the main word—the word which character-izes the meaning of the verse or the word to be rhymed." [13] Mayakovsky had rhythmic headlines, rhythmical impulses when the verse began humming with the yet unexpressed sound as "in the belly of a piano!" All of this was guided by the thematic sail of the word. Playing with a word, that word being very often the rhyme word, Mayakovsky enhanced the rhyme of his verse and gave it tremendous power.

Mayakovsky's rhyme reminds us of the statement by the simple-minded Rozen, which was supported by the wise Pushkin.

Mayakovsky would not tolerate a facile rhyme.

He could not rhyme "rezvost-trezvost" (playfulness-sobri-ety).

The new rhyme, or rather the new concept introduced by the rhyme, had to differ from the initial rhyme, both quali-tatively and emotionally.

In a rough draft of the verses to Yesenin, there was the rhyme "rezvost-trezvost."

It was not good enough.

"Such is the fate of almost all words of the same category: when a verb rhymes with a verb, or a noun with a noun, when both words have the same roots or the same case endings." [14]

Verb rhymes do not constitute rhymes, nor do rhymes on case endings, because these rhymes reflect bare grammatical coincidence without reflecting the meaning.

Mayakovsky couldn't use "rezvost" for another reason: it's a humorous word. That is to say, he needed a meaningful word, and that other word had to be a word of a different quality.

Mayakovsky said: "The rhyme binds the lines together; that is why it must be made of even stronger material than the material used for the rest of the line." [15]

He chose the word "vrezyvayas" (cutting into), which

forced him to change the orchestration of the line so that the "t" and the "st" of the word "trezvost" would have a sound correspondence in the following line.

The word "pustota" (emptiness) appears.

This is an excellent analysis, given by the poet himself.

That a rhyme should convey meaning was already known in Pushkin's time.

In *The Dictionary of Ancient and Modern Poetry,* Ostolopov wrote:

"Rhyme, in our opinion, may have the following merits: first of all, it can give pleasure to the ear that knows how to appreciate it; second, it aids the memory by offering the most distinctive clues for following the train of thought, that is, some lines would be completely forgotten had not the final sound of the following line brought it back to memory; third, rhyme sometimes provokes unintended, startling thoughts which the author could not even imagine in planning his work. One can find proof of this by examining the poetry of the best writers." [16]

Yet, at the same time, the entire image which came to Mayakovsky, "Fly, cutting your way into the stars," is also connected with the image of the flight into heaven in the poem *Man.*

The heaven of separation, the heaven of Mark Twain.

Mayakovsky floated under the great sail of his theme.

We have gotten ahead a bit. The poem "To Sergey Yesenin" was written later.

But Mayakovsky developed so unexpectedly and so irreversibly that it sometimes seems possible to disconnect time when talking about his poetry.

Mayakovsky needed the work of OPOYAZ, the work of Brik—his unfinished "Rhythmico-syntactical Figures."

The Pushkin rhythms had absorbed so many words that they offered ready made word solutions.

Rhythmico-syntactical figures had been predetermining the thought process.

The Symbolist semantics had created new word combinations, but it was exhausted too.

One had to hoist the sail into a new wind.

"Sound Repetitions" was an early work of O. Brik. "The Rhythmico-syntactical Figures" remained in the journal *New LEF*, and were not published as a book.

This book, buried in odd issues of the journal, was needed so that people could surrender to the rhythm of their thoughts.

Mayakovsky could find his way to the new rhythm because he was not learning from poets only.

Of course, he was not alone.

Khlebnikov, Pasternak, Aseyev worked together.

The very syntax of Russian speech was changed.

We used the coordinate clause in our prose; it belongs more to the written language than to dialogue.

The humor and characteristic feature of Leskov's *skaz*,[17] and even the speech of Ostrovsky's characters, are based on the omission of the coordinate clause. Words refuse to form those artificial ranks, and internally keep renewing and changing their meaning in relation to one another.

Mayakovsky turned to parallelism.

It almost seemed as though he were returning to the archaic sphere of solemn ancient Russian prose.

However, the complex interrelationship of parallel sentence structures—partially fortified by rhymes—gave birth to a different cadence, colloquial in its nature.

Pasternak took the coordinate clause, fortified it with rhythm, and used it in his poetry. His poetry proved to be the final subjugation of a fortress taken by storm.

The Acmeists' shortness of breath was finally overcome.

Mayakovsky said, "Pasternak is the application of a dynamic syntax to the revolutionary objective."

In his essay "How Are Verses Made?" he wrote:

"The attitude toward the verse line should be the same as

the attitude toward the woman in Pasternak's sublime quatrain:

> That day, from combs to feet,
> I knew you by heart as a provincial actor knows his Shakespeare,
> I carried you with me,
> wandered about the city, rehearsed my part." [18]

Syntactically, these verses are very complex.

But let us come to a conclusion. What Mayakovsky accomplished was a supreme advance for Russian verse, the broadening of verse semantics.

Russian verse takes many forms.

Mayakovsky's classical verse is not narrative. It is oratorical language.

Oratory has its own syntax. It is usually built on parallelism. Its syntactical structure is often supported by the realization of one given image.

When Mayakovsky, in a poem written shortly before his death, used narrative style, his verse came close to classical verse:

> Deploying in a parade
> > the armies of my pages,
> I pass in review
> > the front of my lines.
> Verses stand
> > lead-heavily,
> ready for death
> > and for immortal fame. [19]

This poem from beginning to end is related to Pushkin's "Monument" and, through it, to Horace.

Mayakovsky was afraid of being applauded by the high priests.

Prose writers and critics, with their shortness of breath, wanted Mayakovsky to repent and return to the fold of orthodox verse before he died.

But Mayakovsky wrote verse in which he used rhythms, old

rhythms, as future poets will use his; as cities drink water from ancient Roman aqueducts.

Mayakovsky succeeded in reforming Russian verse because he aimed at reflecting the new world.

Many people in and around OPOYAZ had the right attitude toward the Revolution.

Even before the October Revolution, Brik asked that the secret treaties be made public. Lev Yakubinsky said the same.

My position differed and, in the journal *Art of the Commune,* I zealously demonstrated Futurism's independence from the Revolution.

In addition, I argued the complete independence of art from the development of life. I had an incorrect theory that poetic genes develop spontaneously.

Now, twenty years later, is not the time to justify myself. I am also to blame for having created a theory narrowed by my attitude at that time, thus making it harder to understand even its correct aspects. The only excuse, or rather comment, that I can make, is that I still bear many very real wounds from that time.

The logic of my letter to *Art of the Commune* can, of course, be explained. But the letter did say that art had nothing to do with politics.

When Wrangel advanced, I fought against him, but at that time I was not a Communist, and I took refuge in a peculiar tower made of method. There had been such an ivory tower on Tavricheskaya Street, and Vyacheslav Ivanov had lived in it. In that tower, they discussed poetry and ate omelets.

This incorrect conception of the world spoiled my theory, or rather, it created an incorrect theory.

It spoiled life.

Because of this incorrect attitude toward the Revolution, I found myself an émigré in Germany in 1922.

PART FOUR

Part Four is composed of three chapters. The first describes how winter kept circling Mayakovsky's house; the second tells about a distant island in the North Sea. The third constitutes a sort of footnote to the Mayakovsky poem.

Chapter **21**

In the Snow

It was the period when Lenin wrote about how to post newspapers. There was a shortage of newspapers. Therefore, they had to be posted on walls so that people could read them. But paste is made of flour, and there was a shortage of flour too. To hammer them down meant nails. And there were no nails. It was suggested that the newspapers be hammered on with small wooden pegs.

Paper was available for books that had a printing of a thousand copies. But the books were small in size.

Mayakovsky, nevertheless, got hold of a lot of paper for IMO, though of poor quality, and published large editions.

It was bitterly cold. The ink stuck to the rollers of the printing presses; it solidified and the roller froze and jumped.

There was nothing to clean the type, either.

[Dead horses lay on the streets. There was nobody to cart them away. They were carried off in pieces, cut up with pocket knives. Mayakovsky writes about this in his poem.[1]

Dogs came later. A weakened city dog is unable to start picking apart a carcass by himself.

Later, when the dogs were completing the work of humans, the bones remained, lying somewhere there on Basseynaya Street.]

Petrograd ate mostly oats. The oats were steamed in pots,

run through a meat grinder and put through a sieve to mash the puffed-up grains; then water was added, and the result was an oats-mash. It was edible.

Frozen potatoes had to be washed before they had thawed. They were sweet and unsavory. We added pepper, if we had any.

As for horse meat, it is generally better fried than boiled. But frying requires something to fry with. One of my acquaintances fried his steaks in soap to which he added vinegar. The vinegar neutralized the taste of soda in the soap.

I am not making this up. The man who did this was a Persian language specialist.

Winter had arrived. A lot of snow fell and accumulated in high drifts. We trampled narrow paths through the snow.

We walked along these paths pulling our sleds behind us; we carried bags over our shoulders.

We wrote a great deal in those days, and OPOYAZ met weekly, I think.

At that time, Boris Eichenbaum, still young, not yet gray, had written a book about the young Tolstoy. And I will say even now that it was an excellent book.

We used to meet at Sergey Bernstein's apartment, or mine, in virtual darkness, by the light of the tiny round yellow flame of a night lamp.

The *burzhuyka*[2] stoves appeared somewhat later.

The World Literature Publishing House[3] was active, and Blok argued with Volynsky on the subject of humanism.

We also met on Liteyny Prospect at the Muruzi house in the former apartment of the former banker Gandelman.

I have already mentioned this apartment. It looked like a Sandunov bathing establishment.

Once, when Yudenich was advancing, a meeting of the literary studio was in progress. Gandelman came in with his wife. We were discussing *Tristram Shandy*. The Gandelman woman walked through us and began lifting the edges of the slip covers on the chairs, to see whether we had cut the leather off the seats.

Later, the Gandelman woman disappeared.

When the thaw came, the city unfroze.

During the thaw, a humid sea breeze blew over Leningrad. It touched the cold skin of the unheated houses, covering them with sweat. In those days, the city was silvery from hoar frost, and it was rare to see dark patches on walls behind which were heated rooms.

This was the time when we were under attack from all sides.

The real world was far away, far away where there are palm trees and birch firewood.

It was almost beyond imagination.

From there arrived once, in a gray suit and with large suitcases, the pale-haired Wells [4] and his son.

It was still fall.

They stayed with Gorky. The son danced a sort of wild jig jingling keys. The father talked about what was going on in England.

The son strolled around town and noticed things that we did not see. He asked: "Where do your flowers come from?"

Indeed there were flowers in the city flower shops; they had not shut down. Somewhere, evidently, there were greenhouses.

He asked why so many people were dressed in leather, inquired about prices and said with deep conviction: "In this country, one ought to speculate."

He spoke several languages, and as far as I can recall, some Russian. The father knew only English, and he explained this as follows: "My father was not a gentleman like me and he didn't teach me languages as I taught my son."

I enjoyed berating this Wells at the House of Arts. Aleksey Maksimovich gleefully told the interpreter:

"Translate all this to him exactly."

And so I travelled from this Petersburg to Moscow, to buy

a tooth brush. At the station, the only thing for sale was jello; red or bright yellow, and wobbling. Nothing else was being sold.

In Moscow, more snow, more bundled-up people and sleds, but there was also the Sukharevka.[5] People were noisy, they were trading, one could buy bread and the aforementioned tooth brush.

The Briks lived on Poluektov Lane, in an apartment they shared with David Sterenberg. The entrance was from the yard, if my memory does not betray me, in a white separate wing of the building. A white wing, three steps, a staircase, and next to the staircase, in the snow, a red-haired dog called Shchen.

Shchen was probably a bastard setter, but nobody asked him what his parents did. He was loved because he was loved.

Dogs are sometimes that lucky.

The Briks' room was small, with a fireplace in one corner. I was asked to buy some firewood, and they warned me: "Don't buy the white kind." I went from Poluektov Lane to the Truba Market. People were trading with whatever they had. There, I found a bundle of birch logs that I bought hastily and immediately carted off. On the way, I realized that the logs were very, very white.

I began chopping them up; I put them in the fireplace and lit the fire—I like to make fires. A sweet-smelling smoke reluctantly enveloped the logs, licked them twice, turned green, absorbed the steam and the fire went out.

Those were the white logs: incombustible.

Of course it was freezing outside. Moscow was filled with snow drifts. Mayakovsky came and consoled me by saying that they would eventually burn up.

No. 2 Lubyansky was then the home of the Moscow Linguistic Circle.[6] A small, narrow room that looked like a blunt-nosed boat, and a fireplace.

This was the little boat in which Mayakovsky was sailing. An unhappy little boat.

There in the fireplace, I burned up cornices and the cases of the butterfly collection, but still did not get warm.

In the Briks' room was a wall rug with a duck embroidered in relief, and warm things were lying about. It was very cold.

There, in Poluektov Lane, Lili, Osya, Mayakovsky and the red Shchen were overcome by fumes.

From there, Volodya used to go to Sretenka, to ROSTA.[7]

There is a play by Pogodin, *The Kremlin Chimes.*

The plot is about a watchmaker (with a capital W), probably a refugee from a Symbolist play, who is tuning up the chimes of the Kremlin on top of the Spassky tower, while the melody is hummed to him by a Red Army soldier. The chimes are tuned to the voice of the people, as it were.

In reality, it was different and more interesting.

There was a competent artist with whom Mayakovsky often worked.

This artist had skilled hands. Artists have preserved in their hands the ancient craftsmanship. They are the last craftsmen in the old sense of the word, and through them has passed, unbroken, the thin thread of a tradition of inspired work.

The artist Cheremnykh could tune tower clocks.

It was he who fixed the Kremlin chimes.

The Kremlin chimes are unrelated to Pogodin's clock. This is another clock. It required a different kind of human skill.

[Cheremnykh is alive, and this question can still be easily answered.] It was this artist who began decorating by hand the ROSTA windows.

In the same way, engravings were being cut on linoleum; great skill often had to be substituted for technical equipment.

[And Mayakovsky had already started on his album *Heroes and Victims of Revolution.* The illustrations by Kozlinsky were engravings on linoleum.]

Mayakovsky had the nature of a highly professional artist. He felt compelled to write; he felt compelled to publish.

Denikin's offensive was under way. It was imperative that the streets should not be silent. The shop windows were blank and empty. They should bulge with ideas. The first Window of Satire was set up on Tverskaya Street in August, 1919. A month later, Mayakovsky began working.

Before Mayakovsky, each window was a random collection of drawings and captions. Each drawing was a separate unit. Mayakovsky introduced central ideas: a whole series of drawings connected by a rhymed text that went from picture to picture.

Each drawing had a textual significance. The text connected the drawings. If those window posters had been printed without drawings, the text would have had to be changed; otherwise, it couldn't have been understood.

Mayakovsky is said to have done 1500 windows, and that is true. There were six drawings to a window, and sometimes more.

There were enough poems for a second edition of his *Collected Works*.

I accompanied Mayakovsky to work. We talked, then we stopped, and he said:

"I have to invent four lines before we reach that house."

I watched him work. It required a tremendous effort. He walked, in a short coat and a small cap pushed to the very back of his head; he walked with a light step. Yet, he not only had to walk and breathe, but to invent as well.

In ROSTA, there was a *"burzhuyka"* stove; the smoke had taken over completely and calmly settled at the level of my rabbit fur cap.

Mayakovsky, working in that smoke, could no longer straighten his back.

The work was done on the floor. Mayakovsky made the posters; the others prepared stencils by cutting out cardboard according to a design; still others used the stencils to make copies.

Lili, in a dress made from green ribbed velvet of a drape and lined with squirrel fur, also painted.

She knows how to work when she wants to.

Brik's main contribution was in theoretical interpretations.

The tall Schieman, who had formerly produced painted scarfs and transrational wails on the harmonium, worked at home.

It was clean at his place—clean paint, clean brushes—and Mayakovsky now respected him for the neatness of his work.

Mayakovsky was right to decorate the ROSTA windows.

The existence of the ROSTA windows was justified, and they stopped existing when the stores reopened.

When Mayakovsky came to Petersburg, he was angered and amused that the old drawings of Vladimir Lebedev with the captions by Flit, had frozen to the window of the Petersburg ROSTA. They were frozen fast and they proclaimed to the street how much things had already changed.

And Mayakovsky wondered why the posters had not been changed. But this was still in 1920–1921. Mayakovsky was working for the Revolution.

He had to move forward, but each step he took was costly. ROSTA meant hard work.

Since I had no money, Volodya wanted to help me. So he suggested that I join the painters. But I lost my way among the innumerable pots of paint that were standing right on the posters.

I overturned a pot and don't remember what they did with the stain, and how it was integrated thematically.

[Mayakovsky worked day and night, and slept with a log under his head to make waking up easier.]

From the window, one could see the Sukharevka, numerous gabled tents, the steam of human breath in the freezing cold and the clock on top of a pillar urging the work along. The famous physicist Arago wrote a biography of the man who laid the foundations of physical astronomy, Kepler.

Kepler was calm and self-confident.

He said that if the universe had waited so many millenia for a man who could understand it, this man could wait a few decades to be understood.

According to Arago, Kepler had had to sell his works directly to the book dealers.

He almost lacked the time to be a genius.

Nevertheless, the laws of physical astronomy are established, and who knows whether a genius ought to be happy?

The only thing we can say is that we would like the genius to be happy.

In the first volume of *Capital*, Marx writes:

"Diamonds are rarely found in the earth's crust, and therefore, their discovery requires, on the average, a great deal of working time. Consequently, their small volume represents a great amount of work. Jacob doubts that gold has ever been priced according to its full value. This applies even more to diamonds."

In the case of paintings, we pay for failures. A Rubens or a Rembrandt is expensive, not because it took so long to paint, but because its value covers the cost of the failures of many painters.

Joint effort is expressed in one individual, and we try to thank him for the success of mankind—usually posthumously.

Even after the artist's death, however, decades may pass in waiting. Mayakovsky gave this a great deal of thought; read the "Conversation with a Tax Inspector." Refining of ore is plainly mentioned there.

Mayakovsky, however, was paid only for quantity.

Life was hard. [Lili Brik did not escape scurvy.]

Mayakovsky worked all his life and was paid by the hour.

And, this great number of lines, these verses, measured in steps—they were difficult.

After the Revolution, Mayakovsky came to love the world.

He loved it from that day and that hour, in February when he said:

Ours is the land.
The air—ours.
Ours the diamond mines of stars.
And we will never,
never!
Allow anyone,
anyone!
To ravage our land with shells,
to tear our air with sharpened spear points.[8]

Blok was wrong to reproach Mayakovsky after *Mystery Bouffe,* that the epitome of happiness there is a roll.

It is our roll.

Mayakovsky became kind toward the world. Had he not already said in his *Tragedy* that maybe things should be loved?

Once, Vasily Rozanov, speaking about an owner coachman who addressed his horses as his "little green ones," rejoiced about this and said that Socialism could do nothing about this love for his "little green horse," named so lovingly.

But Mayakovsky loved air and firewood. Without any dogma whatsoever the word "ours" became for him as tender as the word "my."

We will not leave,
            though
                        to leave
we have
            every right to.
Into *our* cars,
                on *our* tracks,
we are loading
                our
                        firewood.
We could
            leave
                        at about two o'clock,—
but we
            will stay late.

Our comrades
>   need
> *our* firewood:
>   comrades are freezing.[9]

However, Socialism hadn't been achieved yet.
He had to write a lot.

He came to love things; he came to love the day; the old Mayakovsky was no more.

Before, Viktor Khlebnikov had written about him. Miron Levin reminded me of this letter from far away, from Dolossy, above Yalta, where he was dying.

There was snow, endless snow, pine trees, the sea below, the beckoning lights of the city (to which he couldn't descend) and sick people everywhere, everyone suffering from tuberculosis. Levin wrote to me about Khlebnikov. I am quoting from a letter to V. Kamensky, from the year 1914:

"The tiger in the yellow blouse writes: 'In your souls the slave is freed by kisses,' hatred toward the sun, 'our new souls humming like arches,' praise of lightning, 'stroke the black cats,'—also praise of lightning (sparks)." [10]

Yes, these were nocturnal verses. Night and bloodstained cornices. The Strastnoy Monastery by night, night streets.

But when the earth became ours, he began to love people. In 1920, during one of his visits to Moscow, we strolled through the city together.

We dropped into LITO—the Literary Section. A room with many tables. In the room, an elderly man was lecturing on "Turgenev's Dreams and Ideas."

His name was Gershenzon. His hair was already gray and he understood art, but he wanted to squeeze inside it, like through a door, and live on the other side, as Alice had beyond the looking glass.

Everyone was wearing a cap.

We sat on tables in the rear and began taunting Gershenzon. We said that it's better not to jump over a horse when you want to get in the saddle; that art is in the work of art itself, not outside it.

Gershenzon asked Mayakovsky: "And why do you say that? I don't know you."

He answered:

"Then you don't know Russian literature; I'm Mayakovsky."

We talked for a while, then left. Out on the street, Mayakovsky said: "Why did we give him such a hard time?"

[On another occasion, he offended Eichenwald, who was giving a report. In the discussion, Mayakovsky said:

"Yet, Kogan says. . . ."

Eichenwald retorted:

"I am not Kogan."

"You are all Kogans," Mayakovsky said.

Gershenzon was no Kogan to him.]

Later, I learned that Gershenzon had returned home cheerful and content: he had liked Mayakovsky and the entire conversation about art a lot.

[In those days, Mayakovsky liked anybody who wasn't a Kogan.]

It was hard, cold and hard for our country. The poet was sailing in a small boat, 13 meters long. With him were people. He protected them, but on the other hand, he also carried with him a heavy load of art and was responsible for me and many others.

Mayakovsky arrived in Petrograd. Life had already settled down to a routine. There were some relatively warm places, warm in a very conventional and good sense. They were gathering places for writers.

The House of Arts was in a large building that overlooked the Moyka, the Nevsky and the Morskaya. There was a duplex apartment. Formerly, Yeliseyev had lived there with his wife and fourteen servants. He had a dressing room with three windows, and a bicycle.

The bedroom, slightly smaller, a bathtub painted with lilies. There was a separate steam room with another bathtub, a porcelain one, and there was a salon decorated with stucco, and a dining room. And here, the House of Arts was established.

Akim Volynsky used to sit in the kitchen with a cap on his head, reading the church fathers in Greek.

Pyast and I lived downstairs, in the corridor; Slonimsky lived on an upper floor. Later, we began to change places, and to spread out. Olga Forsh, Grin, Zoshchenko and Lev Lunts moved in.

They also lectured on poetry here.

A little old architect would come and sit, keeping his coat on.

In tsarist times, he had built a house and it had collapsed.

His right to build had been revoked. But he did not die. He went off somewhere and was getting old.

During the Revolution, while looking for a heated place, he had wandered into the House of Arts; he slept through the lectures, and even wrote up some short report so that he would not lose his right to sit on a chair in a room where water did not freeze.

Bely spoke here, and for the nth time he wrenched from the air the same words: "Man! Give me Man!"

The jubilee of Mikhail Kuzmin was celebrated on September 29, 1920. Blok came. Looking at Kuzmin, he said softly:

"But you are just as before."

"Two useless angels in the back." [11]

The second line was poetry.

And he kissed Kuzmin.

On the whole, this was a hangout for the Acmeists. But, at the far end of the corridor, behind the bathroom, the Serapion Brothers [12] were already getting underway. The young Mikhail Slonimsky, in his military style jacket fashioned from a soldier's greatcoat, and his black, worn-out felt boots, lay on his bed, covered with a coat, and wondered whether he would be able to graduate from the university and how to fight ornamental prose.

Vsevolod Ivanov was already on the scene, with his short fur coat of singed sheepskin and his red, dry beard, which also looked singed.

Nikolay Tikhonov was an upcoming poet and was writing ballads.

In general, narrative poetry and Kipling were the literary fashion in Leningrad at that time.

Mayakovsky stayed in the big library when he came to town; the library had red bookcases with green glass doors, and very few books.

He would be served one large tray with a whole array of glasses with tea and another tray of pastries.

Many people would come: Eichenbaum, Tynyanov, Lev Yakubinsky and others.

Here, Mayakovsky read his *150,000,000*.

He entered the library.

A servant, left over from the Yeliseyev time, brought in the tea. Mayakovsky went over to him, took his tray, and said:

"Say, your people can't write that way, can they?"

But Yefim had been thoroughly and personally trained by the poets, and his reply was unexpectedly cold.

"Personally, Vladimir Vladimirovich, I prefer the Acmeists."

And he made his exit with great dignity.

Mayakovsky gave no answer, and that evening he heard the ballads and liked them.

And he kept those ballads in mind for his poem *About That*.

Now, let's finish the story of ROSTA.

Volodya had to work in ROSTA, but he should have worked less.

That we understood even then.

ROSTA was hard work, but the hardest work was done by Mayakovsky when he wrote *About That*.

Many people corrected Mayakovsky, directed him and explained at length what was right and what wasn't. They all explained to him that he shouldn't write about love. This conversation had begun in about 1916. He wrote a poem to Lili Brik, "instead of a letter," and this is what happened:

"And that was followed by the long poem 'Don Juan.' I didn't know he was writing it. Volodya recited it to me, unexpectedly, from memory—in its entirety—while we were walking down the street. I lost my temper because, again, it was about love—the same old thing! Volodya jerked the manuscript out of his pocket, tore it up into small pieces, and threw it into the wind along Zhukovskaya Street." [13]

She thought she already knew all the Don Juans.

Perhaps, without her, there would have been more happiness, but not more joy. It is not for us to teach the poet how to live or to change another's life, a very great life—particularly since the poet forbade us to do it.

Meanwhile, Osip Brik was drawing theoretical conclusions about everything that was happening, including the necessity to write too many lines and not to write narrative poems. For everything, he found a justification as precise as it was incorrect.

In 1921, in the month of May, Mayakovsky went to hear Blok.

The hall was almost empty. Mayakovsky later noted:

"I heard him in May of that year in Moscow, in a half-empty hall as silent as a cemetery. He read softly and sadly old lines on gypsy songs, on love, on the beautiful lady. That was the end of the road. Beyond was death. And it came." [14]

He hadn't been able to cross the mountains. And the matter was not that Blok wrote romances.

It's good that he wrote them.

It's not true that poets don't write for the people. Good songs are picked out by the people.

Names disappear, lines are changed, but the song goes on being sung.

It gives birth to a new song, which returns to the poet.

The song, often a gypsy song, about a poor hussar begging for a night's lodging, about evening, about a meadow, about distant, glittering lights, spans all of literature.

And right in the middle, stretching his arm over it, stands Pushkin.

The sea comes. It comes with the Neva, it reaches the rounded steps of the stone stairways, it splashes and murmurs like a suppliant. Private life and love come to poetry with their square meters of living space.

Yevgeny presents a complaint against the Bronze Horseman and threatens him.[15]

Private life comes with the wind and floods the great city of a great literature.

Reconciliation and happiness, a new form of happiness, a culture based on the happiness of man and the realization of his rights: that is what Mayakovsky wanted.

He did not leave his soul behind as one leaves an overcoat in an entrance hall; he elevated the simplest theme and fused it with the theme of the Revolution.

And so, there was ROSTA.

And Mayakovsky, who now felt well disposed toward the entire world, had someone to talk to.

The sun was setting behind the mountains in Pushkino.[16]

It was setting behind the roofs of poor villages.

Over there where the reservoir is now.

It was setting, dropping, and then the poet punned: "Come, drop in on me for a while."

And then they had a friendly chat.

> . . . I sit, chatting ever easier
> with the star.
> Of this
> and that I speak,
> that ROSTA is taking too much out of me,
> but the sun:
> "all right,

take it easy,
look at things simply!
For me, you think,
to shine
is easy?
Go on, try it!—
So, I go on—
That's my job.
I go on—and shine I do!" [17]

But the sun prevailed, thanks to its longevity and, generally, because it got used to it.

Mayakovsky was patient, cheerful.

One had to be clean, disciplined and shaven.

Mayakovsky knew very well what was good and what was bad.[18]

To be clean shaven was good.

But there was no razor. There was a razor at the Lubyansky Passage, in the apartment across the hall.

A Gillette razor.

Vladimir Vladimirovich borrowed the razor from the neighbors.

He would go there, ring the bell, shave and return the razor. But razors wear out.

There were two young men at the neighbors'. They didn't mind sharing the razor with Mayakovsky.

But there was also a Mama—a lady. Her hair combed back, over a roller. She said: "He returns the razor without drying it properly."

So, the next time Vladimir Vladimirovich came for the razor, the lady of the house told him:

"The razor is being used, Vladimir Vladimirovich, and will be for a long, long time to come."

"I understand," answered Mayakovsky, "you are shaving an elephant."

And he left.

In 1921, Mayakovsky organized a "Dyuvlam." The word "Dyuvlam" [19] has gone out of use.

It means a "twelve-year jubilee." Mayakovsky liked such figures.

For instance: 13 years of work.[20]

At the "Dyuvlam," many spoke in his honor.

Mayakovsky replied with respect to Andrey Bely's address, and to that of the Moscow Linguistic Circle, the Moscow equivalent of OPOYAZ.

Then another short man greeted Mayakovsky in the name of the Nothingists.

The Nothingists [21] originated from the Everythingists.

The Everythingists [22] were affiliated with the Futurists.

Everything, to be sure, synthesis, to be sure, so to say.

The Nothingist greeted the venerable Mayakovsky.

Venerable Mayakovsky shook his hand and squeezed it hard. The Nothingist could not pull back his hand, and he was in trouble.

The "Dyuvlam" represented twelve years of work, if one counted from the year 1909, the year of Mayakovsky's prison term. In prison, he wrote his first book of verses. Unpublished. It was confiscated.

And after ROSTA, Mayakovsky painted posters.

Posters that were needed.

And through these posters, he was learning again, experimenting. For him, they served the function of album verses, as Tynyanov used to say then.

But it was a lot of work, hard work.

The poet was never free from care. He has a description of a trip from Sevastopol to Yalta.

A short trip, like life.

On the other side of the Baidar Gates, the sea reveals itself like unexpected love. Life is not the same. Without these clouds, without the bay, without this sea—each bit of which you love—it is utterly impossible to live.

And the road spins, and the sea seems to fling itself from right to left.

And again,
            it is watching,
                        almost
the blanched cheek
                  touches the rocks.
Thus jealousy
            encircles you as
                        rocks—
behind the stone,
                  the outlaw lover.
But farther on—
            calm;
                        peasants toiling
have dressed up the slopes
                        with vines.
Thus
      I, too,
            sprinkling my vineyard
with sweat
            draw my posters.[23]

Chapter **22**

Norderney

I found myself in Berlin. The year was 1922. Berlin is a big city with many parks. Wide streets in the center of town lined with many trees.

And asphalt pavement, a novelty for me at the time.

The subway, its unfaced walls, with its gray hide of concrete.

In the sky, a big bottle of neon lights was pouring wine into a neon goblet.

I was lonely abroad. I went to see Gorky.

I visited him in Freiburg. I crossed Germany at a time when the French Army was invading it with its punitive divisions. I got my trains confused.

Aleksey Maksimovich lived in an empty hotel surrounded by a young pine forest.

Deserted, snow-covered. I was writing *Zoo*.[1]

Mayakovsky and the Briks came to Berlin. Later they left, and Mayakovsky stayed on.

His room was very modest, and there were quite a few wine bottles; a small amount had been drunk from each. He felt only curiosity toward wine.

And next door, there was The House of Arts. That is where the immortal Minsky lived, a grandfather even to the decadents. And then, Pasternak and Yesenin came.

I saw Yesenin for the first time at Zinaida Gippius' house. Zinaida, insistently ladylike, had a lorgnette which she held in her hand ostentatiously.

She looked at Yesenin's feet and inquired:

"What are those gaiters you're wearing?"

"Those are boots."

Zinaida Gippius knew very well that they were boots, but her question was a way of showing her disapproval of this man who had come to the Muruzi House provocatively wearing felt boots.

The story of Sergey Yesenin's appearance, the story of a very lonely man who left his tragic imprint on our poetry—that story is as follows:

I know nothing about Yesenin's childhood, but when I met this handsome man for the first time, he was already familiar with Verhaeren.

Sergey Gorodetsky had created quite a stir at that time, with his publication of *Yar*.[2] It was a very big book. Khlebnikov carried it around with him.

Gorodetsky had opened up new possibilities in poetry, but then he looked at the newly occupied territory with some uncertainty.

One of Yesenin's friends was a man who admired his own shrewdness. He got two pails of paint and two brushes, and went to Gorodetsky's *dacha* to paint the fence. They took the job for little money, the red haired house painter and his apprentice, Yesenin.

When they had finished painting, they went to the kitchen and started reciting poetry. That way, they gave Sergey Mitrofanovich Gorodetsky the pleasure of discovering them.

It was as if a desert island with a motor had floated up to Captain Cook:[3] "Here I am, discover me."

They were indeed discovered; they were displayed in the Tenishev auditorium; they read verses and then played the accordion.

Of course, that was hardly the right occupation for them,

since they were not accordionists. Imagine an intellectual, a poet who, after reading his verses, would play the piano without knowing how.

Yesenin sported a peasant shirt, and Mayakovsky wrote about this as follows:

"I have known Yesenin for a long time—ten or twelve years.

"When I first met him, he was wearing bast shoes and a shirt with some sort of cross-stitch embroidery. It was in one of the fashionable Leningrad apartments. Knowing that a real peasant, as opposed to a decorative one, would have very gladly exchanged his outfit for a pair of boots and a suit, I didn't believe Yesenin. He seemed straight out of an operetta, all theatrical props. All the more so, since his poetry was already popular and, evidently, he could afford the rubles for boots.

"As a man who, in his time, had already worn and given up a yellow blouse, I inquired matter-of-factly about his clothes:

" 'What is all this—for publicity?'

"Yesenin replied, and it was as if the oil of an icon lamp had come to life and started to speak.

"Something to the following effect:

" 'We country folk, we cannot understand your ways . . . we live somehow . . . in our own way . . . plain, as in the days of old.' " [4]

Without knowing poetry, one cannot become a poet; one cannot reveal oneself as a poet.

This conversation with Zinaida Gippius took place with a Yesenin who already wore a jacket. Yesenin was of no use for Gippius.

All in all, she would condescend to rush to join the people.

Just as later, many people rushed to join the proletariat.

But Yesenin's felt boots were a provocation; he wore them with a suit, and they indicated a lack of respect for Gippius.

Gippius was then seriously involved in politics and corresponded with Pyotr Struve.

Eventually, she made an attempt to go into politics; moreover, it had to do with Socialism.

In an open letter to Struve, Gippius wrote: "We believe in the idea of Socialism and in realistic, pragmatic means for its implementation; it is a cause which, under conditions of religious awareness, may become just and godly."

There followed discussions of how the cooperative and religious movements can go hand in hand.

Yesenin, with his felt boots, was disrespectful.

At that particular time, he was expected to come in cheap city shoes, and then Gippius would have contributed toward more expensive shoes.

But Yesenin's life took a different turn; he was writing his poems, writing good poems.

The Yesenists needed him; all sort of Kusikov types [5] who saw in Yesenin an opportunity for a semi-legal opposition. The peasant element, it seems, was in rebellion.

Yesenin was introduced to Isadora Duncan, a woman who also had great talent, who had lived a long life, was not too happy, and was a collector of people.

Yesenin went abroad. He was as boisterous as a recruit hired to take another man's place. I recall, sometime later, a conversation about America, about a red elevator in Chicago and, I think, a black carpet in the Hotel New York. The elevator was of lemon wood, and the rug in the corridor straw colored.

That was all.

But the expression "iron Mirgorod," [6] an expression found from a car with the wind blowing over it, was the right expression.

When I saw Yesenin in Moscow, he gave the impression of peering through oil-smeared glass.

In Berlin, he was already using face powder. He raised Cain and amazed Isadora Duncan with the easy generosity of the Russians.

He didn't like Mayakovsky, and if he found any of his books in his house, he tore them up; yet, at the same time, he was a superb poet who reached his reader.

He was a poet who loved his language. He had baskets containing cards with words. He used to spread out the cards.

Yesenin really was an apprentice to the people, that creator of language.

In Berlin, among the people easily losing their homeland, Andrey Bely, with his mane of gray hair, remained a Russian.

He would walk around Berlin, suntanned, his hands clasped behind his back.

In the summer, he stayed in a small German resort town, Swinemünde.

He ironed his white pants himself, and had completely lost touch with his Anthroposophic crowd. Their talk had no flavor; he had nothing to speak about with them after living in the Soviet country. Bely would sit at home, a tea kettle warming on the alcohol burner in front of him. He would visit Gorky.

He danced in Berlin nightclubs where the lights were deliberately low; he was depressed and drank wine.

He was strong; his eyes seemed lighter than his face; he was young, despite his completely gray hair.

All the wind of Russian poetry was in the Soviet country; and Mayakovsky himself was like a sail.

Yesenin and Bely both felt depressed in Berlin, but in different ways.

All of Berlin closed its doors by 9:00 P.M.

Generally, people stayed home.

I have no idea who frequented the nightclubs; the Berliners spent their evenings at home. At the time, they were trampled upon by the French, who sucked them for two carloads of coal a minute, who placed their engines and diesel motors under steam hammers and who stole their milking cows.

The Germans tried valiantly not to succumb. Americans and Frenchmen flocked to Berlin, to live on devalued money.

The Germans stayed at home, trained their watch dogs and walked them in the evening.

In the suburbs stood grimy factories; there was nothing green in sight. There were still droshkys for hire in those days. They were already disappearing, as plums disappear in wintertime. In the streets were taxicabs with electric motors, but they were also out-of-date by then. The railroad stations in Berlin were huge and old fashioned. The trains left frequently and there was no crowding.

The vast triangular heart of the railroad network was located in Berlin. From here, railroad tracks led to all parts of the world. I boarded a train. The speeding train swayed like a drunkard.

The railroad tracks, fixed on iron cross ties, hummed.

The engine ripped the landscape apart like a piece of calico.

Toward the coast, the ground flattens out, ditches form black stripes on the land, and the trees on the banks of the ditches profit from the relatively dry soil. The banks of the ditches are thickened by discarded soil.

Norderney, as its name indicates, is an island in the North Sea.

It is the product of many sand-bearing waves. It is the product of winds carrying sand from the shore. It is one of a group of islands that stretches in a broken line along the shore.

And so, it is a dune.

Nothing is planted there.

The exposed front side of Norderney forms a slope, paved with stones; in front of this slope, sand extends into the distant, angry, scalding North Sea.

Hotels stand in a tight row. Music is played inside.

The hotels are exactly like city hotels; a narrow alley runs behind them, a clean pavement, a few flower patches and shops selling nothing but the superfluous.

Jewelers, also of a special kind, sell baroque pearls and semi-precious stones. However, that is not my line.

And so the hotels are perched almost on top of the waves. There is just a little sand under their foundations.

A few pale green willows grow on the dunes. Their leaves and branches stretch out in the wind.

The shore side of the island faces a narrow strip of sea and the low coast of the mainland.

From the hotel one can see the high, calm and still waves of the Atlantic Ocean roll in.

The wind blows and burns people a bronze color; that is the highly valued ocean tan. It is imitated in Berlin and sold in bottles for people who can only afford to get their tans at nearby lakes.

Fishing boats go out to sea. On the horizon, somewhere, steamboats pass, heading for Hamburg; there they lower their anchors, dropping a long chain into the river water of the enormous port.

But here the salty sea has no haven.

Swimming in this sea, you can't go too far out: the current carries you away.

This is where we met, Mayakovsky and I.

He was young and looked like a sixteen-year-old boy— cheerful and all windblown.

I was wearing a fancy light beige suit, because I was in love. Mayakovsky's attitude toward this malady was one of sympathy and irony.

We didn't know how to dance.

They danced in the hotel with others.

Behind us hotels which were the same as everywhere else.

Except that they served huge cut-up crabs.

But we were catching crabs in the waves, crabs without any commercial value, just simple citizens of the sea.

We were catching crabs, running after the waves over the sand.

The crabs ran sideways.

We played with the waves, running far out and putting stones in the water.

An ocean wave rolled in, heading up the beach. The triple wave of high tide. One had passed by the shores of Scandinavia; the second by Scotland, and the third had come through the English Channel.

They merged into one high tide.

Later, at low tide, they ebbed away in different directions.

It was windy, the sea spray on our clothing dried fast, leaving gray edges of salt. We would run out on the boat docks pursuing one wave and returning with the next.

The immense sea, which even the sun did not warm, swayed between Europe and America.

The ocean sun warmed us.

The gray—no, not gray—the cream-colored suit (the fancy suit of a man in love, pretending to be as pure as an angel), that easily damaged suit, gave it all the excitement of a game of chance.

Mayakovsky played with the sea like a boy.

Then it was time to leave. We were late for the train, and Volodya ran after the engine, with me following.

We stopped the train, practically grabbing it by the nostrils. We stopped it.

They made the train.

On that occasion, I broke my watch.

Many things were going on then—rejection in love, and nostalgia, and youth.

Memory has selected the sea and the wind.

By that immense, alien sea, with its lip-cutting wind, our youth was ending.

Chapter **23**

"About That"[1]

What I'm writing is neither memoirs nor a research paper.

There's no system, and the writer will not be described exhaustively, and his biography will not be written by me.

> Lubyansky Passage,
> Vodopyany.
> This is
> the view.
> That is
> the background.[2]

Moscow was very different then, and it rang with the clatter of cobblestone pavements.

Mayakovsky—tall, massive—drove around in the narrow Moscow cabs.

The cabbies knew him.

Once, he was arguing with a publisher in a cab as to whether he was a famous writer. The cab driver turned around and said to the publisher:

"Well, everyone knows Vladimir Vladimirovich."

He made this comment, it seems, without having been asked. Mayakovsky, however, was better known as a person, as an action.

At that time, Moscow was all gray and black. In the summer, no one changed into white.

The cab drivers wore hats that widened on top, and wide-skirted coats belted in green.

And the cabs no longer hauled mattresses and cupboards, but people.

The streets were clogged with churches and houses that, unexpectedly, spilled over the sidewalk.

Houses looked as though they had gone out for a walk and, suddenly, had been stopped by the stick of a militiaman in a red cap and black overcoat.

Our globe was relatively peaceful then: it was arming and, on the whole, very poorly equipped to foresee the future.

On Vodopyany Lane: two rooms with low ceilings.

In the foyer was a broken down cornice which had been hanging from one nail for two years. It was dark.

A long corridor. The entrance to the Briks' was directly to the right.

The room was small; it had three windows, but small ones, the old Moscow kind. Directly at the entrance, to the left stood the piano, and on the piano—a telephone.

[The telephone was communal—for the entire apartment; but in the rear, tenants with other names shared the same telephone line.

They could quietly listen to the conversations between Lubyansky Passage and Vodopyany Lane.

In the corner was a stove, badly painted, paint smeared over its air vents. Also in the corner was the bed and above it an inscription: "Nobody is allowed to sit on the bed."

The room was always filled with people. *LEF* was being edited here; Mayakovsky was painting his posters; Rodchenko and Levin, the painter, were always dropping in.]

Outside was NEP.[3] Across the street from St. Paraskeva Church, which had spilled right into the middle of the street, in the low-ceilinged shops of the Okhotny Market, people traded with everything imaginable.

The State Trade Organization was fighting private traders.

Osya's room was behind Lili's; it had a studio couch,

upholstered in a velvet print, a broken-down desk with one remaining lion snout and books.

From the window, one sees a corner of the main post office and a clock.

From that window, I believe, across another building, one could see the *Vkhutemas*—the School of Painting, Sculpture and Architecture—where Mayakovsky and Burlyuk had met for the first time.

Now, a tall red house has been built in that courtyard, and on the top of a staircase overgrown with cats, live Aseyev and Oksana.

Oksana is one of the Sinyakov sisters.

They are friends of Khlebnikov, friends of Pasternak. Aseyev's door was a mass of scribbles—so many inscriptions, complaints and even verses that Selvinsky could have published this door as a separate book.

Aseyev often visited Mayakovsky. They discussed poetry; occasionally they wrote together, and they played cards.

In the morning they would leave; sometimes they bet on the figure appearing on the electric meter or on the number of their cab.

They were together and cared very much for one another. Mayakovsky had finished *About That* and Aseyev was writing *Lyrical Digression*. I lived through those years with the memory of these lines:

> No,
> you are not at all dear to me,
> Beloved ones
> are not like that . . .[4]

And these other lines:

> For this
> living space,
> for this dreary comfort
> they torture you, they kiss you
> and won't let you make a move! [5]

What Mayakovsky wrote about had nothing to do with living space. His destiny was traced not on a blueprint, but on a map. His verse flowed from a mighty stream.

The issue was not that Aseyev, as they alleged, failed to understand the NEP policy then, but that the life style had remained unchanged.

Physiology has a "barrier" concept.

An albino rabbit can be injected with blue dye. The rabbit will take to it. His eyes will turn blue, a very beautiful blue, and his lips will turn blue too; but his brain and his nerves will remain white.

That is due to an inner barrier, a barrier like skin. It has not been established whether this barrier has organs or how it works physiologically. But the general equilibrium of the system is maintained.

The old world had its barrier.

A man could make eyes at the new world, and his eyes would be blue, but at home he would keep his old ways.

So, there was the problem of life and of living space

There was the problem of love and the family which is and always will be, but will be different.

There were telephone conversations about love.

But other things mattered in LEF.

There it was, the question of life styles.

For Marx, for Lenin, [for Stalin,] the revolution is the expression of the entire history of mankind; human thinking is revolutionary in its essence—in its final expression but its revolutionary, Communist spearhead was being broken off.

Marx loved Greece, he loved the art of antiquity; but Dühring said that everything had to be created anew, that the "mythological and other religious apparatus" of the poets of the past could not be tolerated.

Dühring protested against a mysticism toward which, according to him, Goethe had been strongly inclined.

Dühring assumed that new works of art must be created to

correspond to the "higher demands of a fantasy tamed by reason."

Our Proletcultists [6] wanted immediately to create a new poetry, but actually they were satisfied with the banality of the six-foot Alexandrine.

But in *Art of the Commune,* the idea was expressed that essentially there is no such thing as art, and there are no "creators."

The very concept of creative art was put between quotes.

This was an attempt to use OPOYAZ and proclaim its method of literary analysis as a discrowning of literature.

We cheerfully retorted, at the time, that we were not taking the crown off literature, but only taking out its screws.

Futurist paintings had become counter-reliefs. Then they decided to make objects. First, they made spiral monuments of iron, then very economical woodburning stoves, coats with multiple linings and folding beds.

In the tower of the Novodevichy Monastery, one major artist attempted to build a flying machine that would be propelled solely by inspiration: it was supposed to fly on human energy, without a motor, and the flight was to be available even to people with a heart condition.

The wings were built; they were very light, but they did not fly.

Easel painting was rejected altogether; and in the second issue of *LEF,* an appeal was printed.

In all languages.

Let them read!

So-called Stage Directors!
How soon will you and the rats quit messing around with lousy stage props?
Take up the direction of real life.
Become planners for the procession of the Revolution.
So-called poets!
Will you stop these album trills?

Will you understand the stiltedness of glorifying storms you know only through newspapers?

Give us a new "Marseillaise," raise the "International" to thunder the march of the now victorious Revolution!

So-called painters!

Stop applying multi-colored patches on the mousebitten fabric of the time!

Stop decorating the already comfortable life of the NEP bourgeois!

Train the power of artists to take over cities, to take part in all the new construction projects of the world!

Give new colors, new contours, to the earth.

We know that these tasks are beyond the strength and desire of the individualistic "priests of art" guarding the aesthetic borders of their studios.

Here, there are no reservations. Poets, in fact, are all "so-called poets."

LEF always printed poetry and lived by poetry, but it apologized for it somewhat.

We are not priests of art, but craftsmen who fulfill a social command.

The practical examples printed in *LEF* are not "definitive artistic revelations," but only samples of our current work.

Aseyev. An experiment with verbal flight into the future.

Kamensky. The play with words in all its sound potential.

Kruchyonykh. An experiment in using jargon phonetics for the presentation of anti-religious and political themes.

Pasternak. The application of a dynamic syntax to the revolutionary objective.

Khlebnikov. Achievement of maximum expressiveness through colloquial language, cleansed of all poetic artificiality of the past.

Mayakovsky. An experiment with polyphonic rhythms in a poem of broad social and everyday scope.

Brik. An experiment with laconic prose on contemporary themes.

—V. V. MAYAKOVSKY, O. M. BRIK [7]

The artists Rodchenko, Lavinsky, Stepanova and Popova got involved in this movement.

These were talented people. But in art they carried a different intellectual ballast; LEF was less harmful to them than to the poets.

Popova created a construction for the stage which for a long time competed with the old-fashioned box stage, is by now fully accepted by the spectator, and has become an integral part of the play. You can even see it in such a production as *Anna Karenina* at the Moscow Art Theater.

Lavinsky suggested building houses on legs.

A strange suggestion, but that is how Le Corbusier subsequently designed his houses; one of those houses can even be found on Myasnitskaya Street. Only later, the space between its pillars was filled in and the house now stands without an opening for air.[8]

Rodchenko became interested in photography with unexpected foreshortening effects; he painted white on white and black on black. That resulted in a parquet design.

An architecture without decorations came into being.

In destroying the decoration, we often destroyed the construction.

When we introduced bare walls to the theater, the sound became diffused; Rossi's decorations somehow fixed the sound to the architectural forms and strengthened it. It was the sound that was constructive.

We were discovering that it was more difficult and more expensive to make a smooth surface than a decorated one.

Naturally, this does not mean that all the houses built in Moscow now are good; often eight-story buildings pretend to look like three-story buildings thanks to the bossage on the two lower floors, the columns, and the capitals.

But things were relatively easy for the architects. They were building. Painters ceased painting for years on end.

Gan suggested to stage directors that they organize mass festivals.[9] These were very naive proposals for the crowds to march and to take apart some artificial constructions along the way; this would really signify revolution, but, of course, it would have only resulted in a crush.

Now, imagine for a moment the position of the poet. He is at the head of a journal, and this journal opposes poetry. There was no place for Mayakovsky.

With his love, as well as his verses on love.

He loved Aseyev, he loved Pasternak, he loved Blok's poems and the forward movement of Soviet poetry.

At its side, there existed what essentially could be called parody art, ironical art, thriving on the disintegration of old forms.

Sergey Eisenstein, in wide trousers, very young, gay and with a high-pitched voice, brought to LEF his ideas on eccentrism.

Eccentrism meant defamiliarization; it fought against the unnoticed disappearance of the quiet bustle of life.

But eccentrism could also conceal life.

Eccentrism came to us from literature. It came to the motion pictures by way of a cowboy sequence adapted from an American Western: a cowboy galloped down the Moscow streets in a Kuleshov film.

Excerpts from this film—*The Adventure of Mister West*— have been preserved. In it, Moscow is interesting, but the cowboy is terribly dated.

The old art became a pretext for a spectacle.

Hardly absorbed, still alive—it was already disintegrating.

But for the spectator, an "eccentriad" was only an eccentriad because there was no need for him to destroy that which he did not know yet.

Here is what young Sergey Mikhaylovich Eisenstein said about the production of the film *Every Wise Man Has His Folly.*

The montage of attractions is its basis.

An attraction is not a stunt.

"An attraction (in the theater sense) is any aggressive moment in the theater, that is any theatrical element which has an emotional or psychological impact on the spectator (experimentally verified and mathematically calculated for the definite emotional shock it produces on the person exposed). The total of these shocks eventually creates the only possible condition for perceiving the meaning of what is being shown, that is the final ideological conclusion. (The way to comprehension *Through the Living Play of the Passions* is specific to the theater.) [10]

The show went as follows. I will not report all of it, but will list parts of the epilogue:

"1. Expository monologue of the hero.

2. A fragment of a detective film (explanation . . . Theft of a Diary).

3. A musically eccentric scene: the bride and three rejected suitors as best men (one person in the play); a melancholy scene presented in songs: "Your Fingers Scented by Incense" and "Let the Grave Be My Punishment"; the idea was that the bride has a xylophone and is playing on six ribbons of jingle-bells—officers' buttons.

4. 5. 6. Three parallel clown acts, each in two parts (the theme: paying for the wedding arrangements).

7. The appearance of the star (the aunt) and three officers (the theme: delay of the rejected suitors); punning (triggered by the mention of a horse) on a triple vaulting act on a saddled horse because it was impossible to bring a horse into the hall for the traditional act "Three on a Horse").

8. An anti-religious jingle for choir (to the tune of "There Was a Pope Who Had a Dog"), a rubber shape of a priest with a dog's body (the theme: the beginning of the wedding ceremony).

9. An interruption of the action (the voice of a newspaper boy and the exit of the hero).

10. Appearance of a masked villain—an excerpt from a comic film (a summary of the five acts of the play, with transformations. The theme: the publication of the diary)." [11]

A very amusing show.

But these are disconnected comic scenes, of course; it is an art without syntax and without an expressed thought.

You cannot even say that this is form oriented, because the attractions do not have continuity, they do not reinforce one another.

LEF was a phenomenon of extreme diversity. It included Eisenstein, and Aseyev, and Mayakovsky, and the OPOYAZ people with their studies of Lenin's language.

Eisenstein was versatile, too. After *The Wise Man*, he directed *Strike*, which still had many disconnected attractions; then *The Battleship Potemkin*—a film that holds together, expressed in one breath. Here art deals directly with reality instead of propping reality up on attractions which bear approximate resemblance or parody resemblance to reality.

LEF erred in its theory and spoke in a contrived, conspiratorial language; it spoke about art as though apologizing for it, as though justifying itself.

But I believe that, without Mayakovsky's *LEF*, there would not have been such a phenomenon as Eisenstein.

LEF's poetry pointed the way for art.

[Brik was against prose and against poetry.

He said things like: "Poetry is not needed, anyway."

And what is needed? "Newspapers."

A workers' audience answered him.

"Fine, in the morning, a newspaper. But what about the evening?"

"In the evening, an evening newspaper."

But that is wrong because newspapers and novels are not interchangeable. They are two different things.]

The traditional novel and the traditional poem had to be changed because form rules the structure of the work, and the love poem had changed. But Mayakovsky was at his height in those poems and verses where he spoke of what was most important.

One cannot purr a waltz from a cross.

One cannot forget the man who remained on the bridge, there, over the Neva, not alive and yet not killed.

He floats on a pillow, a bear.

Mayakovsky matured, became more European; his shoulders got broader, he stood firm.

But the romances were not over, and the boy in the poem *About That* walks in a halo of moonlight.

> Cotton made snow—
> > the boy walked on cotton.
>
> Cotton in gold—
> > what could be more corny?!
>
> Yet, such sadness,
> > that you must stop
> > > and be wounded by that sadness!
>
> Lose yourself in a gypsyfied romance.[12]

[The gypsy romance is no small matter. Yet, it remained with the man in his room a faithful, lyrical dog.

It must be changed, its very heart should be invaded; the private room must be entered.] One must write about love so that people would not perish or drown in the ripples of scribbling.

The poet doesn't write for himself alone; he does not stand for himself alone.

> On the bridge of years,
> > exposed to contempt,
> > > to laughter,
> > considered the redeemer of earthly love,
> > I have to stand,
> > > for all I stand,
> > for all I'll pay,
> > for all I'll weep.[13]

He wanted to live, he clung to life.

But life had to be changed. To change life is difficult, even when you are living in its future. But you may be the day after tomorrow, yet die tomorrow.

Mayakovsky wrote:

> I shall not give them the joy
> of seeing,
>   that I am silenced by a bullet.[14]

The theme of resurrection returned, but not Fyodorov's mystical nonsense about resurrection of the dead.

Lev Tolstoy wanted to live a long life.

He left home like Natasha Rostova.[15] He made his escape at night through a window of his house; he wanted to begin a new life as a wanderer, an exile.

Aleksey Maksimovich often thought about longevity; every day was precious for him, and he collected information on longevity.

Addressing the science of the future, Mayakovsky wrote:

> I'll shout
>   from this
>   the page of today:
> Don't turn the pages!
>   Resurrect! [16]

He wanted to live in the future, united with the woman by their common love for simple animals.

Mayakovsky said that horses, without the gift of speech, never have heart-to-heart talks, never analyze mutual feelings, and that is why they rarely commit suicide.

And there she was: beautiful, so unquestionable for him, walking in the garden. They would meet, talk about animals.

We read these verses on the day of his memorial.

The future, the thirtieth century, not to be seen, not to be reached—however long your neck may be—the future, the unquestionable one.

The future which will accept our today.

A future without Alexandrine verse, a future with genuine poetry.

Mayakovsky felt that he could master it.

>   Resurrect me—

I want to live out what's due to me!
That there should be no love—servant
of wedlocks,
                 lusts, bread-loaves.
The bed cursed,
                 the comfortable couch abandoned,
love should walk through universe.
For the day,
                 which ages us through sorrow,
you should not beg, in prayers.[17]

Love was set as a distant goal, and the road leading to that goal was the same as the great road itself.

Those were hard times.

A few years later, Mary Pickford visited Russia. She was accompanied by Douglas Fairbanks, who had such full cheeks that they hid his ears.

She drove past the poor, striped fields. Traveling along with her was a camera man who took pictures; pictures of her (no longer young) and of her fat, famous husband, who was already outliving his fame.

The train sped along, past the yellow stations. On the platforms, people shouted.

They waved their caps.

Girls in blouses made of striped silk scarfs greeted Mary. About fifteen thousand people gathered at the station. People hung from the platform pillars. The famous American actress was greeted by middle-aged men, with pants cinched high, by men in suit jackets fastened by one button, in gray cotton shirts.

The crowd ran behind her automobile. Mary sat in the car with her dusty golden hair, hatless.

That night, they went to Red Square. High above, rose the church cupolas, wedged together like bowling pins.

They were admitted into the Kremlin, Douglas climbed into the muzzle of the giant cannon, as Max Linder had once done, but it was no fun in the cannon.

The city was very grave and the actors found it impossible to relax.

In the Labor Palace, Dzerzhinsky argued with the Trotskyites about control figures.

And Mayakovsyk later glorified this life, consumed for the Revolution.

Newspapers discussed the issue of individual farms, of cars versus trucks. In the theater, the play *Zoyka's Apartment* [18] was playing.

In the movie theaters, Dziga Vertov's film *One Sixth of the World* was playing.

In this film, one could see sheep being washed in the sea, and hunters casting spells by bending a knee before shooting a sable. A great country of many cultures and varied, multicolored landscapes passed across the screen. [The reel ended with Stalin's speech on our need for machines to make machines.]

Mayakovsky liked documentaries and praised Dziga Vertov.

He loved poetry; his sail hoisted into the wind of time. He loved his goal, a happy mankind.

He loved Pushkin and felt deeply insulted by Gardin's film *The Poet and the Tsar*.

In it, the poet wrote verse in the following way: he would come in, sit at a table, and immediately scribble something like: "I erected a monument to myself not built by human hands." [19]

But monuments are not erected in this way at all.

Mayakovsky felt insulted for Pushkin as for a fellow writer. On Pushkin Square, next to the large poster, stood two scarecrows representing Pushkin and Tsar Nikolay.

And Mayakovsky would walk through this city, which was not yet entirely a city of the future; he came to Strastnaya Square which was not yet Pushkin Square; he thought about Pushkin and wrote verses about love, jealousy, D'Antes and how hard it was for a poet to work, even with only a small family.

And he went farther along Tverskaya Street, which is now Gorky Street, went toward Petrovsky Park, and headed toward the square which now bears his name.

He was going to a theater.

He was planning to stage a play.

But, first, let's talk about movies.

Mayakovsky liked documentary films, but only when they were organized and had a plot.

He had difficulties with plots. He was a lyric poet and his themes were lyrical; he was the hero of his works.

His theme is the poet crossing the mountains of time.

In the movies, he liked the specifically cinematic properties of films.

He had no intention of toying with the movie camera. On the stage, however, as in all literature, the artist is bound by certain limitations and, when shifting to a new art form, he must try to free himself from these limitations and not drag them along.

Lev Tolstoy liked the transformation scenes in the movies, and did not want to have his *Anna Karenina* filmed.

Mayakovsky liked movies also because cinematic art does not need translation. He loved American films.

". . . Because foreign films found and are using specifically cinematic modes of expression, modes derived directly from film art and capable of being used only in films (the train in *Our Hospitality;* the transformation of Chaplin into a chicken in *The Goldrush;* the shadow of the passing train in *A Woman of Paris* and others).[20]

Mayakovsky dreamt of having a radio station for poets, to transmit his method of reciting, to broadcast the vibrant, new verse.

I once met an editor, an old-timer, who had refused to publish Mayakovsky's work and was among those who kept assuring the poet that he would never, ever, be published.

He came to understand the poet only when his son read the

verse to him, and the son was twenty-one years old, a sailor in the Red Navy.

That is how long one has to wait.

Mayakovsky wanted to introduce poetic images into film.

He needed both the documentary quality and total control over the subject matter; he needed to contrast the different elements, not only to juxtapose them. Characters in a film need not necessarily and always be bound to sex and the seasons.

Mayakovsky—in his dreams in *About That,* when the poet finds himself now in winter, now on the Neva, now on the cupola of the bell tower of Ivan the Great—may have remembered Buster Keaton in *The Possessed.*

He himself was moving films to a different poetic level. Just try convince people! Certainly in motion pictures people have to be convinced to start shooting. The reel doesn't take pictures by itself. And so, Mayakovsky wrote a scenario: "How Are You?" I will remind you of one sequence: Mayakovsky approaches a girl in the street; she tells him: "But I won't speak to you." The girl moves away, turns her head several times, shakes her head negatively.

"And I won't go walking with you, only a couple of steps."

She takes one step with him.

Then, she takes his arm and they walk along together.

Mayakovsky plucks from the pavement a flower, which has sprung up there in some mysterious fashion.

In front of the gate to his house, Mayakovsky says:

"Won't you come in—just for one minute?"

It is winter all around—only directly in front of the house, there is a small garden in bloom, trees filled with birds, and the front of the house is completely covered with roses. The janitor, sitting on a bench in shirtsleeves, wipes off beads of sweat.

"On the Wings of Love." [21]

And that is what Mayakovsky brought to the movies.

On Gnezdnikovsky Lane, there stood a two-story house.

That is where Shvedchikov worked as the director of Sovkino.

The redhead Blyakhin was in charge of the scenario division; he was a man who knew something about films, even then.

Mayakovsky's scenario made you feel as though fresh air had entered the room.

At that time, thousands of monotonously similar airless scenarios had to be read.

Later, the scenario was read by the administrative committee.

What came of it? At that conference or the next, they pardoned Barabbas instead of Mayakovsky—they accepted Smolin's scenario *Ivan Kozyr and Tatyana Russkikh* or, perhaps, *The Voyage of Mister Lloyd*.[22] Later on, they tried to salvage Smolin's scenario with grandiose sets, but unsuccessfully.

The film sank, along with the plywood ship that had Ivan and Tatyana aboard.

But Mayakovsky's conception of a poetic film remained unrealized. Nor are any attempts in that direction made today, not even as an experiment.

The scenario of "How Are You" became the play *The Bedbug*, went on the stage, but in our theaters the word is not the foremost thing. Our performances were bypassing the play and creating a second level.

What Eisenstein had accomplished in *The Wise Man* was only an exaggeration of the usual. With us, the word did not carry full weight; we were unable to produce a play with the emphasis on words. And in the theater, Mayakovsky did not meet a Burlyuk who would have helped him remain true to himself at the footlights.

PART FIVE

It consists of two chapters. The poet is already gray. He has mastered his craft and written many books. These chapters conclude the book.

Chapter 24

The Poet Travels

Once upon a time, the young Mayakovsky wrote the poem "I Love." It's a long poem which tests the course of life. It ended with the following words;

> Solemnly raising my rhyme-fingered verse
> I swear—
> I love
> steadfastedly and truly! [1]

Later, these lines were rhymed with others.

An idea recurs, altered; image recalls image, as rhyme brings back the rhymed word.

In 1930, Mayakovsky concluded the poem "At the Top of My Voice" with the following words:

> I'll raise,
>   like a Bolshevik Partycard,
>   all the hundred volumes
>   of my
>   Party-inspired books. [2]

The image of the oath united love and the Party.
Mayakovsky has another recurrent image:
The boat of days.
The image comes fully equipped.
In 1924, in the poem *Lenin:*

People are boats,
                though on dry land.
While we live
            our
                life,
many, various,
                dirty shells
cling
        to our
                sides.
I am
        cleaning myself
                under Lenin,
in order to sail
        further into the Revolution.[3]

The image of a boat is further developed in the poem *Good!* It becomes a room-rowboat.

Squatting
            amidst crossfire,
quiet
        with my eyes to the casement window,
to have
        a better view,
I sailed
        in a small room-rowboat
                for three thousand days.[4]

People are boats, a room is a rowboat.
Lenin is not only the poem *Lenin*. It is also the poem *Good!*
Mayakovsky has such pairs of poems.
Man goes with *About That*.
Good! goes with *Lenin,* it has the same treatment of time.
    The poet lived in one of the Stakheyev buildings; his room changed very little. In the last years, he had a couch made, set up an American desk, American cabinets, and a camel on the mantelpiece.

Mayakovsky had a ditty:

> The cow has a nest,
> the camel has children.
> But I have no one,
> no one in the whole world.

The camel lived on the mantelpiece.

Mayakovsky wanted to enter Communism with his entire life, with his love, his friends.

[With me, with Aleksey Kruchyonykh.]

He put everyone to the test and led all toward one goal. He rejoiced when Kruchyonykh wrote verses on the Ruhr, and the OPOYAZ people wrote a study of Lenin's language.

He saw people cleansed through Lenin. For him, the city and the Russian language itself were connected with the name of Lenin. He wrote:

> Even if I were
>   a Negro of advanced years,
> yet
>   without discouragement or laziness
> I would have learned Russian
>   just because
> Lenin spoke it.[5]

The Soviet Union is a multi-national country. The Russian language was Lenin's language. And Mayakovsky had all the national pride of a Great Russian.

He wrote poems on the Russian language; he was insulted when he, Mayakovsky, was purposely not understood by people in Tiflis and in Kiev.

He worked these poems over thoroughly, to make them convincing.

"In the second issue of *LEF* appeared my poem 'To Our Young People.' Its central idea (inasmuch as this should be discussed in a poem) is clear. While studying one's own national language, it is pointless to hate Russian, especially as the question arises which other language should be known so that in the future young men, growing up in the Soviet culture, could use their revolutionary knowledge and the forces beyond the boundaries of their land.

"I published this poem in *LEF* and, taking advantage of my lecture tour to Kharkov and Kiev, tested these lines on the Ukrainian audience.

"I spoke with Ukrainian workers and writers.

"I recited the poem at Kiev University and at the Kharkov State Dramatic Theater.

". . . With pleasure and gratitude, I am adding all the suggested corrections for the sake of complete clarity and effectiveness."

He travelled all over the Soviet Union. Traveling was not easy. Trains, and sometimes even sleighs, hotel rooms with water pipes, and forced loneliness.

He travelled so much that he used to say:

"Now, I know how many miles it takes to shave, and how many miles there are in a soup."

Once, he arrived in Rostov at a time when the water and sewage pipes there had become jumbled. One could drink only Narzan mineral water.

Even tea was made with mineral water. And it is difficult to tell when Narzan water starts boiling—the bubbles rise immediately.

In Rostov, Mayakovsky was told that in the local RAPP [6] there was a poetess who had been photographed to look like a peasant. They had put a kerchief on her head and told her: "That's very becoming."

The picture was published with the caption: "Kolkhoz poetess."

And then they stopped publishing her work. [The RAPP people often ruined people in this way.]

The girl obtained a revolver and shot herself in the chest.

In Rostov, Mayakovsky read her verses; they were not bad. He went to see her at the hospital and told her:

"This isn't the way to go about things. You must have some friends? They'll fix things for you. I'll help, too."

He arranged for medical treatment and a convalescence. He asked her:

"Is it bad?"

She answered:

"You know, a shotgun wound doesn't hurt. You feel as though someone suddenly called out to you. The pain comes later."

"What you say isn't nice," said Mayakovsky.

Mayakovsky travelled from city to city, arguing with people, teaching people, lecturing about himself.

Emile Zola once said that he swallowed a toad every morning. Mayakovsky had to swallow a great many toads all through his life.

[There was a poet whom Mayakovsky criticized so often and so hard that he acquired new strength, and came to have an existence of his own, not just as a stereotype. He drew his strength from the many who disliked Mayakovsky.

His book was published by none other than the Poets' Union [7] itself, the same Poets' Union that Mayakovsky despised. The book had a black-and-white cover, like a clean gate smeared with tar. The book consisted of quotations and argued that Mayakovsky was a literary hooligan.

"Mayakovsky's rhymes are very bad. He is monotonous and writes for the *Lumpenproletariat*. His free verse is also no good, it offers no poetic opportunities and, besides, it has already been used by Pushkin and Blok." This booklet came out in 1927.

It has none of the smoothness of the pre-Revolutionary abuse, but the charges are the same. And Mayakovsky answered to the detractor because the latter had an audience, though not a large one.]

This was the period of the poet's travels and wanderings.

Mayakovsky said that, in 1927, his main occupation was "to

transport LEF ideas and verses to all the cities of the Soviet Union."

During this period, he recevied 7000 notes from his audiences. These notes repeated themselves consistently like seasonal changes or the consistent order in which different types of grass grew in a meadow.

Mayakovsky replied to these notes.

One day, a man said to him:

"This is the third city that I've heard you in, and you keep answering with the same jokes."

"So, why do you follow me in my travels?"

As a matter of fact, the repetition was in the audience's comments, and that is why the answers were always the same.

And getting angered by the comments was unnecessary and to no avail.

One had to give answers.

Of course, the critics were in a minority. The audiences loved Mayakovsky.

He went abroad; he wanted to see Paris again, and to travel around the world.

He sailed across the ocean, and saw with his own eyes that Indians really exist.

He wrote about the world in a new prose, and was on the verge of writing a novel, but the theory of fact interfered.[8]

A strong man, of many skills and great vision. Reared by the Revolution, summoned by it long ago, but not yet recognized; he looked at the world through the eyes of the future.

Beautiful islands emerged from the sea, greeting the ship at night with their fragrance.

In the morning, the glitter of some city arose alongside the ship.

Then, the ship left again.

The world proved to be round.

Mayakovsky travelled to exotic countries, but found Latvia.[9]

Men wore tan leather shoes and straw hats. Average men, average women rode in standard model cars amidst botanical miracles.

The world needed change.

The sea is adorned with a rainbow.

The rainbow is mirrored in the sea. The ship sails into a many-hued circle; the rainbow arches from horizon to horizon and yet, that is not so much.

In America, as in Kiev, they do not understand what language is and what it is for.

They understand much less than we do.

Once, before a Russo-European audience, the poet was welcomed in Yiddish, without translation.

He got up, and very seriously replied in Georgian.

Also without translation.

[The meaning was the following: let us use a language that we all understand. You are defending your language in the wrong way.]

Alien people. In America, the country of splendid technology, leading writers had organized a society of "The Green Fishermen."

They sat with fishing rods at the edge of life.

Speaking to them was like speaking through glass. They put their own words, alien to the poet, into the movements of his lips.

People are boats thickly encrusted with barnacles.

The world is beautiful.

Once, Vladimir Vladimirovich became annoyed with me when, questioning him about Mexico, I remained unimpressed by his story about some crested, or perhaps bareheaded, birds.

Paris was extraordinary. Its art was extraordinary. And the very color of its evenings, that aniline color, not yet mastered by the artist.

The poet talked with Cézanne and with Verlaine; he

overcame the impossible by the urgent need of such a conversation. They spoke sadly.

> Let's talk
> > about important trifles,
> about this poor craft of ours.
> Now,
> > bad verses
> > > are trash.
> A good line—
> > > is worth a lot.
> With a good line
> > > I, too, would be ready
> to lay
> > my guts
> > > in the gutter.[10]

This was hardly evidence. The verses were good, and the "poor craft" was poetry and painting.

He loved the world passionately, not only Moscow. The whole world had to belong to his idea.

He wanted to possess that city as a column lovingly dominates the square.

And this entire theme of the world comes back to the theme of love.

> Proletarians arrive
> > at Communism
> > > from down under—
> from the depth of mines,
> > sickles,
> > > and pitchforks,—
> but I
> > from poetry's skies
> > > throw myself into Communism,
> because
> > for me
> > > there is no love without it.[11]

Chapter 25

The Poet Talks to Posterity

They moved to Gendrikov Lane.

This street is behind Taganskaya Square; it's very short, and the houses are low.

The houses are so low that the sky, unlike elsewhere in the city, reaches the earth.

Theirs was a two-story wooden house. The apartment occupied the right half of the second floor.

The house was dilapidated, and it took time to get permission to have it repaired.

In the apartment, there were four rooms — small rooms.

Three cabins, and a ship's messhall: the dining room.

The dining room had two windows curtained with straw shades.

Now, it is a museum, but a well-heated museum, and with a fine entrance. Formerly, all it had was a staircase leading to a narrow hallway.

On both walls were simple cupboards for food.

On Mayakovsky's side, the cupboards were unlocked and contained books.

The foyer was narrow.

It led into a small corridor; to the left, there was a bathroom which, at the time, seemed to us very fancy.

Before *LEF* meetings, I used to shave there.

Mayakovsky did not tell me that the elephant was shaving himself.

Mayakovsky's room was behind the dining room. It had a desk with almost nothing on it, a low couch over which was hung a striped wool Mexican scarf in soft colors and, next to it, a wardrobe built according to the amount of available space.

Here was also the editorial office of *LEF,* the new one.

New LEF [1] was thinner than, simply, *LEF.*

They begrudged us the paper.

But, on the other hand, *New LEF* came out in winter and summer.

It took no vacations.

In the *New LEF* few articles appeared in installments.

Brik's work on rhythmico-syntactical figures began appearing there, but was never completed.

Brik's work remained incomplete; later he didn't collect the installments and, not having collected them, he could not publish it as a book.

New LEF printed not articles, but the cores of articles. Outlines, drafts.

Ideas which were supposed to grow in the reader's mind.

The style of *New LEF* was abrupt; all beginnings and all ends; everything not absolutely essential was squeezed out.

New LEF had a "Notebook" to which Mayakovsky, Aseyev, I, Brik and Pertsov contributed.

We wrote, hoping that our comments would reduce our adversaries to ashes.

No consideration was given as to how they could reply.

That was their problem.

Some famous conferences took place there; the protocol about Polonsky, for instance.

It was a round table discussion.

There was Brik, who formulated it all; Aseyev, who lived dangerously, moving along the road of verse, and Kirsanov, who was deafened by his own verse.

The newspaper idea was still being promoted.

"Art," said Brik, "is nothing but vanity."

I remembered a passage from Dickens. A preacher comes to a debtor's prison and on being offered a drink, replies: "All alcoholic beverages are vanity of vanities."

Samuel Weller calmly persisted: "Which one of the vanities do you prefer?"

The preacher preferred whiskey.

Even when dealing with news items, as soon as one has to establish the format of the column, its limits — one has to determine, select, interconnect the material, and there emerges an attitude to this material, which is basic to all art.

The poem *Good!* was printed in *New LEF,* as well as Aseyev's "Semyon Proskakov," rhymed footnotes to the real biography of a partisan.

Great verse.

LEF existed. They fought LEF; they wanted to split it so as to get at Mayakovsky.

The first attack was against Aseyev. They hounded him with articles entitled "Literary Hackwork."

Later on, there were more attacks against Aseyev.

Still later, they began praising Aseyev, and called him the first poet of the country, greater than Mayakovsky. At a public discussion, Aseyev stood up, next to Mayakovsky, and spoke of the indissoluble friendship of poets.

They started on Pasternak.

For a long time, Mayakovsky had loved Pasternak.

Pasternak broke away.

"They've snatched one," said Mayakovsky.

In *LEF* (not yet *New LEF*), I published an article in which folk riddles were cited. I had taken them from published collections. The magazine was accused of pornography.

They wanted to delete the article. I had those riddles reprinted twice in separate editions, and no one felt offended, nor did people's morals suffer or become lower.

[And later, replying to *LEF*, Polonsky singled me out. "Some writer," he implied.

The objective was to break up LEF.

Everybody was teaching ideology to LEF. Mayakovsky answered and had Iyuda Grosman-Roshchin in mind:

"But why should these unemployed Anarchists from *On Guard*,[2] who run from one literary antechamber to the next, why should they correct the Communist ideology of LEF? I am absolutely unable to understand that. It is clear to me that, in this case, the line of literary labels does not coincide with the line of the essence of literature. We have to throw off the worn out trappings of literary groupings and discard them with the greatest possible firmness."][3]

A great writer is not confined to his works alone. He transcends them. Great writers often turn out to be great editors. Pushkin dreamed all his life of a review, and about a newspaper.

Nekrasov, Saltykov-Shchedrin, Gorky and Mayakovsky were all great editors.

Mayakovsky needed *LEF* because, like Pushkin, he considered working for the arts a matter of national importance. He felt the need to transform life.

He loved his journal, because he was not by nature a factionist.

Therefore, Mayakovsky's attitude to Futurism, and his attitude to *LEF* are phenomena of a different kind.

Mayakovsky needed not art alone, but life.

He needed art to transform life.

[The Academician Williams proved that harvest not only depends on the composition of the soil, but on the structure of the soil, its complex mosaic formation.

Life, as understood through art, acquires a different structure.]

Mayakovsky saw the old way of life as a bunker that had to be stormed.

He deployed his artillery, testing various arms.

In its poetic descriptions, the poem "At the Top of My Voice" is similar to the description of a major offensive.

That is why LEF was over for Mayakovsky.

It's a great thing, a very difficult thing, to relate to the past not only through memories, and not only through love for one's own youth.

Mayakovsky stepped beyond himself.

Yet, at the same time, LEF was a literary salon.

It was the last literary salon.

In it, there were personal problems and even its own "outsiders."

One of these outsiders was Levidov.

LEF was not allowed to bring in new people.

Selvinsky's poems, for instance, were not allowed in *LEF*.

There was an effort to have the Constructivists [4] remain alone.

Mayakovsky knew the danger of LEF. At a discussion of Party policy in the field of literature, on December 23, 1928, Mayakovsky said:

"A writer, when attached to a literary group, does not become a worker for the Soviet Union and the building of socialism, but carries on intrigues for his own group."

LEF was dying, and already this hardly mattered.

[Let's define the time.

It was 1929, the year of Stalin's speech at the conference of Marxist Agricultural Workers.

It was the time of a new offensive. There were many enemies.

The Baptists alone had eleven periodicals — a total of one million printed pages. Those figures were only for the Ukraine.]

The country was short of 500,000 workers in heavy industry, and almost 1,000,000 people in industry as a whole.

The small *LEF* was not up to par.

Mayakovsky aimed at the widest audience.

He remembered ROSTA.

LEF was on its way out.

We began to quarrel easily, and making up was difficult. I quarrelled with L. Brik in the house on Gendrikov Lane about some utterly petty nonsense.

When a person is weak, or a motion is nearing its end, death will come at the slightest provocation.

Literary salons no longer had a reason to exist. We were unaware of this and constantly cross with one another.

The LEFists' home was falling apart.

Later, there was REF.[5] By that time everybody could sit around a table together and have tea, without quarreling. But, all of this was already unnecessary.

LEF—the last Soviet literary group—expired.[6]

[Mayakovsky saw RAPP as a mass literary organization. He had nothing but contempt for the "literary battleline."

It seemed to Mayakovsky that his joining RAPP was the right thing to do for a man serving Communism. Through RAPP, he wanted to make even closer contact with his country.

RAPP, however, was already a dead end.

Magellan sailed along the shore of America, looking for straits.

He sailed into the wide estuaries of rivers, but there he found that it was fresh water. He searched for a passage through the rocks.

But they were bays.

Magellan succeeded in circling America; he succeeded in spanning the two oceans; but he did not return home alive.

Mayakovsky was given recognition in January, 1930, at the reading of his poem *Lenin* at the Bolshoy Theater.

That was the Party's recognition.

But from an organizational standpoint, he belonged to RAPP.

RAPP, however, was a group, a minor school, and it harbored a literary conspiracy within it.]

Mayakovsky sought friends, but there were no friends for him in RAPP.

He sought recognition from his country.

He wanted to talk with it.

Once, he had written:

> I want to be understood by my country,
> and if I am not—
>   never mind,
> I will pass
>   over my native land
> sideways,
>   as a slanted rain passes.[7]

He hesitated printing these verses, and only quoted them two years after they had been written in a short piece in *New LEF*, which was an answer to some poet (the sixth issue in 1928).

That was his last piece in *New LEF*.

It's painful to pass over your country as a slanted rain or to pour down over the sea.

The Party was very busy; mankind had never had more serious business.

[Mayakovsky grew tired in LEF. *LEF*, the old and the new, were no longer needed.] The time for literary experiments, and even literary prognostications, was over.

But LEF had had a literary life; it had been interesting there; its people knew a great deal and where able to appreciate poetry.

[While in the RAPP of those years, it was dull.]

Mayakovsky went to RAPP to get closer to his workers' audience.

He found himself in a stagnant bay, surrounded on all sides by prohibitions and quotations.

Like Pushkin before his marriage, Mayakovsky searched for happiness in the usual ways; he met young playwrights and observed how they lived.

The clock already pointed to Mayakovsky's victory, but the chimes had not rung out yet.

Vladimir Vladimirovich went abroad. There was a woman; there could have been love.

I was told that they looked so much alike, were so suited to one another, that in cafés people smiled gratefully on seeing them.

It is pleasant to see two attractive people together.

But to love a woman, Mayakovsky had to be jealous of Copernicus.[8]

His old love hadn't passed.

In January, 1930, Mayakovsky organized an exhibition of "Twenty Years of Work" in the House of Writers on Vorovskaya Street.

He organized the exhibition himself and was his own collector.

The Academician Pavlov once said that collecting can be a substitute for a purpose in life.

The large rooms were filled with ROSTA posters, books and a flood of Mayakovsky leaflets.

When I got to the exhibition I found out that the poets were not attending.

I gave a lecture on Mayakovsky, on the new lines born in his newspaper verses.

Of all the friends, the quiet Lavut was the only one in the audience.

Then Vladimir came. He was calm, massive, and he stood with his feet slightly apart, in good quality shoes that had metal-reinforced tips and heels.

[His full, finely designed, tired lips. His hair touched with gray at the temples.]

He stood there, calmly, and asked sadly:

"Well, what do you think, did I do enough?"

He waited for the poets. They never showed up.

At that time, his poem, "At the Top of My Voice," had already been written.

It tells what the poet achieved, and what for.

The poem tells how difficult it is to be a poet of the future.

He talks with the stars, with the Milky Way, with objects that are familiar to the poet.

Mayakovsky was tired.

He came down with the flu. [The poet went to the Kremlin Hospital.]

In the hospital, they gave it a name: nervous exhaustion.

Advice: stop working for six months.

The Briks were abroad. In the apartment on Gendrikov Lane, the only living creature, at night, was Bulka, a kindly dog.

On Lubyansky Passage, in the room-rowboat — there was no one.

The camel on the mantelpiece.

Life was not built for its own sake.

Life had built verses ready for death and for immortal fame.

It was spring, a bad spring, April:

> My heart and I never lived to reach May,
> and in this life I've lived
> there is only a hundredth April.

In the journal *Press and Revolution,* [9] they printed his portrait and a greeting from the editors. Mayakovsky was told about this. But on the ninth of April, they came to apologize: Khalatov had ordered the portrait and greeting cut out.

Trifles.

But an infantry must not march in step over a steel bridge; the shocks add up, and the rhythm causes the bridge to collapse.

Mayakovsky wrote verses. He knew the sky very well.

He wrote in one of his last drafts:

> Look, beloved, what stillness in the world.
> Night has covered the sky with a starlit tribute.

    I. At such hours, you grow and you speak
    II. At such hours, you rise and you speak
       to the ages, history, and the universe.

Next to it is written:

The sea's receding,
The sea is going to sleep.[10]

And the sea, with the rain poured down on it, had become tired.

Oh, the sea of Norderney!

The Azores were left behind, and that great love was coming to an end.

The waves parted and receded.

There was no wind in the sail.

The struggle for a future love had ended without victory.

I saw him for the last time in the House of Writers on Vorovskaya Street. The room was lit with spotlights, fixed in the corners of the room, blinding the eyes.

I sat there, and talked with Lev Nikulin about Paris.

One man went by, then another. They carried briefcases. They were on their way to discuss organizational business. A short bald man passed by, pale skin closely stretched over his skull.

He carried a large, shiny, reddish leather briefcase.

The man was in a great hurry: he was on his way to re-educate Mayakovsky.

Vladimir came, stopped for a minute.

He talked.

He began praising life in the communes, which he had never believed in before.

Apparently they had convinced him.

He spoke, wearily, about their box into which everyone puts his money, and from which everyone takes as much as he needs. [Nikulin replied with a joke. Mayakovsky did not argue but smiled and proceeded to the meeting.]

I never saw him alive again.

Of his last days, I know only what I have been told.
Others will write about that, however.
[He was unhappy; he was ill.]
Four years earlier, Mayakovsky had written about Yesenin's
fate; he had written about our having failed the poet, and
going our own way, expecting that "Yesenin's friends, the
Yeseninists, would look after the poet."
At home, there were his verses:

It's past one o'clock,
                    you must have gone to bed.
In the night,
              the Milky Way shines
                          like a silvery Oka.
I'm in no hurry,
              and there is no need in
waking you,
              disturbing you,
                          with the lightning of cables.
As they say,
              the incident is closed.
The love boat
              has crashed against the everyday.
You and I,
          we are quits.
                    And there is no point in listing
mutual pains,
          sorrows,
              and hurts.[11]

He killed himself with the same revolver that had been
filmed in the movie *Not for Money Born*.[12]
There was just one bullet in the cylinder of the revolver.
There had been no friend attentive enough to remove
that bullet, to follow the poet or telephone him.
It was daylight in the Briks' apartment. I usually visited
there in the evening.
It was daytime; it was light, and many, many people.
People were sitting on the backless couches.

Formerly, these people did not associate much.

Aseyev, Pasternak, Katayev, Olesha and newspaper people.

No one from RAPP. They stayed at home, conferring and preparing a resolution.

Mayakovsky, in a light blue shirt, lay there, so close, on the print-covered ottoman, by the Mexican scarf.

The Briks were abroad. A cable had been sent to them.

The physician who had performed the autopsy spoke about a bad case of the flu.

"See, the flu affected the brain. What a huge brain, what deep convolutions! So much more interesting than the brain of the famous professor V.F. Evidently, the shape of the brain is not necessarily decisive."

He was laid out in the Writers' Union.[13] The casket was too small; his shoes with heavy metal tips could be seen.

Outside, it was spring, and a Zhukovsky sky.

He had not planned to die.

At home, he still had several pairs of sturdy metal-tipped shoes.

There was a screen like a slanted black wall over the casket. By the casket, car headlights.

The crowd flowed in a mighty stream from the Red Presnya past the casket and down the Arbat.

It seemed as though the red casket floated uphill by itself toward the beloved Red Presnya.

The city filed by the poet; they came with their children, lifted them up, and said: "This is Mayakovsky."

The crowd overflowed Vorovskaya Street.

The hearse was driven by a non-professional driver; [14] he drove too fast and lost the crowd. The people, who followed the poet, dispersed.

Vladimir died. He had written a letter to "Comrade Government."

He died, having surrounded his death like a disaster area with warning lights; he died, having explained how the love boat crashes, how man perishes, not of unrequited love, but because he has ceased loving.

And so, the list of pains, sorrows and hurts was finished. There remains the poet; the books remain.

History accepts the life which has been lived, and the love that is essential for us.

History accepts Mayakovsky's words:

I know the power of words,
                    I know the tocsin of words.
They are not those
                    that make theater boxes applaud.
Words like that
                    make coffins break out
make them
            pace
                    with their four oak legs.
It happens—
            they are thrown out,
                            not printed, not published.

But the word gallops,
                    its saddle girth tightened,
it rings through the ages
                    and trains creep nearer
to lick
        poetry's
            toil-hardened hands.[15]

RITTER LIBRARY
BALDWIN-WALLACE COLLEGE

Transliteration

Below is the system of transliteration used. The generally accepted spelling of familiar names is retained even if it differs, as in cases like Chaliapin (not Shalyapin), Eisenstein (not Eyzenshteyn), etc. Anglicized spelling is also used for originally non-Russian names, as in cases like Eichenbaum (not Eykhenbaum), Mach (not Makh), Eichenwald (not Aykhenvald).

ALPHABET		TRANSLITERATION
А	а	a
Б	б	b
В	в	v
Г	г	g
Д	д	d
Е	е	e, ye[1]
Ё	ё	yo
Ж	ж	zh
З	з	z
И	и	i[2]
Й	й	y
К	к	k
Л	л	l

---

[1] "Ye" initially, after vowels, and after ъ, ь. "E" with dieresis in Russian (ё) is transliterated as "yo."

[2] Omitted if preceding a "y," e.g. Vasily (not "iy"; not "ii"). Combinations ый and ий are transliterated as "y."

ALPHABET		TRANSLITERATION
М	м	m
Н	н	n
О	о	o
П	п	p
Р	р	r
С	с	s
Т	т	t
У	у	u
Ф	ф	f
Х	х	kh
Ц	ц	ts
Ч	ч	ch
Ш	ш	sh
Щ	щ	shch
Ъ	ъ	—[3]
Ы	ы	y
Ь	ь	—[3]
Э	э	e
Ю	ю	yu
Я	я	ya

[3] Generally omitted. Before vowels transliterated as "y."

Notes

Preface

1. Viktor Shklovsky, *Tetiva* [Bow-String] (Moscow, 1970), p. 708.

2. For a comprehensive study of Formalism, see: Victor Erlich, *Russian Formalism: History-Doctrine* (The Hague: Monton, 1969).

3. Viktor Shklovsky, *Khod Konya* [The Knight's Move] (Moscow-Berlin: Helikon, 1923) p. 39.

4. Viktor Shklovsky, *O Mayakovskom* [About Mayakovsky] (Moscow, 1940), p. 88.

5. Viktor Shklovsky, *Sentimental Journal*, translated by Richard Sheldon (Ithaca: Cornell University Press, 1969).

6. *Zoo, or Letters Not About Love*, translated by Richard Sheldon (Ithaca: Cornell University Press, 1971.)

7. See Chapter III, footnote 3.

8. Nadezhda Mandelstam, *Hope Against Hope* (New York: Atheneum 1970), pp. 346–348.

9. Boris Pasternak, *I Remember* (New York: Pantheon 1959), p. 101.

10. Viktor Shklovsky, *Dnevnik* [Diary] (Moscow, 1939).

11. *O Teorii prozy* [On the Theory of Prose], (Moscow: "Federatsiya," 1929) p. 178.

12. Vladimir Mayakovsky, "Lilichka! Instead of a Letter"; *Works*, Vol. I; pp. 107–108; for edition, see Chapter One, footnote 1.

13. A. Fadeyev, *Sobraniye Sochineny* [Collected Works] (Moscow, 1971), Vol. V, p. 333.

14. M. Charny, "About Mayakovsky or About Shklovsky," *October*, 1940, No. 8, pp. 189–191.

15. Viktor Shklovsky, *Zhili-byli* [Once Upon a Time] (Moscow, 1964). This is the 2nd edition that is subsequently referred to.

Part One

1. Futurism—movement of Russian poets and artists who rebelled against all traditions and established rules in literature and art. The movement was composed of different groups. Mayakovsky belonged to the Cubo-Futurists. In 1912, they issued their first manifesto, "A Slap in the Face of Public Taste," signed by Mayakovsky, Burlyuk, Khlebnikov and Kruchyonykh. In their writings, they experimented with transrational language, new syntax, new rhythms, new typographical form; in painting, they created new abstract art forms of expression. Their interest in urban imagery and technology brought them close to Italian Futurism but they remained an independent, specifically Russian movement. They scandalized the world of literature and art before the Revolution, but wanted to become the official spokesmen for the arts under the new regime. After being supported for a short time by the People's Commissariat of Education, they lost favor with the authorities and, in 1923, united with other avant-garde writers and artists to form LEF, Left Front of Art, under the leadership of Mayakovsky. For a comprehensive study, see Vladimir Markov, *Russian Futurism*, (Los Angeles: University of California Press, 1968).

Chapter 1. Introduction

1. V. Mayakovsky, from "Man" [Chelovek], *Works*, Vol. 1, p. 246. Citations from Mayakovsky in the text refer to *The Complete Works of Vladimir Mayakovsky in 13 Volumes* [Polnoye sobraniye sochineny Mayakovskogo v 13 tomakh] ed. by V. Katanyan (Moscow: Gosudarstvennoye izdatelstvo khudozhestvennoy literatury, 1955–1961)—hereafter cited as *Works*.

2. Ilya Muromets, popular hero of Russian epic folklore. He was strong and overpowered all his enemies. Allegedly, he sat immobile for the first thirty years of life before carrying out his deeds of valor.

Chapter 2. The Landscape

1. Robert Grant and Jacques Paganel are characters in Jules Verne's *Les Enfants du Capitaine Grant* [Captain Grant's Children].

Chapter 3. Moscow Was Rusty

1. Butyrki, name of a prison in Moscow.

2. Cell No. 103—Mayakovsky, arrested twice in 1909, spent five months in solitary confinement in this cell.

3. LEF, Left Front of Art [Levy front iskusstva], iconoclastic literary group formed by Mayakovsky, Aseyev, Khlebnikov, Brik and others in 1923. It united Futurists, Formalists, Constructivists and individual writers. Their journal *LEF* began appearing in 1923 and became the center for experimental new art. *LEF* was criticized and stopped publication in 1925. Publication was resumed under the name *New LEF* in 1927. In 1928, *New LEF*, too, ceased to exist.

4. Sadovayas—a series of boulevards that form a ring around the central city of Moscow.

5. "Falsified inscription" refers to the fact that the Tsarist censorship had changed some of the original lines of the poem "Monument" by A. Pushkin.

6. V. Mayakovsky, from "I Love" [Lyublyu], *Works*, Vol. IV, p. 89.

Chapter 4. Painting Reinterpreted

1. AKhRR, Association of Artists of Revolutionary Russia [Assotsiatsiya khudozhnikov revolutsionnoy Rossii] (1922–1928), an organization that encouraged artists to use realistic methods in art.

Chapter 5. David Burlyuk

1. Shklovsky refers sometimes to "Leningrad" when actually, at that period, the city was called Petrograd (Petersburg changed to Petrograd in 1914, and to Leningrad in 1924).

2. *The World of Art* [Mir iskusstva] (1899–1904), richly illustrated bi-weekly, later monthly, journal; published by S. Diaghilev and A. Benois. It was the mouthpiece of a very influential movement in Russian art that introduced French Impressionism to Russia, opposed the trend of utilitarian, realistic art and advocated an art for art's sake attitude. It also published the writings of major Symbolists, like Bely, Bryusov and Rozanov.

3. The Therapont Monastery—(built around 1400) is famous for its frescoes, dating from about 1500, in the chapel of the Nativity.

4. "The Wreath" [Venok], title of three exhibitions of Russian avant-garde art (1907, 1908, 1909). Its contributors rebelled against the naturalism, realism and symbolism of the preceding period and developed new, extremist modes of artistic expression. Among the exhibitors were Goncharova, Larionov, Burlyuk and others.

5. "Donkey's Tail" [Osliny khvost] (1912), exhibition of avant-garde artists, organized by Goncharova and Larionov, which showed works by major artists of the Rayonnist and Suprematist schools: Malevich, Chagall, Stepanova, the brothers Burlyuk and others.

6. *New Time* [Novoye vremya] (1868–1917), pre-revolutionary, reactionary daily newspaper with a wide circulation, published by A. S. Suvorin.

7. *Niva* [Russian word for a field before harvest, sometimes translated as *The Field*, or better, *The Harvest*] (1870–1918), illustrated weekly magazine with a wide circulation. The complete collected works of Russian classics, Tolstoy, Turgenev, Leskov and others, were published by the journal as separate supplements.

8. *Hatchery of Judges* [Sadok sudey], 1910 almanac in which the group of poets who later came to be identified as the Russian Futurists (Burlyuk, Khlebnikov, Kamensky and others) appeared for the first time. A *Hatchery of Judges II* was published in 1913, but did not have the same impact.

9. Guild of Poets [Tsekh poetov] (1911–1914), literary circle founded by

N. Gumilyov and S. Gorodetsky. It became the cradle of a new approach to poetry, Acmeism.

10. Viktor (Velimir) Khlebnikov, *Teacher and Pupil* [Uchitel i uchenik], published by Burlyuk (Kherson, 1912).

Chapter 6. Neighbors

1. Russian Symbolism—a literary and philosophical movement which brought about a new flowering of Russian poetry (about 1890–1910). Inspired by the poet-philosopher Vladimir Solovyov, Russian Symbolists created a new approach to metrics, imagery and lyrical themes. In contrast to the French Symbolists, whose poetry they admired, Russian Symbolists combined their new aesthetics with elements of mysticism and sought for additional metaphysical meaning in symbols, words and even sounds. Their greatest poet was Aleksandr Blok. Other major Symbolist poets were: Balmont, Bely, Sologub, Bryusov, and Ivanov.

2. In the 2nd edition, a phrase is added and the sentence reads: "Vyacheslav Ivanov's art relied entirely on substitution of one series for another, and when he died, he was the curator of the Vatican Library."

3. In the 2nd edition, a phrase is added and the full sentence reads: "Beyond Blok's symbolism, a second theme emerged, a theme not from religion, but from everyday life, a theme that was replaced by the theme of the Revolution."

4. Aleksandr Blok, from an untitled poem (1914), *Collected Works in Eight Volumes* [Sochineniya v vosmi tomakh] (Moscow-Leningrad, 1960–1966), Vol. III, p. 221. Hereafter cited as *Works*.

5. In the 1st edition, this sentence reads: "In these pre-war years the gypsy romance had not yet made its appearance in Blok's poetry." This was obviously a mistake.

6. Anna Akhmatova, from "A Walk" [Progulka], *March of Time* [Beg vremeni] (Leningrad, 1965), p. 49.

7. *Ibid.*, from "In the Evening" [Vecherom], p. 52.

8. *Ibid.*, from *Evening* [Vecher], p. 20.

9. Acmeism—Movement in modern Russian poetry (initially headed by N. Gumilyov) which arose in reaction to the abstractness and mysticism of Symbolist poetics. The Acmeist poets demanded clarity, concreteness, precision of images and of words. The most important poets of the group were A. Akhmatova and O. Mandelstam. Their main publication was the *Apollon*. As a literary movement, Acmeism ceased to exist after the Revolution.

Chapter 7. More Neighbors

1. Rayonnism—A school of abstract painting created by Larionov and Goncharova that was influential in Russia during the period 1911–1915.

2. *Baranki* are rolls made with wheat flour in the form of doughnuts, with a larger hole.

3. "Jack of Diamonds" [Bubnovy valet] (1910–1918), name of a very im-

portant group of Russian avant-garde artists. Their exhibitions included the works of Larionov, Goncharova, Tatlin, Kandinsky, Malevich, etc. Initially closely connected with the Futurists, they were later attacked by them for their "conservatism."

4. Valery Bryusov's drama discussed here is "The Earth" [Zemlya], *Complete Works* [Polnoye sobraniye sochineny i perevodov] (St. Petersburg, 1914), Vol. XV, pp. 8–54.

5. *The Satyricon* and *New Satyricon* (1906–1917), the most famous among the many magazines devoted to political and social satire at that time, it produced a school of humorous writers. It was closed by Soviet authorities because of its anti-Soviet attitude.

6. Nadkin, an imaginary person whose parodies of well-known writers appeared in the magazine.

7. A cartoon which pictured the censor's red pencils as prison bars.

8. V. Mayakovsky, from "Hell of the City" [Adishche goroda], *Works*, Vol. I, p. 55.

9. Pyotr Potyomkin, from "Beauty Parlor Doll" [Parikmakherskaya kukla], *Poets of the Satyricon* [Poety Satirikona] (Moscow-Lenigrad, 1966), p. 65.

Chapter 8. David Burlyuk Finds a Poet

1. Volodya, diminutive of Vladimir.

2. V. Mayakovsky, from "Night" [Noch], *Works*, Vol. I, p. 33.

3. V. Mayakovsky, from "Morning" [Utro], *Works*, Vol. 1, p. 34.

4. Allusion to the fact that Kamensky was an aviator.

5. V. Mayakovsky, from "Morning" [Utro], *Works*, Vol. I, pp. 33–34.

6. V. Mayakovsky, from "A Few Words About Myself" [Neskolko slov obo mne samom], *Works*, Vol. I, p. 48.

7. V. Mayakovsky, *Vladimir Mayakovsky, a Tragedy, Works*, Vol. I, p. 156.

8. V. Mayakovsky, *Vladimir Mayakovsky, a Tragedy, Works*, Vol. I, p. 162.

9. V. Mayakovsky, from "Cloud in Pants" [Oblako v shtanakh], *Works*, Vol. I, p. 184.

10. V. Mayakovsky, from "Cloud in Pants", *Works*, Vol. I, p. 190.

11. Raskolnikov, the hero of Dostoyevsky's *Crime and Punishment.*

Chapter 9. Women

1. V. Mayakovsky, from "After a Woman" [Za zhenshchinoy], *Works*, Vol. I, p. 44.

2. Rocambole, the hero of a series of novels by Vicomte Pierre-Alexis Ponson du Terrail (1829–1871). The main attraction of these novels were their intricate plots dealing with adventures and fast action.

3. Gleb Uspensky, *Collected Works* [Sochineniya] (Kiev, 1876), pp. 198–199.

4. Genrikh Tasteven, *Futurism*, (Moscow, 1914), Appendix, p. 14.

5. "Lawyers" is meant in an ironic sense, symbolizing establishment intellectuals.

6. Elsa K.—see glossary under Triolet-Aragon, Elsa.

Chapter 10. Already About the Briks
and More About the Circle

1. *Russian Thought* [Russkaya mysl] (1880–1918), a literary and political monthly. From 1905 on, it was edited by P. Struve and became the journal of the liberal Constitutional Democratic Party. After 1918, publication was continued in Prague by P. Struve.

2. Konstantin Balmont, "Departing Shadows" [Ukhodyashchiye teni].

Part Two

1. "The Stray Dog" [Brodyachaya sobaka]—café, nightclub and cabaret, where the literary and artistic elite of pre-Revolutionary Petersburg met. All non-artists were contemptuously called "pharmacists" by the insiders as they came to mingle with the fashionable Bohemians to listen to their debates, poetry readings and lectures.

Chapter 11. Petersburg

1. *The Speech* [Rech] (1906–1918)—newspaper of the moderate and anti-Marxist Constitutional Democratic Party.

2. *Apollon* [the Russian form for Apollo],—a Petersburg monthly devoted to literature and the arts, with very fine reproductions. It was connected with the Symbolists and later became the mouthpiece of the Acmeists. The manifesto of the Acmeists was published in *Apollon*.

3. *Russian Wealth* [Russkoe bogatstvo] (1876–1918), an influential liberal Populist monthly journal dealing with literature, art and social issues.

4. V. Mayakovsky, from *Vladimir Mayakovsky, a Tragedy, Works*, Vol. I, p. 162.

5. Shklovsky refers here to Andrey Bely's novel *St. Petersburg*.

6. Shklovsky refers to Valery Bryusov's novel *Fiery Angel*.

7. Aleksandr Blok, from *Puppet Show* [Balaganchik], *Works*, Vol. IV, p. 15.

Chapter 12. On Criticism

1. "Theater for oneself"—one of the experimental concepts advocated by the playwright and theatrical personality, Yevreinov, who attacked the commercial theater.

2. *The Hedgerose* [Shipovnik], publishing house and literary almanac by the same name (26 issues), in existence from 1906 to 1918.

3. *Hedgerose Almanac* [Shipovnik] (1914), Vol. XXII, p. 107. The last line of the quotation is untranslatable as it is written in transrational language, which was widely used by Kruchyonykh. Usually his name appears as Aleksey Kruchyonykh, but occasionally as Aleksandr.

4. V. Mayakovsky, from "A Few Words About Myself" [Neskolko slov obo mne samom], *Works*, Vol. I, p. 48.

5. *Hedgerose Almanac* [Shipovnik] (1914), Vol. XXII, p. 124.
6. *Ibid.*, Vol. XXII, p. 150.

Chapter 13. Kulbin/"The Stray Dog"/Debates

1. Union of Youth [Soyuz molodyozhi] (1910–1913), a group of modernist painters and Futurists formed in Petersburg in 1910. It held two exhibitions a year, began publishing a magazine in 1912, sponsored many public discussions in Moscow and Petersburg, produced Futurist plays.
2. "B" is probably A. Byelenson, one of the editors of the almanac *Archer*.
3. A. Akhmatova, untitled poem written in January 1913, *Works*, [Sochineniya] (Munich: Inter-Language Literary Associates, 1965), pp. 87–88.
4. V. Mayakovsky, from *I Myself* [Ya sam], *Works*, Vol. I, p. 22.

Chapter 14. The War—The Years 1914 and 1915

1. A. Blok, from an untitled poem dated September 8, 1914, *Works*, Vol. III, p. 278.
2. St. George the dragonkiller was especially revered in the Orthodox church; "Lvov" probably refers to a victory over the Germans in the first year of World War I.
3. These are the last lines in a short poem by Nikolay Nekrasov, written in 1877. N. A. Nekrasov, *Complete Works and Letters*, [Polnoye sobraniye sochineny i pisem] (Moscow, 1948–53), Vol. II, p. 433.
4. *Archer* [Strelets], the name of three almanacs which were published in 1915, 1916 and 1923. The first issue caused a sensation because it contained, side by side, writings by major Futurists and Symbolists.
5. This line refers to Francesca and Paolo da Rimini in Dante's *Inferno*, Canto V, line 138.
6. V. Mayakovsky, from "About Various Mayakovskys" [O raznykh Mayakovskikh], *Works*, Vol. I, p. 344.
7. *Journal of Journals* [Zhurnal zhurnalov] (1905–1917), weekly literary magazine.

Chapter 15. About Love and Man

1. V. Mayakovsky, from *Vladimir Mayakovsky, a Tragedy*, *Works*, Vol. I, p. 159.
2. In the 2nd edition, this sentence is replaced by the following: "There are many friends."
3. V. Mayakovsky, from "Cloud in Pants," *Works*, Vol. I, p. 185.
4. V. Mayakovsky, from "Backbone Flute" [Fleyta-pozvonochnik], *Works*, Vol. I, p. 207.
5. In the first edition, Lenin's letter starts with the words "Dear friend" and ends with "Friendly shake hands!" in English; in the 2nd edition these phrases do not appear.
6. Letter of V. I. Lenin to Inessa Armand, January 17, 1915.

7. These are the words of the first line of Khlebnikov's poem "Menagerie."

8. *Argus* (1913–1918), illustrated monthly popular magazine, edited by V. Reginin.

9. Probably the famous ballerina Tamara Karsavina, as indicated by Shklovsky in his *Diary* [Dnevnik] (Moscow, 1939), p. 105.

10. Ego-Futurism—literary group, formed in 1911 around Igor Severyanin and Ivan Ignatyev, which aimed at creating a completely new poetry characterized by strong individualism and a certain preciousness of expression. It failed to produce great poetry and its popularity was short-lived.

11. *Zem-gusars*—an ironic reference to the young men who belonged to voluntary organizations created by the war effort. They wore para-military uniforms.

12. V. Mayakovsky, from "You There!" [Vam!], *Works,* Vol. I, p. 75.

13. *The Chronicle* [Letopis] (1915–1917), monthly Petrograd journal founded and edited by Gorky, dealing with literature, social issues and politics.

14. Imaginists (1919–1924)—a short-lived movement in Russian poetry (which took its name from Ezra Pound's Imagists). Their main emphasis was on the primary importance of imagery in poetry. Their greatest poet, who really did not fit into any group, was Yesenin. One of its founders was Vadim Shershenevich.

15. *Took: A Futurists' Drum* [Vzyal: Baraban futuristov] (Petrograd, 1915), published by Osip Brik. Slim booklet of 16 pages with poetry and critical essays by Mayakovsky, Pasternak, Shklovsky, etc.

16. N. Aseyev, "Lyrical Essay" [Lirichesky felyeton], *New LEF* [Novy LEF], No. 11 (1928), p. 3.

17. From A. Pushkin's little tragedy, "Mozart and Salieri," in which Salieri, envying Mozart's effortless facility and genius, poisons him.

18. V. Mayakovsky, from "Man" [Chelovek], *Works,* Vol. I, p. 257.

19. V. Mayakovsky, from "Man", *Works,* Vol. I, p. 268.

Chapter 16. February—The Years 1917–1918

1. *Tyotka*—a Russian card game.

2. In his autobiographical collection *Once Upon a Time,* Shklovsky names Larisa Mikhaylovna Reisner as the girl in love with Mayakovsky. She was a Bolshevik Commissar during the Civil War, a talented journalist and a well-known beauty.

3. V. Mayakovsky, from "Good!" [Khorosho!], *Works,* Vol. VIII, p. 263.

4. This is a reference to Jack London's novel *Martin Eden.*

5. V. Mayakovsky, from "Our March" [Nash marsh], *Works,* Vol. II, p. 7.

6. In the 2nd edition, it is explicitly stated that "the poet played with a revolver, a small Spanish Browning, but not with the one whose bullet ended his life."

Chapter 17. On Blok

1. The *Aurora* was a cruiser which on November 7, 1917, opened fire on the Winter Palace. Its role in the victory of the Revolution has become a legend in the Soviet Union.

2. Khlestakov, the impostor in Gogol's play *The Inspector General*.

3. The Socialist Revolutionaries, an influential Russian Marxist political party which emphasized the role of the peasantry. Its right wing opposed the use of terror and did not collaborate with the Communists when they came to power, while its left wing worked with the Communist government from December 1917 to March 1918.

4. Blok referred to two lines in Mayakovsky's *Mystery Bouffe* (first version); Mayakovsky, *Works*, Vol. II, p. 233.

Chapter 18. I Continue

1. TEO [Teatralny otdel], Theater Section of the People's Commissariat for Education.

2. *Art of the Commune* [Iskusstvo kommuny] (1918–1919), official weekly publication of the People's Commissariat for Education, edited by O. Brik and N. Punin, to which Mayakovsky and other Futurists contributed.

3. IZO, Section of Visual Arts of the People's Commissariat of Education (1918–1921), headed by D. Sterenberg in Petrograd. In these years, Futurists, Mayakovsky among them, were very influential within this section.

4. IMO [Iskusstvo molodykh] Art of the Young, publishing house organized by Mayakovsky in 1918 with the support of the People's Commissariat for Education.

5. In the 2nd edition, this sentence reads as follows: "Aleksey Maksimovich was not given the name of the comrade, and he wrote a few words to L. Brik on the back of her letter to him, saying that he had been unable to obtain that address, after all."

Chapter 19. OPOYAZ

1. OPOYAZ, Society for the Study of Poetic Language [Obshchestvo po izucheniyu poeticheskogo yazyka]—a group of linguistic scholars and poets formed by V. Shklovsky, L. Yakubinsky and E. Polivanov, around 1915, which became one of the two centers of Russian Formalism.

2. Here Shklovsky misquotes Potebnya, who actually wrote that he regarded the image as the constant predicate of a changeable subject.

3. R. Avenarius in *Poetics* [Poetika] (Petrograd, 1919), pp. 103–104.

4. V. Mayakovsky, from "Order to the Army of Art" [Prikaz po armii iskusstva], *Works*, Vol. II, p. 14.

5. Lev Tolstoy, *Diaries, Complete Works* [Polnoye sobraniye sochineny] (Moscow, 1953), Vol. LIII, pp. 141–142.

6. N. P. Pavlov, *Twenty Years of Objective Study of the Higher Nervous Activity (Behavior) of Animals* (Moscow: Biomedgiz, 1938), p. 722.

7. Maxim Gorky, *Collected Works in Thirty Volumes* [Sobraniye sochineny v 30 tomakh] (Moscow: 1949–55), Vol. 17, pp. 16–17.

8. *Ibid.*, p. 16.

9. V. Mayakovsky, from "Cloud in Pants", *Works,* Vol. I, pp. 181–182.

Chapter 20. Mayakovsky's Verse

1. In the 2nd edition, this sentence reads: "They should be published though unfinished."

2. Andrey Bely, *Epopee* [Epopeya], No. 1 (Berlin, 1922), p. 220.

3. Aleksey K. Tolstoy, letter to Turgenev, *Complete Works* [Polnoye sobraniye sochineny] (St. Petersburg, 1908), Vol. IV, p. 182.

4. Andrey Bely, *Beginning of the Century* [Nachalo veka] (Moscow, 1933), p. 425. In this excerpt, Merezhkovsky speaks to Bely and, at the end of the quote, he addresses him as "Borya," the familiar form of Bely's real first name which is Boris [Bugayev].

5. Vladimir Trenin, *In the Workshop of Mayakovsky's Verse* [V masterskoy stikha Mayakovskogo] (Moscow, 1937), p. 108.

6. A. S. Pushkin, from *Ruslan and Ludmila.* In Russian, lines 1, 3, 5 and 7 rhyme, as well as lines 2, 4, 6 and 8.

7. P. A. Vyazemsky, *Complete Works* [Polnoye sobraniye sochineny] (St. Petersburg, 1878), Vol. I, p. 42.

8. *The Contemporary* [Sovremennik] (1836–66), progressive literary and political journal, one of the most important Russian periodicals. It was founded by A. S. Pushkin; in 1847, Nekrasov became its editor. In the 1850s and 1860s it was the central organ of liberal and radical thought. In 1864, Saltykov-Shchedrin became its editor and, in 1866, the Tsarist government closed the journal.

9. *Song of Igor's Campaign,* anonymous epic poem of the 12th century, considered a masterpiece of Old Russian literature.

10. Baron Rozen, *The Contemporary,* Vol. I (1836), p. 143.

11. *Ibid.*, p. 154.

12. V. Mayakovsky, from "How Are Verses Made?" [Kak delat stikhi?], *Works,* Vol. XII, p. 105. Translated and annotated by G. M. Hyde (London: Jonathan Cape, 1970).

13. *Ibid.*, p. 100.

14. *Ibid.*, p. 106.

15. *Ibid.*, p. 106.

16. Ostolopov, *Dictionary of Ancient and Modern Poetry* [Slovar drevney i novoy poezii] (St. Petersburg, 1821), Part III, pp. 24–25.

17. *Skaz,* a style developed by 19th century Russian writers; the term is widely used in Formalist stylistics to describe a narrative manner that reproduces the speech patterns and tone of a fictional narrator.

18. V. Mayakovsky, from "How Are Verses Made?", *Works,* Vol. XII, p. 93. The lines quoted are from Pasternak's poem "Marburg." Some words are misquoted by Mayakovsky.

19. V. Mayakovsky, from "At the Top of My Voice" [Vo ves golos], *Works*, Vol. X, p. 282.

Chapter 21. In the Snow

1. V. Mayakovsky, "Two Rather Unusual Events" [Dva ne sovsem obychnykh sluchaya], *Works*, Vol. II, pp. 78–82.

2. *Burzhuyka*, a roughly put together metal stove which came into use during the Civil War because all other heating systems had broken down.

3. World Literature (1919–1927), publishing house founded by Maksim Gorky. Its aim was to publish great works of world literature from the 18th century to the present. It provided work for many Russian intellectuals of that period.

4. H. G. Wells' visit to the Soviet Union at that time was a great event.

5. *Sukharevka*, a market which became a center for trade, speculation and exchange during the Civil War period.

6. Moscow Linguistic Circle, group of linguistic scholars and poets formed by R. Jakobson and P. Bogatyryov around 1915, which became one of the two centers of Russian Formalism.

7. ROSTA, Russian Telegraph Agency. In the early days after the Revolution (September 1919–February 1922), it published posters for mass propaganda and the dissemination of information. A special technique of poster art was developed by Mayakovsky and other artists who drew the pictures and wrote the text.

8. V. Mayakovsky, from "Revolution: a Poet's Chronicle" [Revolyutsiya: poetokhronika], *Works*, Vol. I, p. 139.

9. V. Mayakovsky, from "Good!", *Works*, Vol. VIII, p. 271.

10. Viktor Khlebnikov, *Collected Works* [Sobraniye proizvedeny] (Leningrad, 1933), Vol. V, p. 303.

11. Mikhail Kuzmin, from "My Portrait" [Moy portret], *Seti* (Petersburg-Berlin: Petropolis, 1923), p. 33.

12. Serapion Brothers, a group of young Soviet prose writers, formed in 1921 (the name was taken from the romantic writings of E. T. A. Hoffmann). The main credo of the group was that the artist needed artistic freedom and that the ideology of each individual member had to be respected. Some of the most talented Soviet writers started their career in this group: V. Kaverin, E. Zamyatin, M. Zoshchenko, K. Fedin, V. Ivanov, L. Lunts, etc.

13. Lili Brik, "From Recollections" [Iz vospominany], *Almanac with Mayakovsky* (Moscow, 1934), p. 76.

14. V. Mayakovsky, from "Alexsandr Blok Has Died" [Umer Aleksandr Blok], *Works*, Vol. XII, p. 22.

15. Yevgeny is the hero of Pushkin's poem "The Bronze Horseman."

16. Pushkino, a country place about 50 miles from Moscow where Mayakovsky stayed in the summer.

17. V. Mayakovsky, from "An Extraordinary Adventure that Happened to Vladimir Mayakovsky in Summertime at a *Dacha*" [Neobychaynoye priklyucheniye, byvsheye s Vladimirom Mayakovskim letom na dache], *Works*, Vol. II, p. 37.

18. "What is Good and What is Bad," title of a poem for children by Maya-kovsky.

19. *Dyuvlam*, word formed from the first letters of "Twelfth Jubilee of Vladimir Mayakovsky" [*Dvenadtsety Yubiley Vladimira Mayakovskogo*].

20. *Thirteen Years of Work*, title of a collection of Mayakovsky's writings, in two volumes, published in 1923.

21. Nothingists [Nichevoki]—one of the many minor avant-garde groups which emerged after the Revolution in Russia. All of them wanted to create something completely new in art or to transform the concept of art itself—little, however, was achieved.

22. Everythingists [Vseki]—Larionov and Zdanevich worked out the new aesthetics which were going to be the base for this new artistic grouping. Apparently, however, they were not very successful because Zdanevich has been called the only Everythingist by his contemporaries.

23. V. Mayakovsky, from "Sevastopol-Yalta," *Works*, Vol. VI, pp. 66–67.

Chapter 22. Norderney

1. *Zoo* — the author is referring to his own experimental autobiographical novel in the form of letters: *Zoo; or Letters Not About Love* [Zoo, ili pisma ne o lyubvi] (Berlin: Helikon, 1923); translated by Richard Sheldon (Ithaca: Cornell University Press, 1971).

2. *Yar* [Brightness], Gorodetsky's first collection of poems, (Petersburg, 1907).

3. Captain Cook, probably James Cook the English sea captain and ex-plorer of the 18th century.

4. V. Mayakovsky, from "How Are Verses Made?," *Works*, Vol. XII, pp. 93–94.

5. Kusikov-types — Shklovsky's contemptuous reference to Boris Kusikov, a minor Imaginist "peasant poet" who left the Soviet Union in 1924.

6. "Iron Mirgorod"—Mirgorod, the name of a provincial town in Gogol's writings, came to represent, in Russian usage, a backward provincial town.

Chapter 23. "About That"

1. *About That* [Pro eto], Mayakovsky's great personal lyric poem, deal-ing with his love, his doubts, his despair. Written in 1923. It has been trans-lated and annotated by Herbert Marshall in *Mayakovsky*, (New York: Hill and Wang, 1965).

2. V. Mayakovsky, from "About That," *Works*, Vol. IV, p. 140.

3. NEP, New Economic Policy (1921–1929), introduced by Lenin to allow the country to regain stability. The Civil War and War Communism had brought economic chaos and the new policy, allowing for more private in-itiative and limited profit, was to restore the Soviet economy. Mayakovsky feared the reappearance of any form of bourgeois mentality.

4. Nikolay Aseyev, from "Lyrical Digression" [Liricheskoye otstupleniye], *Complete Works* [Polnoye sobraniye sochnineny] (Moscow, 1963–1964), Vol. I, p. 396.

5. *Ibid.,* p. 390.

6. "Proletkult" (1917–1923), abbreviation for "Proletarian Culture", the name of a cultural and educational organization headed initially by A. Bogdanov. This group encouraged the development of the arts and literature for and by the proletariat.

7. *LEF* (1923), No. 1.

8. In the 2nd edition, this sentence reads: "Later, the space between the pillars was filled in, but it should have been left 'as it was'; there isn't enough room for the cars in the streets."

9. Mass festivals — Spectacles reenacting revolutionary events. The most famous spectacle was the "Storming of the Winter Palace" (1920), produced by theater professionals but with the participation of at least 10,000 people in the crowd scenes.

10. *LEF* (1923), No. 3.

11. *Ibid.*

12. V. Mayakovsky, from "About That," *Works,* Vol. IV, p. 155.

13. *Ibid.,* p. 172.

14. *Ibid.,* p. 179.

15. Natasha Rostova, the heroine of Tolstoy's *War and Peace.*

16. V. Mayakovsky, from "About That," *Works,* Vol. IV, p. 182.

17. *Ibid.,* p. 184.

18. *Zoyka's Apartment* is a satirical play by Mikhail Bulgakov, written in 1926.

19. This is a line from A. Pushkin's famous poem "The Monument."

20. V. Mayakovsky, from "Alarm!" [Karaul!], *Works,* Vol. XII, p. 136.

21. V. Mayakovsky, from "How Are You?" [Kak pozhivayete?], *Works,* Vol. XI, p. 144.

22. The scenario of *Ivan Kozyr and Tatyana Russkikh* was written by the playwright Dmitry Petrovich Smolin (1891–1955); *The Voyage of Mister Lloyd* was made by Aleksey Aleksandrovich Utkin (1891–1965).

Chapter 24. The Poet Travels

1. V. Mayakovsky, from "I Love," *Works,* Vol. IV, p. 94.

2. V. Mayakovsky, from "At the Top of My Voice," *Works,* Vol. X, p. 285.

3. V. Mayakovsky, from "Lenin," *Works,* Vol. VI, pp. 233–234.

4. V. Mayakovsky, from "Good!", *Works,* Vol. VIII, p. 284.

5. V. Mayakovsky, from "To Our Young People," [Nashemu Yunoshestvu], *Works,* Vol. VIII, p. 17.

6. RAPP, Russian Association of Proletarian Writers [Russkaya assotsiyatsiya proletarskykh pisateley] (1925–1932), Soviet writer's organization which developed from the Proletkult and, in the 1920s, spoke for the Communist Party, stressing realistic art in the service of the Party. With the tightening of controls a stricter organization of literature became necessary and, in 1932, RAPP, along with all other literary groups, was dissolved by a decree of the Central Committee of the Communist Party.

7. Poets' Union [Soyuz poetov], All-Russian Union of Poets, an apolitical organization of poets in the 1920s.

8. Theory of Fact, a new concept set forth by the LEF group, mostly in *New LEF*. It asserted that in the new society there was no need for purely creative literature; literature should deal with facts only.

9. Latvia as a symbol of petty bourgeois capitalist society, is mentioned in Mayakovsky's poem, "Mexico," *Works,* Vol. VII, pp. 41–48.

10. V. Mayakovsky, from "Verlaine and Cézanne," *Works,* Vol. VI, p. 206.

11. V. Mayakovsky, from "Homewards" [Domoy], *Works,* Vol. VII, p. 93.

Chapter 25. The Poet Talks to Posterity

1. *New LEF* (1927–28), journal of the LEF group, a revival of *LEF* which had been discontinued in 1925.

2. *On Guard* [Na postu] (1923–1925), later renamed *On Literary Guard* [Na literaturnom postu] (1926–1932). Influential magazine of the Association of Proletarian Writers. It attacked dissenting writers for any deviation from the official literary line. Mayakovsky and LEF were its favorite targets.

3. V. Mayakovsky, from "Speech at the Meeting of the Federation of Associations of Soviet Writers" (1928), *Works,* Vol. XII, p. 367.

4. Constructivists (1924–1930)— a group of Soviet poets around Igor Selvinsky that stressed the importance of using language and imagery reflecting a specific subject matter. In contemporary themes, they introduced a wide use of technical vocabulary.

5. REF, Revolutionary Front of Art [Revolyutsionny front iskusstva], name of the group Mayakovsky formed in 1929 with a few friends to succeed LEF.

6. In the second edition, the following two sentences replaced the long deleted passage: "Now, there was RAPP. Mayakovsky joined RAPP."

7. V. Mayakovsky, from "Homewards," *Works,* Vol. VII, p. 489.

8. A reference to a line in Mayakovsky's poem "Letter from Paris to Conrade Kostrov on the Nature of Love." [Pismo tovarishchu Kostrovu iz Parizha o sushchnosti lyubvi], *Works,* Vol. IX, pp. 381–385. This poem is dedicated to Tatyana Yakovleva, the girl Mayakovsky fell in love with in Paris.

9. *Press and Revolution* [Pechat i Revolyutsiya] (1921–1930), an influential monthly edited by A. Lunacharsky and V. Polonsky.

10. V. Mayakovsky, from unfinished drafts, *Works,* Vol. X, p. 337.

11. V. Mayakovsky, from untitled last poem, *Works,* Vol. X, p. 287.

12. In the second edition, this sentence reads as follows: "He killed himself with one shot from a revolver, in the same way as Ivan Nov in the movie *Not for Money Born.*"

13. Writers' Union [Soyuz pisateley], the only officially recognized organization of Soviet writers, formed in 1932 after all other literary groups were dissolved by a decree of the Central Committee of the Communist Party. It is closely controlled by the Party.

14. In the 2nd edition, the driver's name is given: Mikhail Kolstov, a Soviet journalist (1898–1942).

15. V. Mayakovsky, from untitled last poem, *Works,* Vol. X, p. 287.

A Chronology of the Career
of Vladimir Mayakovsky

1893   Vladimir Vladimirovich Mayakovsky is born in Bagdadi (now renamed Mayakovsky in the Georgian SSR). Has two older sisters, Ludmila and Olga.

1906   Mayakovsky's father dies and family moves to Moscow.

1908   At the age of fourteen, Mayakovsky joins the Russian Social Democratic Workers' Party (Bolsheviks).

1908–09   Mayakovsky works in high school underground organization; is arrested three times. At his final release faces choice: Party work or acquire artistic craftsmanship. Leaves Party, turns to painting, then also to poetry.

1910–12   Meets David Burlyuk in Art Institute, forms with him first Futurist group, becomes its leading proponent and signs its manifesto, "Slap in the Face of Public Taste."

1913–14   Mayakovsky's first collection, *I*, is published; his first play, *Vladimir Mayakovsky, a Tragedy*, is performed; he travels all over Russia to speak out for a new art, a new life style, a new society. He is expelled from the Art Institute, and not accepted for military service.

1915–17   Friendship with the Briks: Osip Brik becomes his life-long friend and publisher: Lili Brik—the great love of his life. More of his poems appear in the journals and his long poems (*Cloud in Pants, Backbone Flute, War and the Universe, Man*) are published. Gorky meets Mayakovsky and recognizes his talent.

1917–22   Mayakovsky greets the Revolution enthusiastically; devotes himself—his painting and his poetry—to it: his work in ROSTA and his contributions to some work of the People's Commissariat of Education involve him directly in the new society, his play *Mystery Bouffe* celebrates the new spirit.

1922   First trip abroad—to Latvia, Germany, France.

1923   The New Economic Policy and the reality of Soviet society make Mayakovsky again attack in his poetry his old foe: philistinism. He also returns to personal-lyrical themes in *About That.*

He gathers his friends to create his own platform, the journal *LEF.*

1924–27   Mayakovsky travels abroad (Mexico, United States, Germany, France); goes on lecture tours and poetry readings all over the Soviet Union. In 1925, publishes his long poem *Vladimir Ilyich Lenin.* Nevertheless, he and *LEF* are constantly attacked by Marxist literary critics for not being close enough to the proletariat. *LEF* stops publication in 1925. In 1927, he publishes a long poem, on the occasion of the anniversary of the Revolution, *Good!.*

1927–28   *New LEF* resumes publication, but only for about a year. Mayakovsky works on movie scenarios, starts publication of his *Collected Works,* still lectures and writes articles.

1929–30   Mayakovsky writes his two satyrical plays, *The Bedbug* and *The Bathhouse;* and his unfinished poem "At the Top of My Voice." The *Bedbug* is performed at the Meyerhold Theater (1929), with music by Shostakovich; but the reception is cool. *The Bathhouse,* produced in Leningrad in 1930, is a complete critical disaster. His exhibition "Twenty Years of Work" is ignored by all the important writers and critics.

April 14, 1930   Mayakovsky shoots himself.

1930–35   A period when both the poet and his work are either ignored or criticized.

1935–54   After Stalin's remark that he considers Mayakovsky "the most talented Soviet poet," Mayakovsky is streamlined and glorified, but editions of his works are deleted and his plays are not performed. Streets, cities, airplanes, even mountain peaks are named after him, but his role is limited to being "the drummer of the Revolution."

Since Since the Khrushchev years, Mayakovsky's plays are being
1954 performed, his influence on young poets is felt not only in the sphere of revolutionary zeal but in poetic style; reminiscences of personal friends are being published.

English Translations
of Mayakovsky's Works

The Bedbug and Selected Poetry, translated by Max Hayward George Reavey, edited by Patricia Blake (New York: The World Publishing Co., 1960).

Mayakovsky, translated and edited by Herbert Marshall (New York: Hill and Wang, 1965).

The Complete Plays of Vladimir Mayakovsky, translated by Guy Daniels (New York: Simon & Schuster, 1968).

Russian Plays, translated by F. D. Reeve (New York: Random House, 1963).

Poets on Street Corners, edited by Olga Carlisle (New York: Random House, 1970).

The Penguin Book of Russian Verse, introduced and edited by Dimitri Obolensky (Harmondsworth: Penguin Books, 1962).

How Are Verses Made?, translated and annotated by G. M. Hyde (London: Jonathan Cape, 1970).

A Biographical Glossary

We have provided basic biographical information on persons discussed or mentioned in the text whenever we have felt that they may be unfamiliar to the American reader. It is assumed that such major figures as Tolstoy, Lenin, Karl Marx, Goethe or Isadora Duncan do not fall into this category.

Altman, Natan Isayevich, (1889–   ). Russian painter, illustrator, sculptor and stage-designer, a contributor to avant-garde exhibitions. After the Revolution, he helped organize festivals, propaganda trains and street art for the government. In 1918, he was appointed professor of the Petrograd Free Art Studio.

Akhmatova, Anna Andreyevna (real name: Gorenko), (1880–1966). Major Russian poetess. Akhmatova began writing lyric verse in 1907 and gained wide recognition with her first collections, *Evening* (1912), *Rosary* (1914). She and her husband, N. Gumilyov, founded the Acmeist movement. He was shot in 1921 for plotting against the government. She was divorced in 1918; her second marriage to the Assyriologist V. Shileyko also ended in divorce. In the 1930s, her third husband, N. N. Punin, and her son, Lev Gumilyov, were deported. From 1923 to 1940, Akhmatova hardly wrote poetry. During the war, she resumed writing and published the long poem "Poem Without a Hero" (issued abroad; it appeared only in a censored version, later, in the Soviet Union). In 1946, she was severely criticized and excluded from the Writers' Union. She returned to poetry during Khrushchev's "thaw," but her major poem, "Requiem," dedicated to Stalin's victims, is still banned in the Soviet Union. Akhmatova is considered one of the greatest Russian poets of this century; she was awarded an honorary Doctorate from Oxford University (1964) and the Etna-Taormina Poetry Prize.

Aksakov, Sergey Timofeyevich, (1791–1859). Major Russian realist novelist of the 19th Century whose fictionalized reminiscences recreate the atmosphere of his society.

Andreyev, Leonid Nikolayevich, (1871–1919). Russian novelist and playwright. Andreyev gained fame with his realistic short stories; later he turned to symbolism and allegory. After the unsuccessful 1905 Revolution, he lost faith in man and reason, and turned to the themes of suicide, alienation and sexual obsession. He left Russia soon after the 1917 Revolution and died in Finland.

Apukhtin, Aleksey Nikolayevich, (1840–1893). Russian lyric poet, popular in the 1880s. His themes are grief and dissatisfaction with life, treated romantically. Some of his poems are versed monologues, others are gypsy songs; many were set to music by Tchaikovsky and other composers.

Arago, Dominique Francois Jean, (1786–1853). French physicist, discoverer of the principle of the development of magnetism by rotation.

Armand, Inessa Fyodorovna, (1885–1920). Leading Bolshevik revolutionary, a close friend and confidante of Lenin, one of the first members of the Bolshevik Party. After her death, Lenin and his wife, Nadezhda Krupskaya, became the guardians of her daughter, Inna.

Artsybashev, Mikhail Petrovich, (1878–1927). Russian novelist and playwright. He became famous with the publication of his novel *Sanin* (1907) which discussed sex in an unusually frank manner. He was expelled from the Soviet Union in 1923 and went to live in Poland where he wrote anti-Communist articles.

Aseyev, Nikolay Nikolayevich, (1889–1963). Russian Futurist poet, close friend of Mayakovsky and co-founder of *LEF*. Later, he conformed to the Party line on literature, writing patriotic poems during World War II and, still later, anti-American verse. In 1940, he wrote a long poem on Mayakovsky for which he was awarded the Stalin Prize.

Avenarius, Richard, (1843–1896). German philosopher, who formulated a theory of knowledge known as empirio-criticism. This philosophy became a matter of controversy among Russian Marxists: Bogdanov-Malinovsky, a follower of Avenarius' teachings, was sharply attacked by Lenin in that connection.

Averchenko, Arkady Timofeyevich, (1881–1935). Russian humorist, publisher and editor of *The Satyricon*. He left Russia after the Revolution and directed his satire against the Soviet regime.

Bagritsky, Eduard Georgiyevich (real name: Eduard Dzyubin), (1895–

1934). Russian lyric and epic poet, translator of Rimbaud, Burns and Scott. He romanticized the Revolution and the Civil War; his later poems are filled with love of life and nature. He was one of the first to form a group of "proletarian" writers; later, he joined the RAPP. His poetry is still very popular in the Soviet Union.

Balmont, Konstantin Dmitriyevich, (1867–1943). One of the early Russian Symbolist poets, immensely popular between 1904 and 1910 for the sonorous and musical quality of his verse, but considered a minor poet today. He translated poetry, prose and drama; his translation of Shelley's writings introduced Shelley to the Russian public. Balmont opposed the Revolution and settled in France in 1918.

Baudouin de Courtenay, Jean, (1845–1925). Shklovsky's teacher; a leading Slavic philologist and professor at the Petersburg University; one of the originators of modern phonology.

Bely, Andrey (real name: Boris Nikolayevich Bugayev), (1880–1934). Major Russian Symbolist poet, novelist and critic. He was one of the creators of Symbolist theory, which he endowed with a mystical and religious meaning. In 1912, he joined the Anthroposophic movement and lived abroad for several years. He returned to Russia in 1916 and, at its beginnings, welcomed the Revolution. His poems are constructed like musical compositions, some of which he called "symphonies"; his fictional prose is extremely original and experimental, combining elements of fantasy and reality, symbolism and narrative. His best-known novel is *St. Petersburg* (1913). He is also the author of important critical studies, like *The Craftsmanship of Gogol* (1929) and reminiscences, like *Between Two Revolutions* (1934).

Benois, Aleksandr Nikolayevich, (1870–1960). Russian painter, stagedesigner, art historian and critic, publisher (together with S. Diaghilev) of the influential journal, *The World of Art*. He greatly contributed to the renaissance in Russian aesthetics at the turn of the century and during the pre-World War I years. He was sharply critical of Futurism. In 1926, he emigrated to France and continued to design for the stage, particularly for the Diaghilev ballet productions.

Bernstein, Sergey Ignatyevich, (1892–   ). Russian philologist. In the 1920s, he was associated with the Formalists. His major field was phonetics and he made recordings of poetry readings by Mayakovsky, Yesenin and others.

Blok, Aleksandr Aleksandrovich, (1880–1921). One of Russia's greatest lyric poets, also a playwright and critic. A Symbolist with mystical and romantic tendencies, his verse expresses both his personal experience and the "music" of his time. His early work (1898–1906) is dominated by an idealized vision of the "eternal feminine," the "Beautiful Lady." Then follows a period of greater social consciousness, passion, doubts, and forebodings (1906–1918). Blok hailed the Revolution and in 1918 it inspired his two most famous poems: "The Twelve," in which Christ is seen leading the revolutionary forces, and "The Scythians," an appeal to the West for understanding and nonintervention. In the years following the Revolution, Blok felt increasingly depressed, isolated and disappointed.

Blyakhin, Nikolay Vasilyevich, (1886–1961). Writer and chief of the story department of the Soviet Motion Picture Industry (Sovkino) in the 1920s.

Boehm, Elisabeth, (1843–1914). Minor Russian painter of aquarelle imitations of Russian folk art, often reproduced on postcards.

Bogdanov, Aleksandr Aleksandrovich (real name: Malinovsky), (1873–1928). Russian physician, economist and political scientist, the author of standard works on Marxist economics. He joined Lenin in 1904. Influenced by Mach and Avenarius, he was a co-founder, with Lunacharsky and Gorky, of the School for Revolutionary Russian Workers in Capri, and a co-publisher of the journal *Forward*— both of which were disapproved of by Lenin and hence short-lived. After returning to Russia in 1917, Bogdanov became one of the creators of the Proletkult, and, later, the director of the Medical Institute for Experimental Research in Moscow. He died testing a new type of blood transfusion on himself.

Borovikovsky, Vladimir Lukich, (1737–1825). Russian portraitist and painter of miniatures and icons. He was the first to break with the tradition of the 18th century and belongs to the beginnings of the Russian school of Romantic painting.

Breshko-Breshkovsky, Nikolay Nikolayevich, (1874–1934). Russian journalist and minor novelist. He contributed to popular conservative publications; his novels were of little literary value and dealt with the obscure and the violent.

Brik, Lili Yuryevna, (1892–   ). Wife of the Formalist critic, Osip Brik; sister of Elsa Triolet, through whom she met Mayakovsky. The Brik home became the Futurist salon and Lili Brik's affair with Mayakovsky was the theme of many of his poems, among which *The Backbone Flute, I Love,* and *About That.* Though this menage à trois had its ups and downs, in his suicide note, Mayakovsky asked that his last unfinished verses be given to the Briks and, probably, they were addressed to Lili.

Brik, Osip Maksimovich, (1888–1945). Russian writer, literary critic and theoretician; a leading exponent of Futurism and one of the founders of the Formalist group, OPOYAZ. An early admirer of Mayakovsky's poetry, he became his close friend, literary associate and publisher. He helped form the LEF group, created many of its concepts and fought its literary battles. In the 1930s and 40s, he wrote movie scripts and *opera libretti*.

Bryusov, Valery Yakovlevich, (1873–1924). Russian Symbolist poet, critic and novelist. His translations of the French Symbolist poets and his own early poems, published in *Russian Symbolists* (1894–95), marked the beginning of the Symbolist movement. He became the spokesman and theoretician of the Moscow Symbolists and the editor of their review *Balance* (1904–1909). He predicted and supported the Revolution; he set up and directed the Moscow Institute of Art and Literature, which was renamed after him.

Bunin, Ivan Alekseyevich, (1870–1954). Russian prose writer and poet, a follower of the 19th century realistic tradition. In 1920, he emigrated to Paris, and became the leading Russian émigré writer. He was awarded the Nobel Prize for Literature in 1933.

Burlyuk, David Davidovich, (1882–1967). Russian painter and poet, a leading figure in the Russian Futurist movement. Burlyuk rebelled against all established artistic dogma and introduced the revolutionary concepts of disharmony, dissymmetry and disconstruction into art. Together with Khlebnikov, Kruchyonykh, Larionov, Mayakovsky and others, he formed the first Futurist groups, published Khlebnikov's and Mayakovsky's first books and organized exhibitions of Futurist painters. Burlyuk left the Soviet Union in 1918, and after living in Japan for a short while, settled in the U.S.A. in 1922, where he was known as a painter and the publisher of the magazine, *Color and Rhyme*.

Burlyuk, Nikolay Davidovich, (1890–1920). Russian prose writer and poet, brother of David Burlyuk. He contributed to the early Futurist publications, signed its first manifestos and was a militant fighter for the new art. He was a talented impressionistic writer, but left only a slim body of work behind; he was probably killed in the Civil War.

Chaliapin, Fyodor Ivanovich, (1873–1938). Famous Russian bass opera singer. He left the Soviet Union in 1921, became a French citizen and performed all over the world.

Chekrygin, Vasily Nikolayevich, (1897–1922). Russian painter of the Expressionist school. He studied icon painting in Kiev and stressed the spiritual and mystical content of art. Chekrygin contributed four illustrations to Mayakovsky's first published collection of poems, the cycle *I*.

Cheremnykh, Mikhail Mikhaylovich, (1890–1962). Russian illustrator, painter and cartoonist, the first to use a new kind of poster for the "Satire Windows of the Russian Telegraph Agency." It combined slogans, ditties and instructions with expressionistic illustrations. More recently, he was a contributor to the magazine *Crocodile*.

Chukovsky, Korney Ivanovich, (real name: Korneichuk), (1822–1969). Eminent Russian literary critic, writer of children's books and translator. Before World War I, he was very active in avant-garde literary circles. Today, he is highly regarded for his popular children's books, his studies of Nekrasov (*Mastery of Nekrasov*, 1952) and his translations of Dickens, Kipling, Wilde, Twain, Whitman and Chesterton.

Chulkov, Georgy Ivanovich, (1879–1930). Russian Symbolist poet, literary critic and translator. He was an influential member of the Vyacheslav Ivanov circle of the St. Petersburg Symbolists.

Chyorny, Sasha (real name: Glickberg, Aleksandr Mikhaylovich), (1880–1932). Talented Russian writer of satirical verse and children's stories. He worked with Mayakovsky on *The Satyricon* and is credited with having had an influence on him. He emigrated in 1920 and settled in France.

Danilov, Kirsha. Allegedly the first compiler of Russian oral folklore. The first collection, *Old Russian Poetry*, came out in 1804.

D'Anthès, Baron George Charles, (1812–1895). The French officer who fatally wounded Pushkin in a duel.

Denikin, Anton Pavlovich, (1872–1947). Russian general, Commander-in-Chief of the White Army in the South of Russia during the Civil War. In 1920, after suffering heavy defeats by the Red Army, he resigned in favor of General Wrangel and fled to Constantinople. He settled in France, but came to the United States in 1946.

Diaghilev, Sergey Pavlovich, (1872–1929). Famous Russian ballet producer and impressario, co-founder of *The World of Art*. He moved to Paris in 1907, where he created the celebrated Russian Ballet.

Dühring, Eugene Karl, (1833–1921). German philosopher and political economist.

Dzerzhinsky, Feliks Edmundovich, (1877–1926). Polish and Russian Communist and revolutionary. He helped plan the Bolshevik takeover in November 1917, and in December 1917 became the first head of the Cheka, the Soviet secret police, later renamed GPU.

Eichenbaum, Boris Mikhaylovich, (1886–1959). Leading Russian Formalist critic and literary scholar. An early member of OPOYAZ, he was more interested in a new analysis of literary technique than in Futurist experimentation. His major early (1919) study, "How Gogol's 'Overcoat' is Made," was a brilliant example of the new

Formalist analysis. He was associated with LEF, but under the growing pressure of official critics, began including biographical and sociological material in his literary studies. His books on Tolstoy, Gogol, Blok and other writers are considered classics. After being denounced in 1946 for his favorable attitude toward Akhmatova, he disappeared from the literary scene until the late 1950s.

Eichenwald, Yuly Isayevich, (1872–1928). Russian literary critic, influenced by the Symbolists. His favorable articles on N. Gumilyov (who had been shot for counterrevolutionary activity) led to his arrest and expulsion from the Soviet Union in 1922.

Eisenstein, Sergey Mikhaylovich, (1898–1948). Internationally known Russian film director and producer. He directed *The Battleship Potemkin* (1925), *Aleksandr Nevsky* (1938) and *Ivan the Terrible*, Parts I and II (1944, 1945). He was awarded the Stalin Prize and the Order of Lenin. A member of LEF, he introduced original and advanced techniques into film making. In the 1930s, he was accused of Formalism for his film *Bezhin Meadow* (1937).

Fet, Afanasy Afanasyevich (real name: Shenshin), (1820–1892). Russian lyric poet who exerted a strong influence on the Russian Symbolists. His very personal lyrics on nature and love reveal a pantheistic view of the universe, colored by a sensual love for life. The impressionistic quality of his verse, its rhythmical variety and musicality, found followers in Blok and Balmont.

Filonov, Pavel Nikolayevich, (1883–1942). Russian painter, stage designer and illustrator, a founder of the Union of Youth. He was a leading figure in the Futurist movement, illustrated Futurist publications and made stage designs for their theatrical productions. Later he created and headed the school of "Analytical Painting" (1925–1928). He died during the siege of Leningrad.

Filosofov, Dmitry Vladimirovich, (1872–1940). Russian Symbolist literary critic of the Merezhkovsky circle. He attacked Shklovsky's article in defense of Futurism (1915), and stated that the Futurist movement had already reached its peak.

Flit, Aleksandr Matveyevich, (1891–1954). Russian poet-parodist.

Forsh, Olga Dmitryevna, (1873–1961). Russian novelist and author of popular biographical and historical novels.

Fyodorov, Nikolay Fyodorovich, (1828–1903). Russian mystical philosopher who worked as a librarian and wrote on the side. His only book, *Philosophy of the Common Cause,* expresses the belief that man's salvation depends not only on God but on man himself. According to him, modern science and technology were proof of man's divine powers, and by devoting himself to the common cause, man could eventually bring about the resurrection of all and eternal life. These ideas influenced Tolstoy and Dostoyevsky, and apparently influenced Mayakovsky as well.

Gan. Aleksey Mikhaylovich, (1895–   ). Russian writer and critic, member of the Constructivist group.

Gardin, Vladimir Rotislavovich, (1897–1965). Russian actor and leading film director. He successfully directed films before the Revolution; in 1919, he became the founder of the first State School of Cinema; in 1921, he directed *Hammer and Sickle* and, in 1925, *Cross and Mauser*. He organized the movie industry in the Ukraine in the 1920s. After his film, *Kastus Kalinovsky* (1928), was banned and he himself severely criticized, he gave up directing to become a full-time actor.

Gershenzon, Mikhail Osipovich, (1869–1925). Russian historian, literary critic and essayist. He was highly regarded as a literary critic and considered a foremost Pushkin scholar.

Gippius, Zinaida Nikolayevna, (1869–1945). Russian poetess, novelist and essayist, the wife of Merezhkovsky, whose creed she preached all her life. Both she and Merezhkovsky were Symbolists and developed, together with Filosofov, a new religious philosophy. Their salon in St. Petersburg was an important literary center (1905–1917). They emigrated in 1920 and continued to write anti-Soviet articles and poems abroad.

Gofmann, Viktor Viktorovich, (1884–1911). Minor Russian Symbolist poet and short story writer. He committed suicide in Paris.

Goncharova, Natalya Sergeyevna, (1883–1963). Major Russian painter, illustrator and stage designer. She worked in close association with her husband Larionov. Turning away from Impressionism, she drew her inspiration from icons and folk art and became one of the leading figures in Russian avant-garde art and Futurism. In 1915, she and Larionov moved to France to work with Diaghilev.

Gorky, Maksim (real name: Aleksey Maksimovich Peshkov), (1868–1936). Major Russian novelist, short story writer and playwright. His literary reputation was well established before the Revolution with such major works as *Foma Gordeyev* (1899), *Lower Depths* (1902), *Mother* (1907), and *Childhood* (1913). Gorky was inspired by the Revolutionary cause and, for his prose-poem *Stormy Petrel*, was arrested in 1901, and again in 1905. In 1906, he visited the United States to collect money for the Bolsheviks. In 1907–13, Gorky lived mostly in Capri, Italy, where he founded with Bogdanov the School for Revolutionary Russian Workers. He returned to Russia in 1913 and, after the Revolution, was openly critical of some of the excesses. Nevertheless, he appealed to writers to support the new regime and initiated World Literature, a publishing house that helped many writers to survive the difficult years of the Civil War. It was through his personal intervention that Shklovsky was allowed to return to the Soviet Union in 1923. From 1921 to 1929, Gorky lived again abroad, due to ill health. When he returned, he was used as the mouthpiece for official literary policy. He created the concept of "Socialist Realism," criticized Futurism and Formalism, and, in 1932, became Chairman of the Soviet Writers' Union. His death is surrounded by mystery; during the Stalinist purges, an alleged conspiracy that included Yagoda and Gorky's secretary Kryuchkov, as well as some doctors, was uncovered; its members were charged with Gorky's "medical murder."

Gorodetsky, Sergey Mitrofanovich, (1884–   ). Russian poet and translator; one of the organizers of the Acmeist Poets' Guild. He hailed the Revolution in his poetry and wrote patriotic poems during the Civil War and World War II. He translated Bulgarian, Polish and Ukrainian poetry.

Goryansky, Valentin Ivanovich (real name: Ivanov), (1888–1940). Russian poet, a leading contributor to the *The New Satyricon*. After the Revolution, he emigrated to France.

Grammont, Maurice, (1886–1946) French linguist and literary scholar who studied and classified the use of vowels and consonants in poetic language, and their emotional meaning.

Grigoryev, Boris Dmitriyevich, (1886–1939). Russian painter who studied in Paris, adopted Cubist techniques and became an exponent of Russian Expressionism. He later emigrated to Paris.

Grin, Aleksandr Stepanovich (real name: Grinevsky), (1880–1932). A very popular Russian writer of romantic love stories and fantasy novels, who had been active in the revolutionary movement before World War I.

Grinevskaya, Izabella Arkadyevna, (1864–1944). Minor Russian poetess and playwright.

Grosman-Roshchin, Iyuda Solomonovich, (1883–1934). Russian literary critic and journalist, a member of RAPP and an advocate of proletarian literature. In his polemics against the members of LEF, he stressed the ideological content of art above all. The reference to "Anarchists" is meant to recall his past affiliation with the Anarchist movement.

Gumilevsky, Lev Ivanovich, (1890–   ). Russian prose writer and playwright. His novel, *Dog's Alley* (1927), became a controversial subject because of its naturalist description of sexual mores during the NEP period. He is also the author of children's books and biographies of scientists.

Guro, Yelena Genrikhovna (real name: Notenberg), (1877–1913). Russian writer and poet; trained as a painter, she wrote original Impressionist prose and some poetry. She was interested in Futurism, signed some of the early Futurist manifestos and contributed to their publications.

Herzen, Aleksandr Ivanovich, (1812–1870). Russian writer, publicist and editor, the founder of Russian Populism. After 1847, he lived in London where he published the famous émigré journal, *The Bell*.

Ignatyev, Ivan Vasilyevich, (1882–1914). Russian literary and drama critic, essayist and minor poet, the promoter, financial backer, organizer and editor of the Ego-Futurists. He slashed his own throat on the second day of his marriage.

Ivanov, Georgy Vladimirovich, (1894–1959). Russian Acmeist poet who emigrated to Paris after the Revolution and gained recognition as an émigré poet.

Ivanov, Vsevolod Vyacheslavovich, (1895–1963). Russian novelist, short-story writer and playwright. In the 1920s, he was a member of the Serapion Brothers. His early writings are vivid descriptions of his unusual and often dangerous experiences. Later, he conformed to "Socialist Realism." His play, *Armored Train*, was produced by Stanislavsky in 1922.

Ivanov, Vyacheslav Ivanovich, (1866–1949). Major Russian Symbolist poet and philosopher. A scholar of classical antiquity, his poetry was inspired by mysticism and religion. He formulated the theory of Symbolism and became the leader of the St. Petersburg Symbolists during the period 1905–1911. He moved to Italy in 1924, converted to Roman Catholicism and taught classical literature at the University.

Kamensky, Vasily Vasilyevich, (1884–1961). Russian poet, novelist and playwright; a very colorful personality who dabbled in painting, was a travelling artist and an aviator. He joined the Futurist movement at its beginnings, experimenting with transrational language neologisms. His 1915 novel, *Stenka Razin*, combines prose and songs (some of the latter are written in an imaginary Persian language). He belonged to the inner circle of LEF, but contributed little to their journal. A close friend of Mayakovsky, in 1940 he wrote *Life with Mayakovsky*.

Kandinsky, Vasily Vasilyevich, (1886–1944). Russian painter. In 1910, he met the Burlyuks, Larionov and Goncharova; he was the first Russian painter to turn to abstract art; he exhibited with the Futurists at the "Jack of Diamonds" and "The Donkey's Tail." From 1920 to 1922, he worked for IZO and other government projects.

In 1922, he left the Soviet Union, joined the Bauhaus in Weimar and later settled in France.

Katayev, Valentin Petrovich, (1897–   ). Russian novelist, short-story writer and playwright, a personal friend of Mayakovsky. After Stalin's death, he was the editor of *Youth,* a liberal periodical.

Kelin, Pyotr Ivanovich, (1877–1946). Russian Realist painter, of whom Mayakovsky said in his autobiography: "Drew well. Very good teacher. Strict."

Kepler, Johannes, (1571–1630). German astronomer, whose studies prepared modern dynamical astronomy.

Khalatov, Artemy Bagratovich, (1896–1938). Head of the State Publishing House from 1927 to 1932.

Khlebnikov, Velimir (real name: Viktor Vladimirovich), (1885–1922). Russian poet, with Burlyuk and Mayakovsky, a founder of Futurism. He experimented with words, images, rhythms, neologisms and transrational language, using his wide knowledge of Slavic linguistics and folklore to create highly original poems. His best known poem is "Incantation by Laughter" (1910).

Khodasevich, Valentina Mikhaylovna, (1894–   ). Russian painter and stage designer, the niece of the poet Vladislav Khodasevich.

Khodasevich, Vladislav Felitsyanovich, (1886–1939). Russian poet and critic, a Symbolist and arch-enemy of the Futurists. In 1922, he emigrated to Paris and became a central figure in émigré literary circles; he was considered their leading poet.

Kirsanov, Semyon Isaakovich, (1906–   ). Russian poet and translator, whose first poems appeared in 1924. He was close to Mayakovsky, and a member of LEF until it was dissolved. He translated works by Pablo Neruda, Louis Aragon and Berthold Brecht. During the Khrushchev "thaw," he published a poem "Seven Days of the Week," sharply critical of Stalinism, but was later forced to recant.

Kogan, Pyotr Semyonovich, (1872–1932). Russian literary historian and critic, a member of the *On Guard* group of proletarian writers. He attacked Mayakovsky for clinging to his bohemian, bourgeois past. He later became President of the Moscow Academy of Arts.

Korolenko, Vladimir Galaktionovich, (1853–1921). Russian writer and journalist, one of the leaders of the Liberal Populists and a co-editor of their publication, *Russian Wealth.*

Kozlinsky, Vladimir Ivanovich, (1891–   ). Russian illustrator. He illustrated some of Mayakovsky's books.

Kruchyonykh, Aleksey Yeliseyevich, (1886–   ). Russian Futurist poet. Originally a school teacher of art, he met the Burlyuks in 1907 and became a writer. One of the most radical innovators of the

Futurist group, in his poems, he used sound images, typographical effects and no punctuation. He signed all the Futurist manifestoes, and came to represent Futurism both through his creative work and theoretical essays. He joined Mayakovsky in the LEF, but only a few of his poems were published in *LEF* or *New LEF,* because they were considered too extreme. In the 1930s, Kruchyonykh virtually ceased writing, although he did try to bring jazz rhythms to poetry, and wrote some bibliographies. In 1934, he apparently went back to teaching art in a high school.

Kryuchkov, Pyotr Petrovich, (1890–1938). Gorky's secretary and literary manager, a highly controversial figure. From 1921 to 1936, he enjoyed the confidence of Gorky, his friends and his family, but in 1938, was arrested and implicated in the trial against Yagoda and two doctors. They were all accused of having killed Gorky and his son; Kryuchkov confessed and was executed. Now, he is being "rehabilitated" in some memoirs.

Kulbin, Nikolay Ivanovich, (1868–1917). Russian professor at the Military Medical Academy; an organizer, sponsor and promoter of avant-garde art and Futurist poetry. His own attempts at painting were of minor significance, but he was very close to the artists and poets of the new art, and gave them moral, as well as occasional financial, support. Because of his obsession with the ideas of the new art, he was nicknamed "the mad doctor."

Kuleshov, Lev Vladimirovich, (1899–   ). Russian film director, who introduced revolutionary new techniques into movie making. He stressed the psychological impact of film. He directed *The Unusual Adventure of Mr. West in the Land of the Bolsheviks* (1924), and his best film, *By the Law* (1926), was written in collaboration with Shklovsky. A teacher at the Moscow Film Institute from 1921 to 1930, he was attacked for Formalism in the late 1920s, only to be rehabilitated in 1940 for his film on Stalin, *The Siberians.*

Kuzmin, Mikhail Alekseyevich, (1875–1936). Russian poet, prose writer and playwright. He began as a Symbolist, but later became very influential in the formation of Acmeism.

Larionov, Mikhail Fyodorovich, (1881–1964). Russian painter, illustrator and stage designer, very influential in the rise of the Russian avant-garde art movement. After breaking away from the influence of the French Impressionists, he turned to non-objective, expressionistic techniques, and developed a theory called "Rayonnism." He and his wife, Goncharova, were closely associated with the Futurists. In 1915, they moved to France to work with Diaghilev's Russian Ballet.

Lavinsky, Anton Mikhaylovich, (1893–   ). Russian artist who designed a town built on springs (1921).

Lavut, Pavel Ilyich, (1898–   ). The organizer of Mayakovsky's lecture tours from 1926 to 1930. In 1963, he published *Mayakovsky Travels All Over the Union.*

Lebedev, Vladimir Vasiliyevich, (1891–1967). Russian painter and illustrator, who made numerous ROSTA posters in Petrograd. He is also a well-known illustrator of children books. In 1967, he became a corresponding member of the USSR Academy of Art.

Le Corbusier (real name: Charles Edouard Henneret), (1887–1965). World famous French architect and designer. He built the Ministry of Central Economic Planning in Moscow, in 1925–1929.

Ledentu, Mikhail, (? –1917). Russian avant-garde artist, who was the hero of an experimental drama by Ilya Zdanevich, *Ledentu as a Beacon* (1923).

Leskov, Nikolay Semyonovich, (1831–1895). Russian novelist and short story writer, noted for his vivid, idiomatic and humorous narrative style. He influenced some of the Russian writers of the 1920s.

Levidov, Mikhail Yulyevich, (1892–1942). Russian journalist and critic, a foreign correspondent of TASS. He belonged, for a while, to the LEF group.

Levin, Aleksey Sergeyevich, (1893–   ). Russian painter who worked with Rodchenko.

Levin, Miron Pavlovich, (1918–1940). Russian literary scholar.

Levitsky, Dmitry Grigoryevich, (1735–1822). Major Russian portrait painter, influenced by Western art.

Linder, Max (real name: Gabriel Leuvielle), (1883–1925). French comic actor considered the king of burlesque cinema before 1914. He visited St. Petersburg in 1913 and gave live performances.

Lomonosov, Mikhail Vasilyevich, (1711–1765). Russian scientist, scholar and poet, considered the founder of modern Russian culture. Aside from his notable scientific contributions, his reforms in the field of grammar, style and prosody led to the development of modern literary Russian. His adoption of the syllabo-tonic system of versification has dominated Russian poetry ever since.

London, Jack, (1876–1916). American novelist. A romantic adventurer and self-made man, his novels express a belief in social progress and socialism.

Lunacharsky, Anatoly Vasilyevich, (1875–1933). Russian man of letters and critic; a theoretician of proletarian art, and a leading Bolshevik. From 1917 to 1929, he was the Commissar for Education.

Lunts, Lev Natanovich, (1901–1924). Russian playwright and short story writer, a disciple of Shklovsky, a spokesman and theoretician of the Serapion Brothers.

Lyubavina, Nadezhda Ivanovna. Russian painter.

Mach, Ernst, (1838–1916). Austrian physicist and philosopher. His philosophical position and the theory of empirio-criticism were attacked by Lenin.

Malevich, Kasimir Serafimovich, (1878–1935). Russian painter, the founder of Suprematism. He was influenced by the French Impressionists, turned to Russian Expressionism, assimilated Fauvism and Cubism, and finally created his own synthesis which he called Suprematism. He exhibited at Futurist exhibitions, illustrated their publications and designed their stage sets. Mayakovsky collaborated with him on his Suprematist manifesto (1915). In the 1920s, he applied his art to industrial designs, in later years, he devoted himself to teaching and writing.

Marinetti, Filippo Tommaso, (1876–1944). Italian poet and novelist, the leader of Italian Futurism. His visit to Russia, in 1914, revealed the rift between European and Russian Futurism.

Merezhkovsky, Dmitry Sergeyevich, (1865–1941). Russian novelist, poet and essayist. He was one of the main founders and theoreticians of the Symbolist movement; he and his wife, Zinaida Gippius, attempted to create a "religious-philosophical" group. His historical novels are known even outside Russia. In 1919, the Merezhkovskys fled from the Soviet Union, settled in France and remained permanent enemies of Communism.

Mikhaylovsky, Nikolay Konstantinovich, (1842–1904). Russian writer, literary critic and sociologist, a leading theoretician of Russian Populism and an editor of *Fatherland Notes*.

Minayev, Dmitry Dmitriyevich, (1835–1889). Russian poet, publicist and translator. A socially concerned writer, a master of satire and parody, he apparently influenced Mayakovsky.

Minsky, Nikolay Maksimovich (real name: Vilenkin), (1855–1937). Russian writer who protested against the lack of aesthetic appreciation in 19th century Russian criticism. He is considered one of the first precursors of Russian Symbolism.

Nagrodskaya, Yevdokiya Apollonovna, (1866–1930). Minor Russian novelist and short story writer, who exploited the problems of women, free love and sexuality as early as 1910, when her novel *Anger of Dionysus* became a best seller. She emigrated in 1917.

Nekrasov, Nikolay Alekseyevich, (1821–1878). Major Russian poet, whose foremost subject was the suffering of the Russian peasantry. A publisher and editor of *The Contemporary* and, later, *Fatherland*

Notes, he was a very important literary figure and a leading member of the progressive circles of Russian society.

Nikulin, Lev Veniaminovich, (1891–1954). Minor Russian poet, novelist and playwright, a member of the Mayakovsky circle in the 1920s. In 1940, he became a member of the Communist Party.

Nyrop, Kristoffer, (1858–1931). Danish linguistic scholar, professor at the University of Copenhagen. His major work was in Romance languages.

Olesha, Yury Karlovich, (1899–1960). Russian novelist, short story writer and playwright. In 1927, he became famous with *Envy,* a novel dealing with the problems of the intellectual in the new society. Olesha's style was influenced by Formalism; both the content and style of his novel were attacked, and he was made to recant. He is also the author of short stories and plays, and in later years turned to writing film scenarios, literary criticism and reminicences. His last autobiographical novel, *A Line for Every Day,* was published in 1965.

Olimpov, Konstantin Konstantinovich (real name: Fofanov), (1880–1940). The son of the well-known Symbolist poet Konstantin Fofanov, a poet of the Ego-Futurist group. In the years 1913–1922, he wrote hyperbolic and self-glorifying poems, then disappeared from the literary scene.

Ostolopov, Nikolay Fyodorovich, (1782–1833). Russian poet, translator and literary theoretician. For a long time his *Dictionary of Ancient and Modern Poetry* was the only source in Russia for the study of poetical terminology.

Ostrovsky, Aleksandr Nikolayevich, (1823–1886). Major Russian playwright, considered the founder of modern Russian drama. He wrote about forty plays in prose and eight in blank verse, portraying, for the most part, the uneducated merchant class in a colorful and colloquial language. *The Storm* is considered his masterpiece.

Panina, Varvara Vasilyevna, (1872–1911). Popular Russian singer of gypsy songs.

Pasternak, Boris Leonidovich, (1890–1960). Russian poet and novelist who was awarded the Nobel Prize for Literature in 1958 for *Doctor Zhivago.* A member of the Futurist movement from 1914 to 1920, he later contributed to *LEF;* he described his relationship with Mayakovsky in his autobiographical sketch, *I Remember.*

Pavlenkov, Florenty Fyoderovich, (1839–1900). Russian publisher of cheap editions of Russian and foreign classics, of a popular science series, of writers' biographies and, also, of a very widely used *Encyclopedic Dictionary.*

Pavlov, Ivan Petrovich, (1849–1936). Famous Russian physiologist, who formulated the theory of conditioned reflexes. He was awarded the Nobel Prize for Medicine (1904) and the Copley Medal (1915). His teachings, absolute dogma under Stalin, are still the main basis of Russian physiology.

Pertsov, Viktor Osipovich, (1898–   ). Russian literary scholar and critic. A member of the LEF group in the 1920s he edited, together with Aseyev, Serebryansky and Mayakovsky's sister, a twelve-volume edition of Mayakovsky's complete works (1939–1949). In 1957, he published *Mayakovsky, His Life and Work*.

Petrov-Vodkin, Kozma Sergeyevich, (1878–1939). Russian painter who never belonged to any specific school of painting. After 1918, he was one of the most influential professors of the Leningrad Art Academy.

Pisarev, Dmitry Ivanovich, (1840–1868). Russian Nihilist leader, a socially concerned literary critic and publicist. His most important work of criticism was written during his imprisonment in the Peter and Paul Fortress. An extreme utilitarian, he valued scientific knowledge more than art.

Pogodin, Nikolay Fyodorovich (real name: Stukhalov), (1900–1962). Russian playwright. His central theme is the education of man in Soviet society; his style is Socialist Realism. He was awarded the Stalin Prize in 1941. Two of his most popular plays are *The Aristocrats* (1934) and *Man with a Gun* (1937).

Polonsky, Vyacheslav Pavlovich, (1886–1932). Russian Marxist literary critic and historian, an editor of *New World*. He assailed all the Futurists violently, particularly Mayakovsky, for being too obscure.

Polonsky, Yakov Petrovich, (1819–1898). Russian poet and prose writer. Some of his poems, in the form of folk ballads and gypsy romances, were put to music by Tchaikovsky and Rubinstein.

Popova, Lyubov Sergeyevna, (1889–1924). Russian artist who belonged to the Constructivist school, a group which emphasized applied art and technique. She was connected with *LEF*, to which she contributed illustrations. In 1922, she began to work at the First Textile Factory in Moscow as a textile designer.

Potebnya, Aleksandr Aleksandrovich, (1835–1891). Russian philologist, the founder of a new school of linguistics. Though some of his basic concepts were rejected by the Formalist critics, his general approach to literary analysis anticipated Formalist literary theory.

Potyomkin, Pyotr Petrovich, (1886–1926). Russian writer, playwright, critic and translator. From 1908, he was a permanent contributor to *The Satyricon*, and later became one of its editors. He emigrated in 1920.

Pronin, Boris. Founder and owner of "The Stray Dog" cafe. He was also an actor and theatrical director.

Prutkov, Kuzma. A joint pseudonym used by Aleksey K. Tolstoy (1817–1875) and his two cousins, Aleksey and Vladimir Zhemchuzhnikov, to write satirical verse and witty parodies.

Punin, Nikolay Nikolayevich, (1888–1953). Russian critic and art historian, the third husband of Akhmatova. A Futurist since the Revolution, he worked for *Art of the Commune* and IZO and was a friend of Mayakovsky. He was arrested and deported in the 1930s.

Pyast, Vladimir Alekseyevich, (1886–1940). Minor Russian poet, a friend of Blok. In 1929, he published his memoirs, an interesting account of the preceding years.

Radakov, Aleksey Aleksandrovich, (1879–1942). Russian painter and caricaturist, a leading collaborator on *The Satyricon*. Later, he contributed to Soviet satirical journals, including *Crocodile*, and illustrated a number of children's books.

Radishchev, Alexsandr Nikolayevich, (1749–1802). Russian poet and prose writer, often regarded as Russia's first revolutionary writer. His *Voyage from St. Petersburg to Moscow* (1790), published through an oversight of the censors, described the horrors of serfdom and Russian autocracy. Radishchev was sentenced to hard labor in Siberia. Rehabilitated and released in 1797, he committed suicide five years later.

Rakitsky, Ivan Nikolayevich, (? –1942). A charming, cultivated friend of Gorky's household, who moved in "accidentally" and remained about twenty years, as a companion to Gorky's son and granddaughters.

Redko, A. Russian literary critic who wrote for the liberal Populist journal, *Russian Wealth*.

Remizov, Aleksey Mikhaylovich, (1877–1957). Russian novelist and essayist. A brilliant stylist, he introduced important innovations into Russian prose. Influenced by Gogol, Leskov and Dostoyevsky, his heroes are lonely and alienated, while part of his inspiration is derived from Russian folklore. He left Russia in 1921, lived in Germany until 1923 and then settled in France, where he continued to write.

Repin, Ilya Yefimovich, (1844–1930). Leading Russian painter of the Realist school. For the most part, he painted portraits, scenes from peasant life and historical subjects. From 1909 to his death, he lived in Kuokkala, the Finnish resort.

Rodchenko, Aleksandr Mikhaylovich, (1891–1956). Russian painter, illustrator, stage designer and photographer. A member of the Constructivist school, in 1921 he turned to industrial and applied art.

He designed revolutionary posters with Mayakovsky, and from 1923 to 1925, also collaborated on *LEF,* making title pages and photo-montage illustrations for Mayakovsky's poems. When LEF was dissolved and Socialist Realism became the official artistic dogma, Rodchenko was allowed to continue his work in graphic design and photography.

Rossi, Karl Ivanovich, (1775–1849). Russian architect of Italian origin. As the chief architect of Alexander I, he is responsible for some of the most beautiful buildings in St. Petersburg.

Rozanov, Vasily Vasileyvich, (1856–1919). Russian philosopher, essayist and critic. He had highly original ideas on sex, and mystical religious views, which he presented in an utterly new prose style. He exerted a strong influence on Shklovsky, who wrote a study of Rozanov in 1921.

Rozanova, Olga Vladimirovna, (1886–1918). Russian painter, illustrator and poet. She introduced letters and words into her Cubist and Suprematist paintings. In 1912, she married Kruchyonych, dedicated her art to the Futurist movement and worked in IZO. She died of diphtheria.

Saltykov-Shchedrin, Mikhail Yevgrafovich (real name: Saltykov), (1826–1889). Russian novelist, publicist and editor. A writer of social and political satire, the novel *The Golovlyov Family* is considered his masterpiece. A leader of the radical intelligentsia, he edited *The Contemporary* from 1863 to 1864 and then *Fatherland Notes,* with Nekrasov, from 1868 to 1884.

Schieman, Eduard Gustavovich, (1885–1942). Germain painter belonging to the Kandinsky group.

Selvinsky, Ilya Lvovich, (1899–1968). Russian poet and playwright, leader of the Constructivists. In his work in the 1920s, he criticized experimental orthography, punctuation, etc. Later, he conformed to official policy.

Serov, Valentin Aleksandrovich, (1865–1911). Major Russian realist painter, famous for his portraits and landscape paintings, also a member of *The World of Art* group.

Severyanin, Igor Vasilyevich (real name: Lotarev), (1887–1941). Russian poet, leader of the Ego-Futurists. For a few years his books, *The Thunder-Seething Cup* (1913), *Pineapples in Champagne* (1915), won him the popularity of a movie star. In 1919, he emigrated to Estonia, and when the Soviets occupied Estonia in 1940, he had poems published in the Soviet Union. He died under the German occupation.

Shekhtel, Lev Fyodorovich (real name: Zhegin), (1892–   ). Russian painter and illustrator. In Mayakovsky's cycle, *I,* he contributed four illustrations. In 1970, under the name L. Zhegin he published, together with B. Uspensky, *The Language of a Pictorial Work,* a structuralist study.

Shengeli, Georgy Arkadyevich, (1894–1956). Russian poet, critic and translator. He wrote a series of textbooks for aspiring writers. Mayakovsy attacked Shengeli in some of his public lectures and Shengeli's book, *Mayakovsky Life-Size,* represents an insulting and distorted view of the poet.

Shershenevich, Vadim Gabrielevich, (1893–1942). Russian poet and translator. He espoused Symbolism, then Ego-Futurism, and finally became the main theoretician of Imaginism.

Shileyko, Vladimir Kazimirovich, (1891–1930). Russian poet and Assyriologist, the second husband of A. Akhmatova. A great scholar and translator of Babylonian literature.

Shvedchikov, Konstantin Matveyevich, (1884–   ). Soviet bureaucrat, head of Sovkino, the organization of the Soviet motion picture industry, from 1924 on. Mayakovsky spoke out against him and his incompetence. In 1935, he received the Order of the Red Banner of Labor as "former organizer and chairman of Sovkino."

Sinyakova, Mariya and Oksana Mikhaylovna, (1898–   ) (1900–   ). Both sisters were very much a part of Futurist circles; Mariya illustrated Futurist publications, signed Futurist manifestos, and was courted by Pasternak; Oksana became the wife of N. Aseyev.

Skobelev, Mikhail Dmitriyevich, (1843–1882). Russian general who distinguished himself during the Russian-Turkish war of 1877–1878.

Slonimsky, Mikhail Leonidovich, (1897–   ). Russian novelist and short-story writer, one of the founders of the Serapion Brothers. He was influenced by Shklovsky, but in the 1930s, conformed to the official line in literature.

Sologub, Fyodor Kuzmich (real name: Teternikov), (1863–1927). Russian Symbolist poet, novelist and playwright. His best-known works belong to the period before the Revolution; they deal with the problem of evil and the attempt to escape into the imaginary. He did not support the Communist regime, but stayed in the Soviet Union, where little of his work was published or even mentioned.

Steiner, Rudolph, (1861–1925). Austrian social philosopher, the founder of Anthroposophy, a doctrine which postulates the existence of a spiritual world accessible to man's higher faculties. Its headquarters were in Switzerland.

Stepanova, Varvara Fyodorovna, (1894–1958). Russian Constructivist artist, stage-builder and illustrator, the wife of Rodchenko. She was a permanent contributor to *LEF*.

Sterenberg, David Petrovich, (1881–1948). Russian painter and graphic designer. He lived in Paris from 1907 to 1917; in 1918, he was appointed head of IZO, the Section of Visual Arts of the Commissariat for Education.

Struve, Pyotr Bernardovich, (1870–1944). Russian economist, publicist and political leader. He was a representative of "legal" Marxism, edited several publications and was active in the Social Democratic movement. During the Revolution, he fought with the White Army; later he emigrated to Czechoslovakia and then to France.

Sudeykin, Sergey Yuryevich, (1882–1946). Russian painter of *The World of Art* group. He emigrated after the Revolution and worked for Diaghilev in Paris; eventually, he became an American citizen, and designed sets for the Metropolitan Opera and Radio City Music Hall.

Sumarokov, Aleksandr Petrovich, (1718–1777). Russian playwright and poet. In his plays, he combined the classical French form with Russian themes. His poetry stands out for its simplicity and lucidity, its varied themes and meter.

Sumtsov, Nikolay Fyodorovich, (1854–1922). Ukranian ethnographer and literary scholar, a disciple of Potebnya. He wrote literary studies on Ukrainian writers of the 16th and 17th centuries, and on Pushkin (1900).

Suvorov, Aleksandr Vasilyevich, (1730–1800). Great Russian general, the originator of Russian military strategy. He scored famous victories against the Turks (1789–1790) and against the French (1799).

Tatlin, Vladimir Yevgrafovich, (1885–1953). Russian painter, sculptor and stage designer, the leader of the Constructivist artists who saw themselves as artists-engineers and worked with industrial material. Tatlin's reliefs and counter-reliefs of 1913–14, already attempt to destroy pictorial illusion through the spatial use of real material. After the Revolution, he headed the Moscow IZO (Section of Visual Arts of the Commissariat of Education), designed workers' clothes and stage sets and worked in a factory. He is well-known for his utopian monument to the Third International (1919–20).

Tikhonov, Aleksandr Nikolayevich (real name: Serebrov), (1880–1956). Russian editor and publisher. In his journal *Russian Contemporary* appeared some of Pasternak's poems; he also worked with Gorky to create the World Literature publishing house.

Tikhonov, Nikoloy Semyonovich, (1896–   ). Russian poet, novelist and short story writer, a member of the Serapion Brothers in the 1920s. His powerful verses on the Civil War were influenced by the Acmeist poets, as well as Khlebnikov and Pasternak. He survived the siege of Leningrad during World War II and was named Chairman of the Soviet Writers' Union in 1944. In 1946, he was criticized for not attacking the "Formalists" and lost his position. In the 1950s he took part in the campaign against Pasternak.

Tolstoy, Count Aleksey Konstantinovich, (1817–1875). Russian poet, playwright and novelist. A distant cousin of Lev Tolstoy, he was an extremely versatile writer who fought for full freedom in art. He invented the fictitious character Kuzma Prutkov.

Tolstoy, Aleksey Nikolayevich, (1882–1945). Russian novelist, poet and playwright. He fought the Red Army during the Civil War and emigrated to Paris in 1919; but he returned to the Soviet Union in 1929, to become one of the most popular Soviet writers. His trilogy, *The Road to Calvary*, earned him the Stalin Prize in 1942. His unfinished novel, *Peter the First* (1929–1945), is probably his most powerful work.

Tredyakovsky, Vasily Kirillovich, (1703–1796). Russian poet, translator and philogogist. He was the first poet to introduce accentual verse into Russian; his *New and Brief Method for the Composition of Russian Verses* (1735) represents his main contribution to Russian literature as a theoretician.

Trenin, Vladimir Vladimirovich, (1904–1941). Russian literary critic and scholar.

Triolet-Aragon, Elsa Yuryevna, (1896–1970). Russian and French novelist, the daughter of a prominent Russian lawyer, Yury Kagan, and the sister of Lili Brik, to whom she introduced Mayakovsky. After her marriage to André Triolet, a Frenchman, ended in divorce, she married Louis Aragon, the famous French Surrealist and future resistance leader, in 1939. She shifted to writing her novels in French, and was awarded the Goncourt Prize. She also translated Mayakovsky's poetry and prose.

Tynyanov, Yury Nikolayevich, (1894–1943). Russian Formalist critic, novelist and biographer. A leading Formalist theoretician, his comparative studies and historical novels are considered classics. His major work belongs to the 1920s, e.g., "Gogol and Dostoyevsky" (1921), *The Problem of Verse Language* (1924). He translated Heine.

Uspensky, Glev Ivanovich, (1843–1902). Russian prose writer, close to the Populists. Uspensky was committed to radical ideals of social justice, and wrote humane, sober and humorous sketches of the Russian peasantry and lower classes.

Vengerov, Semyon Afanasyevich, (1855–1920). Russian literary historian, critic and professor at Petersburg University. The future Formalist critics, B. Eichenbaum, B. Tomashevsky and Y. Tynyanov, took part in his seminar course.

Verbitskaya, Anastasya Alekseyevna, (1861–1928). Russian writer of popular novels for women, without any literary value, dealing with free love, the contemporary family, etc.

Verhaeren, Emile, (1855–1916). Belgian poet, a champion of the Impressionist painters. He influenced the Russian Symbolists.

Verne, Jules, (1828–1905). Famous French science fiction writer whose novels were very popular in Russia.

Vertinsky, Aleksandr Nikolayevich, (1889–1957). Russian minor poet and popular singer. After the Revolution, he emigrated; performed all over the world with great success among Russian émigrés, and returned to the Soviet Union in 1943.

Vertov, Dziga (real name: Denis Kaufman), (1896–1954). Major Russian film maker, theoretician of the "camera-eye." He introduced new techniques of editing and filming in the documentary genre. In 1926, he made two full-length films, *One Sixth of the Earth* and *Forward Soviet*. He was influenced by Futurist and Constructivist aesthetics, and contributed to *LEF*. In the 1930s he was denounced as a Formalist and did not return to movie making until 1942.

Veselovsky, Aleksandr Nikolayevich, (1838–1906). Russian literary historian, a professor at Petersburg University. An authority on comparative literary history, he established a system of historical poetics, which contributed many concepts to the Formalist theory. In 1947, he was denounced as an originator of Formalism, but his name was "rehabilitated" in 1956.

Voloshin, Maksimilyan Aleksandrovich, (1877–1932). Russian Symbolist poet, translator and painter, a friend of all the major Symbolist poets. He opposed the Revolution, but remained in the Soviet Union, where he is now almost unknown as a poet.

Volynsky, Akim Lvovich (real name: Flekser), (1863–1926). Russian Symbolist literary critic and art historian. In his articles, he violently opposed the critical traditions of the 19th century, with its emphasis on civic and social content, and won many new followers for the "new" art.

Vostokov, Aleksandr Kristoforovich, (1781–1864). Important Russian philologist, Slavicist and poet. His studies on the Russian tonic versification system were highly valued by Pushkin. He also studied Russian songs and proverbs, collected material for an etymological dictionary and wrote a grammar book of Church Slavonic.

Vyazemsky, Prince Pyotr Andreyevich, (1792–1878). Russian poet, a close friend of Pushkin; their correspondence is remarkable for its wit and literary insights. His poetry is romantically inspired, but classical in style.

Williams, Vasily Robertovich, (1863–1939). Outstanding Soviet soil agronomist, a member of the Academy of Science since 1931. His studies examine soil structures; he was awarded the Order of Lenin.

Wrangel, Baron Pyotr Nikolayevich, (1878–1928). Russian general who followed Denikin as Commander-in-Chief of the White Army in the South of Russia during the Civil War (1920). In the same year, he and his troops were evacuated to Turkey.

Yakubinsky, Lev Petrovich, (? –1946). Russian Formalist literary critic, linguistic scholar and member of OPOYAZ; he contributed to their first collection, *Studies in the Theory of Poetic Language* (1916), and later wrote very technical studies of Russian prosody.

Yeliseyev. The wealthy owner of Petersburg's most fashionable delicatessen store where exotic fruits and pastries were sold. When he fled the country after the Revolution, his apartment was used by the Serapion Brothers.

Yesenin, Sergey Aleksandrovich, (1895–1925). Russian lyrical poet. His peasant background was reflected in his early poetry. He welcomed the Revolution, endowing it with a mystical power. His first collection (1916) brought him immediate recognition; later, he joined the Imaginists, and became known as the most talented "peasant poet." After his unsuccessful marriage to Isadora Duncan (1922–23), Yesenin's poetry expressed disillusionment, melancholy and defiance. He took to drink and his life was surrounded by scandal and debauchery. On December 27, 1925, he hanged himself in a Leningrad hotel. Yesenin is very popular in the Soviet Union. His poetry is considered by many to belong to the best written in Russian in this century.

Yevreinov, Nikolay Nikolayevich, (1879–1953). Russian playwright, historian and theoretician of the theater, an active member of the theatrical avant-garde. In 1922, he was expelled from the Soviet Union.

Yudenich, Nikolay Nikolayevich, (1862–1933). Russian general and Commander-in-Chief of the White Army in the Baltic area. He led an unsuccessful offensive against Petrograd in 1919, and had to retreat to Estonia. He emigrated to France.

Yushkevich, Semyon Solomonvich, (1868–1927). Minor Russian writer of sentimental novels and plays, that were popular in 1910–12, but are now forgotten. *Miserere* was performed by the Moscow Art Theater. He emigrated after the Revolution.

Zdanevich, Ilya Mikhaylovich, (1894–   ). Russian Futurist poet, playwright and critic. He worked in close collaboration with Larionov and Goncharova to formulate their Rayonnist theories. He was one of the most radical innovators among the Futurists, and used transrational language in many of his poems and plays. When he emigrated to Paris, he became a member of the Dada movement.

Zenkevich, Mikhail Aleksandrovich, (1891–   ). Minor Russian poet and translator. He belonged to the Acmeist group, but hailed the Revolution. His translations are very important, and include Victor Hugo, Walt Whitman, Shakespeare and contemporary Western poets.

Zhukovsky, Stanislav Yulyanovich, (1873–1944). Russian neo-Realist painter of landscapes and still lifes, a student of Levitan. He left the Soviet Union in 1923.

Zoshchenko, Mikhail Mikhaylovich, (1895–1958). Russian humorist and master satirist of language, a member of the Serapion Brothers. In 1946, he was severely criticized and excluded from the Writers' Union for his "vulgar parody" of Soviet life. In 1956, he reappeared on the literary scene when some of his skits were performed at the Hermitage Theater.

Index

RITTER LIBRARY
BALDWIN-WALLACE COLLEGE